# JOURNAL FOR THE STUDY OF THE NEW TESTAMENT SUPPLEMENT SERIES
## 199

*Executive Editor*
Stanley E. Porter

Sheffield Academic Press

# Pauline Persuasion

## A Sounding in 2 Corinthians 8–9

Kieran J. O'Mahony

Journal for the Study of the New Testament
Supplement Series 199

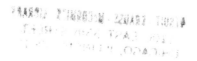

For my parents

Copyright © 2000 Sheffield Academic Press

Published by
Sheffield Academic Press Ltd
Mansion House
19 Kingfield Road
Sheffield S11 9AS
England

http://www.SheffieldAcademicPress.com

Typeset by Sheffield Academic Press
and
Printed on acid-free paper in Great Britain
by Antony Rowe Ltd
Chippenham, Wiltshire

British Library Cataloguing in Publication Data

A catalogue record for this book is available
from the British Library

ISBN 1 84127 149 7

# CONTENTS

In the Pauline corpus, Second Corinthians is both relatively neglected and highly controverted. It is neglected in comparison with research into First Corinthians. It is controverted as regards the integrity of the letter. Originally, my own investigations led me to look at all of Second Corinthians, but when the amount of work envisaged became clear, it became likewise obvious that such an enterprise would be well beyond the limits of a single monograph. The 'amount of work envisaged' means the approach adopted here using detailed delimitation, identification of all figures and rhetorical analysis, leading to a rhetorical synthesis and finally an engagement of the broader discussions. During a four-month stay in Jerusalem, it was decided to confine the study to chapters 8 and 9 of Second Corinthians, intended as a *sounding* in Pauline persuasion.

In recent years, scholars have turned to rhetoric to help deepen our understanding of the world of the biblical text. Two difficulties have to be faced by anyone employing rhetoric: the first is the general question of the applicability of the canons of rhetoric to these texts; the second is the particular question of a methodology.

The first Chapter of the present book discusses the applicability, use and abuse of rhetorical categories to texts of St Paul. It takes into account the various objections raised against rhetorical criticism and at the end proposes a methodology. This methodology involves two steps. The first is a delimitation of the text according to modern literary criteria, against which any rhetorical division of the material is to be tested. The second step involves using the stages proposed by the rhetorical manuals for the construction of a speech in reverse order, beginning that is with the end product, with the final artefact, and working backwards to see how the rhetorical analysis can lay bare the persuasive strategies of the writer.

Before putting this methodology into practice, it will be necessary necessary to review the history of rhetorical readings of 2 Corinthians

8–9. The writers in question are John Chrysostom, C.G. Heinrici, H.D. Betz, F. Young and D. Ford (joint authors), F.W. Danker and Ben Witherington III. H.D. Betz is the most influential of these writers and a full comparison of his work with this research is postponed until the final Chapter. Chapter 2 concludes with a schematic outline of the rhetorical *dispositiones* according to the authors discussed.

Chapter 3 undertakes the task of delimitation, and at the end of the Chapter, units of discourse are suggested, subject to confirmation from a rhetorical point of view. This chapter, however, discusses not just delimitation, but also takes into account the cultural background of the vocabulary (especially that of benefaction) which is so significant for what Paul wishes to achieve in chapters 8 and 9.

The rhetorical analysis proper is undertaken in Chapters 4 and 5. Chapter 4 employs the three stages for the construction of a speech in reverse order, that is, firstly, examining the surface of the text for figures of speech and figures of thought (*elocutio* or style*).* Following on the *elocutio*, the next step is to examine the *dispositio* (structure) and, only then, the *inventio* (the arguments discovered). Chapter 5 follows through directly from Chapter 4 and is a rhetorical exposition of 2 Corinthians 8–9, in an attempt to relate the various observations touching style, structure and content. The commentary is intended as a close reading of the text, with a view to laying bare the persuasion and strategy of Paul.

Chapter 6 takes this close rhetorical reading back into the wider world of Pauline scholarship. The first part offers a comparison between the results of this thesis and the rhetorical analysis of H.D. Betz. The second part comments on Paul's education and holds that—if his skill in rhetoric is a sound indicator—he enjoyed a solid, relatively extensive, Hellenistic education.

This study grew from an interest in rhetoric first awakened by Professor Jean-Noël Aletti SJ of the Pontifical Biblical Institute, Rome. To him a debt of gratitude is owed for his help and patience in guiding my first stumbling steps in rhetorical analysis, made in 1990. In 1995, some time was spent at the École Biblique in Jerusalem. There I took part in a seminar on classical rhetoric conducted by Professor Paolo Garuti OP. Without his rich insight into rhetoric, both classical and modern, shared during the weekly seminar in the autumn and winter of 1995, this book would have been a far poorer affair. My thanks in particular go to my confrère Fr J.F.M. Smit OSA, from Utrecht in The Netherlands, who read the work with great care and precision and made many useful suggestions and observations. It was very beneficial to hear the comments of such an expert in Pauline rhetoric. This study is the adapted version of a thesis submitted to the University of Dublin under the supervision of Professor Séan Freyne.

It is a pleasure to acknowledge the generous support of my friends and colleagues and in particular that of Séan Goan LSS and Dr Carmel McCarthy, who kindly and thoroughly proofread the manuscript. Likewise, I thank most sincerely Tina D. Nilsen of the Milltown Institute of Theology and Philosophy, who painstakingly checked all the Scripture references and greatly improved the accuracy of the text. All the remaining inaccuracies are my own responsibility.

The members of the Augustinian Order in Ireland, especially the leadership, have supported me unstintingly during my research. I am happy to acknowledge the active encouragement our former Provincial, Fr John Byrne OSA who freed me from my duties as province secretary to spend that semester in Jerusalem. Jerusalem was indeed a 'city of peace' for me and I have the happiest memories of my time there, especially of the warm hospitality of the academic community of the École Biblique.

I dedicate this book to my parents.

Kieran J. O'Mahony OSA

ABBREVIATIONS

| | |
|---|---|
| *ABD* | David Noel Freedman (ed.), *The Anchor Bible Dictionary* (New York: Doubleday, 1992) |
| BAGD | Walter Bauer, William F. Arndt, F. William Gingrich and Frederick W. Danker, *A Greek–English Lexicon of the New Testament and Other Early Christian Literature* (Chicago: University of Chicago Press, 2nd edn, 1958) |
| BDF | F. Blass, E. Debrunner and R.W. Funk, *A Greek Grammar of the New Testament and Other Early Christian Literature* (Cambridge: Cambridge University Press, 1961) |
| *DIB* | R.J. Coggins and J.L. Houlden (eds), *A Dictionary of Biblical Interpretation* (London: SCM Press, 1990) |
| *EDNT* | H. Balz and G. Schneider (eds.), *Exegetical Dictionary of the New Testament* (3 vols.; Grand Rapids: Eerdmans, 1990) |
| *EEC* | A. Di Berardino (ed.), *Encyclopedia of the Early Church* (2 vols.; Cambridge: James Clarke & Co, 1992) |
| *GELNTSD* | J.P. Louw and E.P. Nida (eds.), *Greek–English Lexicon of the New Testament according to Semantic Domains* (2 vols.; New York: United Bible Societies, 1989) |
| ICC | International Critical Commentary |
| *JBL* | *Journal of Biblical Literature* |
| KJV | King James Version |
| NAB | New American Bible |
| NIV | New International Version |
| NJB | *New Jerusalem Bible* |
| *NJBC* | R.E. Brown, J.A. Fitzmyer and R.E. Murphy (eds.), *New Jerome Biblical Commentary* (Englewood Cliffs: Prentice Hall, 1990) |
| *NovT* | *Novum Testamentum* |
| NPNF | Nicene and Post-Nicene Fathers |
| NRSV | New Revised Standard Version |
| *NTS* | *New Testament Studies* |
| REB | Revised English Bible |
| SBL | Society of Biblical Literature |
| SBS | Stuttgarter Bibelstudien |

*TDNT*                Gerhard Kittel and Gerhard Friedrich (eds.), *Theological Dictionary of the New Testament* (trans. Geoffrey W. Bromiley; 10 vols.; Grand Rapids: Eerdmans, 1964–)

*ZNW*                *Zeitschrift für die neutestamentliche Wissenschaft*

Chapter 1

INTRODUCTION AND METHODOLOGY

> The order of ideas is emotional rather than logical; a subject is not taken
> up, dealt with, and disposed of, but, like some strain in a piece of impas-
> sioned music, occurs, is lost in a maze of crowding harmonies, and recurs
> again and again.
>
> A. Robertson (quoted in Hastings 1898: I, 497a)

In the course of the last hundred years, the context in which to study the figure of St Paul has undergone a sea change. Early in the century, scholars emphasized the Hellenistic inheritance of Paul, exemplified in the works of Bultmann and the history of religions school. More recent-ly, however, the Jewishness of the apostle has been rediscovered and recovered, especially in the light of the work of E.P. Sanders (1977). Indeed, it has become clear that one cultural context is simply too nar-row to comprehend, not to say exhaust, the founding theologian of Christianity. He inhabited several 'worlds', not only the Jewish and Hellenistic worlds, but also the emerging world of the Christian faith.[1] The complex of issues raised by the question of appropriate interpret-ative context touches problem areas in New Testament studies which include (a) the Paul and the Law discussion; (b) the *extent* to which Paul was influenced directly and indirectly by the Graeco-Roman world; (c) the difficult question of normative Judaism and the Judaisms of antiquity; and (d) the interpenetration of Judaism and Hellenism (Lemmer 1996: 161-62). Within these broad discussions, the question of Paul's use of Hellenistic rhetoric arises: the origin, extent and use of

1.    Though he himself would not have seen Christianity as an off-shoot of Jud-aism, but rather, its full realization (see Ziesler 1990: 69). 'This is why in becoming a Christian, Paul did not think he was converted from Judaism—he never left it—but was rather converted to being a true Israelite and a true child of Abraham (it was probably not until after the Jewish war of 66–70 that Christians began to see themselves as outside Israel).'

Hellenistic rhetoric in his writings. The related question of rabbinic rhetoric cannot be ignored, but it is difficult precisely because the sources are late and because, unlike Classical and Hellenistic rhetoric, rabbinic rhetoric appears to have generated very little theoretical formulation (Lemmer 1996: 166).

In terms of the context in which to read Paul, the purpose of the present study is to investigate the potential of Hellenistic rhetoric for our understanding of Pauline persuasion, using as a test case 2 Corinthians 8–9.[2] The study is about 'how' Paul argues. By rhetorical analysis I intend the use of classical rhetorical texts and handbooks for the purpose of examining the world of the text of Paul in a historical frame. We are fortunate that, just as in architecture we have Vetruvius to help in understanding the remains of classical buildings, in rhetoric we have the rhetorical manuals for understanding extant remains of the spoken and written word. The goal of the thesis is, then, to cast an eye, metaphorically, over the 'edifice' which is a Pauline text and, so to speak, to discover not only where the eye is carried by the lines of the building and arrested by the embellishments, but to go on to imagine the architectural outline and even the foundations of the whole persuasive construct, not normally immediately apparent.

Our rhetorical analysis does not pretend to be a commentary on 2 Corinthians 8–9, but rather the propedeutic to, or foundation for, a commentary. The goal is to investigate the means of persuasion (the 'how' question), with a view to a clearer idea of the content (the 'what' question). Content can be presented in a variety of ways and the chosen mode of presentation can be revealing with regard to what the speaker/writer wishes to emphasize, and how she or he understands both the audience and the audience's attitude towards the speaker/writer. While bearing in mind that the distinction of 'how' and 'what' is itself artificial, nevertheless, the emphasis here will be on the 'how', to lay bare the persuasive strategies of Paul. The use of classical rhetoric has the potential for unravelling the argumentative sequence and gauging persuasive power of a text in order simply to make the often foreign sequence of thought more comprehensible.

In spite of the more recent tendency in Pauline studies—which has been to valorize his Jewish background—and even his substantial con-

---

2.   For a very brief account of the reasons for the revival of rhetoric, see Wuellner 1995.

tinuity with Jewish religion,[3] there are scholars who still situate Paul firmly within the Greek milieu, not only from the point of view of language, but also of ideas and even philosophy.[4] This is a question which is not without significance for the analysis here, and, in the last chapter this important question of appropriate cultural context will be taken up.

This introductory chapter sets out to review first of all the appropriateness of using rhetoric to read Paul and second to propose a specific methodology.

## 1. *The Appropriateness of Rhetorical Analysis*

People understand different things by rhetorical analysis.[5] Rhetoric as such can be ancient or modern, historical or universalist, Hellenistic or

---

3.    Ziesler 1990: 9-23. The Reformation optic on the antithesis faith-works (based, it seems, on a misreading of Palestinian Judaism in the light of late medieval Catholicism) has been shown to falsify Paul's understanding of that antithesis.

4.    An example would be A.J. Malherbe 1989. Malherbe is firmly within the long German tradition of using classical studies to appreciate Paul.

5.    Muilenburg 1969 is often regarded as the start of the current interest in rhetoric in biblical studies. Cohen 1994 provides a useful overview of the current interest in classical rhetoric. On p. 69, he writes: 'The past three decades have witnessed a remarkable resurgence of interest in rhetorical theory. This interest has, however, taken a number of distinct forms. Some theorists, for example, have sought to extend traditional understanding of rhetoric as a methodology for the study of argument. On the other hand, others have paid little heed to rhetoric's historical parameters as they have reconceptualised rhetoric as the analysis of fictional narrative. Still others have attempted to overcome the ancient antagonism between philosophy and rhetoric by construing rhetoric as the framework for a philosophy of discourse. Finally, in recent years post-modernist thinkers have turned to rhetoric precisely because of its repudiation of philosophical conceptions of knowledge and truth'. Cf. also Anderson: 'It ought to be noticed, however, that what is termed "rhetorical criticism" by New Testament scholars today, is slightly different from what Muilenburg himself envisaged. Muilenburg saw rhetorical criticism as a form of literary criticism that dealt with stylistics, whilst New Testament scholars, as we shall see, have tended to emphasises rhetoric in terms of argumentation' (1966: 19). Cf. Anderson 1996: 23: 'But rhetorical criticism seems to have concentrated not on the historical discipline of evaluating New Testament argumentation within its own time framework, but on evaluating it for ourselves today. Of course we no longer have access to the original audiences of the New Testament documents, so it is impossible to survey their reactions. Yet modern evaluation is quite possible. The only problem here is that modern evaluation all too frequently uses modern canons of acceptability determined by modern philosophy.'

rabbinic. Rhetorical analysis itself can be primarily historical or primarily literary.[6] A choice has to be made between using rhetoric as a general literary approach employing both ancient and modern theory and using rhetoric as a tool of historical investigation. For this study, rhetorical criticism is taken to belong fundamentally to the historical critical method, in other words, using the literary and rhetorical conventions *of the time* to unravel the persuasive strategies and structures of a text. This is not to deny the usefulness of modern rhetorical theory,[7] which is very rich: it is simply to distinguish the methodologies.[8] Although understood here to be part of the historical critical method, a rhetorical reading can lead to results which challenge or support diachronic readings.[9] Because of the possible variety of approaches and results, the use of classical rhetoric in New Testament studies has not gone unchallenged. Before presenting in detail the methodology proposed for this research, it is necessary first of all to attend to these challenges.

 

    6.    Classen 1991: 2-3 in an *apparent* concession writes: 'Die Frage, ob die Kategorien der antiken Rhetorik sinnvoll zur Erklärung der Paulus-Briefe herangezogen werden können, gibt Anlaß zu einer grundlegenden Feststellung: Das Instrumentarium der griechisch-römischen Rhetorik kann mit Gewinn zur Analyse jedes geschriebenen oder gesprochenen Textes verwendet werden'.

    7.    For example, Group μ 1981.

    8.    Anderson 1996: 171: 'It is unfortunately a rather extreme example of disturbing trends in recent rhetorical studies, namely, the confusion of ancient and modern rhetorical theory, and the misuse or misunderstanding of ancient terminology and texts' (this is a point he makes several times in his very useful survey).

    9.    Dozeman 1992 alludes to this issue, while claiming that the disciples of Muilenburg have abandoned the diachronic aspect, which Muilenburg himself did not wish to abandon. Cf. Betz's comment in Betz 1992: 718a: 'The rhetorical criticism based on the principles of classical rhetoric has a historical perspective and thus directly complements traditional historical criticism.' Cf. Anderson 1996: 27. 'Such a historically conditioned application of ancient rhetorical theory would indeed be a valid and significant contribution to biblical studies. Does ancient rhetoric supply us with specific forms, patterns of argumentation, and proofs that show up in the New Testament and therefore help us understand its rhetoric in its own historical setting? This to my mind is the question that application of ancient rhetoric should answer, and it is precisely this question that a universal rhetoric cannot be expected to satisfy. Despite the fact that all societies to some extent engage in "rhetoric", use metaphors, similes, etc., our interest here must be not in these general phenomena themselves, but in the specific ways in which they are used and applied in ancient rhetoric.'

Not everybody agrees that the application of classical rhetoric is helpful and the use of rhetoric has been challenged both generally and specifically. In a trenchant and well-researched article, C.J. Classen lays down a challenge before those who would employ this approach.[10] In the course of his objections, he makes the following points.

1.    The use of rhetoric is *not* new; on the contrary it is part of a long tradition, ignored, apparently, by contemporary users of the method.

---

10.  Classen 1991: 6-7. It should be said that the article is chiefly a negative evaluation of the work of H.D. Betz on Galatians (Betz 1979), a work widely criticized elsewhere, including by those who do not doubt the value of rhetoric as a tool. The article concludes with an equally demanding programme for those who would use classical rhetoric, which I report here in full because of its importance. '1. Wer Paulus' Briefe im Licht der griechisch-römischen Rhetorik liest und feststellt, daß der Apostel zahlreiche Regeln der Theorie beachtet, sollte nicht vergessen, daß a) gerade die *dissimulatio artis* zu den zentralen Forderungen der Theorie an jeden Praktiker gehört, die Forderung also, die Beachtung der *praecepta* nicht spürbar werden zu lassen, so daß die deutlich erkennbare Verwendung der Regeln als Zeichen mangelnder Erfahrung oder Fähigkeit wirken muß, jedenfalls im Bereich der *dispositio* und *locutio*; b) das viele Autoren im Einklang mit den Ratschlägen der Theorie schreiben oder reden, ohne sie zu kennen (wie denn die Praxis älter ist als die Theorie), und daß ohnehin nicht zu bezweifeln ist, das "Paul of Tarsus, the young Pharisee, developed his masterly rhetorical style, in which rabbinic exegesis and popular philosophy accompany an apocalyptic view of the world". 2. Wer Paulus' Briefe—oder auch andere Teile der Bibel—mit Hilfe der Kategorien der antiken Rhetorik und der antiken Epistolographie zu verstehen und zu interpretieren sucht, wird sich zunächst mit Gewinn deutlich machen, wie pagane Autoren die Regeln der Theorie beim Abfassen von Reden oder Briefen oder anderen Gattungen handhaben (nämlich mit um so größerer Selbständigkeit, je begabter und erfahrener sie sind), und er wird sich für die Exegese die antiken Erklärer oder Melanchthon zum Vorbild nehmen, d.h. wer wird sich einerseits auf diejenigen Vorschriften und Ratschläge beschränken, die sich ohne weiteres auf die in der Bibel vorkommenden literarischen Genera anwenden lassen, also vor allem die Regeln zur *inventio* und zur *elocutio*, während er sich zur *dispositio* daran erinnern wird, daß die Theorie zwei Arten unterscheidet: *unum ab institutione artis profectum, alterum ad casum temporis adcommodatum* (RhetHer 3, 16), also nicht einmal für alle Reden nur eine Struktur empfohlen wird, und er wird weiter bedenken, daß für Briefe besondere Empfehlungen überliefert sind; andererseits wird er sich nicht auf die antike Rhetorik und die humanistische Exegese beschränken, sondern einbeziehen, was seither an theoretischen Überlegungen angestellt und an Erkenntnissen gewonnen worden ist' (Classen 1991: 31-32).

2.  The categories of classical rhetoric can be used to read any text or speech. The later tradition developed and improved on the classical insights.
3.  There is no good reason to use only classical rhetorical categories to read texts of St Paul, although Paul does have access through his knowledge of Greek to literary work shaped by rhetoric.
4.  Letters are a special form of communication and even within that form there are different kinds of letters.
5.  Letter-writing was not part of ancient rhetoric. Indications of good style in letter-writing have nothing to do with the production of speeches.
6.  Letter-writing is a distinct area of study, with a great variety in form, structure and tone. Anyone who wants to interpret letters needs to be familiar with such epistolary traditions.

One might further ask:

1.  Can letters, almost unnoticed in the handbooks on rhetoric, be properly analysed using approaches designed for speech?
2.  Were the texts intended as rhetorical?
3.  Does Paul's rejection of 'fair speech' preclude an analysis using an approach he himself eschewed?
4.  Did Paul receive a rhetorical training?
5.  Finally, do the problems surrounding the redaction history of 2 Corinthians make such an undertaking not only dubious, but impossible?

The objections in Classen's list do not all have the same force. For example, the first one—ignoring the use of rhetorical categories in the exegetical tradition—can be met by attending to the exegetical tradition which has actually used classical rhetoric, for instance in the work of C.F. Georg Heinrici in the last century or in the commentaries of John Chrysostom in the patristic period. The second objection is that (a) ancient rhetorical theory may be used for any text and (b) later rhetorical theory improved on the earlier. The first part is a two-edged sword—if any text, then also Paul! The second part is largely true, but that hardly hinders us from using the theory available at the time, if this can be established on historical grounds, in order to make a historical analysis. In fact, Anderson in his excellent study *Ancient Rhetorical Theory and Paul* is at pains *not* to confuse ancient and modern rhetoric, or even classical, Hellenistic and Byzantine rhetoric, precisely for the sake of historical clarity. The third objection (confining analysis to rhetoric) must of course be conceded: there is no reason at all to say that rhetoric is the only route. That still allows a place for the specific use of ancient rhetoric within a historical frame. The fourth and fifth objections (to do with the theory of letter-writing) are substantial and I deal with them separately below. The sixth objection is also substantial—but I hope to show that 2 Corinthians 8–9, like 1 Corinthians 15, is very much like a speech which Paul must often have given, albeit adapted to the particular circumstances of the Corinthian audience. Classen's interrogation of the use of rhetoric helps to establish part of the agenda of the present research. Chapter 2 attempts to synthesize the work of those who have used the categories of classical rhetoric. For the moment, we return to the question of letters and speeches.

### 1.1. *Letters and Speeches*
It is clear that the rhetorical handbooks were there to help people construct speeches, not analyse them.[11] It seems an unwarranted extrapolation to use techniques designed for the *creation* of *speeches* for the *analysis* of *letters*.[12] Furthermore, the methodology of using rhetorical

---

11. A *caveat* registered by Anderson 1996: 256. 'One important caution ought to be borne in mind. Rhetorical theory was designed to help men *write* speeches, not, in the first place, to analyse them. We need, therefore, to be careful in applying such theory retrogressively for the purposes of analysis. Many of the theorists themselves admitted that practice was often removed from theory. This consideration should highlight the need for a certain sobriety in our analysis, and also the need to couple our use of rhetorical theory with knowledge of contemporary rhetorical practice. But this does not mean that rhetorical theory ought to be ignored, not even for the purposes of considering the letters of the apostle Paul. If the reader has gained any insight from our rhetorical analysis of the letters to the Galatians and Romans, then the effort will not have been in vain.'

12. Reed 1992: 299-300: 'The ancient epistolary genre allowed the individual to handle a variety of situations with a variety of types of letters. Therefore, it is no surprise to find types of letters which parallel the three subgenres of rhetoric. Such parallels do not prove, however, a direct borrowing from rhetorical categories. Rather, the similarities are probably due to common communicative practices in the culture. In other words, argumentation is universal as well as culture-specific, that is, developing from the beliefs and behaviors of individual societies. Groups within the society (lawyers, for example) may have adapted common rhetorical practices to their unique needs, but on the broader schema, judicial, deliberative, and epi-deictic "types" of rhetoric, including the letter, would have been used in various

categories is not always without limitations. J. Murphy-O'Connor, who otherwise thinks Paul a brilliant rhetor (both in his book on Paul the letter-writer and in his recent biography of the apostle) warns us against the rigid use of the rhetorical arrangements of texts, because the manuals themselves recommend flexibility and, in any case, Paul's purpose was not the creation of perfect rhetorical specimens. And he specifically warns against a particular abuse of the rhetorical schema:

> Refusal to acknowledge the truth of what Quintilian said...has led to the use of the rhetorical schema for an end for which it was never intended, namely, to demonstrate the limits of a literary unity with a view to establishing its original independence (Murphy-O'Connor 1995: 79).[13]

These are serious *caveats* against the use of rhetorical theory and, as is well known, each point opens on to a vast research literature. To present a thorough response to each area would take us into several monographs. For our purposes, it must suffice to show that (a) our methodology is designed precisely to avoid the arbitrary misuse of ancient rhetoric and (b) it is possible to meet the substantial objections listed by Classen and others and to establish the possibility and usefulness of ancient rhetoric in analysis of Paul.

Can *letters* be analysed as *speeches*?[14] The evidence here is complex and the scholarly literature on ancient epistolography is extensive.[15] The main objection to using rhetoric for reading letters is that the handbooks on rhetoric did not include a treatment of letters until the fourth century with Julius Victor[16] and, therefore, rhetorical theory is irrele-

Graeco-Roman contexts. But what exactly do the theorists and the letter writers say about the rhetorical types as they pertain to letters?' Reed 1992: 301: 'Since the epistolary theorists did not systematize a purely rhetorical typology of letters, the reasonable conclusion can be drawn that Paul probably did not.'

13. Quintilian writes: 'If the whole of rhetoric could be thus embodied in one compact code, it would be an easy task of little compass: but most rules are liable to be altered by the nature of the case, circumstances of time and place, and by hard necessity itself. Consequently, the all-important gift for an orator is a wise adaptability since he is called upon to meet the most varied emergencies' (2.13.2).

14. Cf. Classen 1991: 13: 'Zunächst sind Rhetorik und Epistolographie nach antiken Verständnis zwei verschiedene Dinge, die Betz nicht so klar trennt, wie es notwendig ist.'

15. For a general overview and basic bibliography see *ABD* 4: 282-93 under 'Letters'.

16. Even a cursory glance at modern manuals of rhetoric such as Lausberg or Mortara Garavelli shows the paucity of treatment—the later has no entry under

vant to the study of Paul's *letters.* One might add according to epistolary theory letters should be short, whereas Paul's are generally much
longer than classical examples.[17]

The question of length can be treated first. Paul's letters formally
resemble Hellenistic letters.[18] However, by convention letters were
brief and it was conventionally conceded that there were some matters
unsuitable for letter writing. But Paul's letters *are* long and conventional epistolary theory is limited in its use for these texts.[19]

'letters' and the former has three negligible references. Malherbe 1988: 3 writes,
'The first rhetorician to discuss the subject as part of the *ars rhetorica* was Julius
Victor (fourth century). At the end of his handbook he adds two appendices, *de
sermocinatione* and *de epistulis*, in which he uses material from traditional rhetorical instruction. While epistolary style is here, then, part of a rhetorical system, it can
nevertheless be argued that its relegation to an appendix shows that it does not
properly belong in a discussion of rhetoric.'

17.  Anderson 1996: 97 notes, 'Whilst this fact appears to bring Paul close to
"literary" letters, yet at the same time it shows that Paul thereby flaunted one of the
cardinal literary rules for writing letters, namely, that letters should be brief (cf.
Isoc. *Ep.* 2.13; Demetr. *Eloc.* 228; [Lib.] *Ep. Char* 50)—a rule closely followed, for
example by Pliny (cf. *Ep.* 2.5.13; 2.11.25).'

18.  Not only in formal structure, but in the commonplaces. Bailey and Vander
Broek 1992: 25  comment 'As one might expect in communication between two
parties, Paul's letters contain several themes or topics common in Hellenistic
letters: the health of the sender or recipient (2 Cor. 1.8-11; Phil. 2.15-30; Eph. 6.21-
22), business matters (2 Cor. 8, 9; Phil. 4.14-18), and talk of a future visit (Rom.
15.14-33; 1 Cor. 4.14-18; 16.1-11; Gal. 4.20; Phil. 2.19-30; 1 Thess. 2.17-3:13)'.

19.  Aune 1988: 160: 'Yet while nearly all the papyrus letters are relatively brief,
many early Christian letters are quite lengthy. Their very length suggests a
comparison with the longer literary and official letters of antiquity preserved in
epistolary collections, embedded in literary narratives or inscribed on stone.' Doty
1973: 5, makes a similar point: 'In many cases these types (*scil.* of letters in
epistolary theory) are of little direct relevance to the study of primitive Christian
letters, since they are representative of more commercially and politically oriented
situations than those found in the earliest Christian letters. Precisely for contrast and
context, however, they are worth our attention'. See also Aune 1988: 160-61:
'Earlier Graeco-Roman rhetorical handbooks have little to say about the art of letter
writing. The two most important treatments of epistolary theory are *On Style* 4.223-
235 (c. first century BC), incorrectly ascribed to Demetrius of Phalerum, and
*Epistolary Styles* (fourth to sixth centuries AD), erroneously ascribed to Proclus or
Libanius. Cicero's familiarity with Greek epistolary theory indicates that handbooks on epistolography were circulating during the first century BC. Also important is Pseudo-Demetrius' *Epistolary Types* (first century BC or later), and an

Furthermore, there were in antiquity letters which were in reality speeches.[20] It is sufficient to establish in antiquity the possibility that some letters were really speeches to leave open the question of rhetoric as a tool for analysing the Pauline corpus. Letters were considered a substitute for presence (παρουσία). It is clear that Paul's presence and entire apostolic role is precisely as preacher, and it follows that if his letters are a substitute for his usual mode of παρουσία, then it is not surprising that, in part, they would have sometimes resembled speeches.[21] We may add further that the education of the time included not only rhetoric but also letter-writing, which even without the theoretical connection, must have influenced each other.[22] The later episto-

appendix entitled "On Letter Writing" in the *Rhetorical Arts* of Julius Victor (fourth century AD)'.

20. Anderson 1996: 105: 'There are, however, certain letters from antiquity which may profitably be analysed in terms of a rhetorical *speech*. J.A. Goldstein has shown, for example, that the first four letters of Demosthenes, written in exile to the assembly in Athens, are effectively deliberative speeches. Demosthenes states that were he present he would address the Athenians himself, but because of his situation he must write his thoughts in a letter, *Ep.* 3.35: ταῦτα δ', εἰ μὲν παρῆν, λέγων ἂν ὑμᾶς ἐδίδακσον· ἐπειδὴ δ' ἐν τοιούτοις εἰμί, ...γράψας ἐπέσταλκα. What is important is the fact that the letters he wrote are structured using rhetorical methodology. Demosthenes *might* just as easily have made the same points in a more informal and epistolographical way. He didn't.'

21. 2 Cor. 10.10; Phil. 2.12.

22. 'It is more likely that the handbooks were used in the training of professional letter writers. Their occupations required them to be familiar with other official and rhetorical styles, and the comparative similarity that does exist in their letters suggests that they had received instruction in the subject. The criticism by Philostratus of Lemnos of [*scil.* by] Aspasius, when compared with other theorists, further shows the degree to which the observance of rhetorical niceties was expected of them. It is natural to assume that such instruction of these professional writers as did exist took place under teachers of rhetoric' (Malherbe 1988: 7). Malherbe is supported in this by Aune 1988: 158: 'First, oratory was very important in the Graeco-Roman world and rhetoric occupied a central role in ancient education. Though primarily connected with oral delivery, rhetoric had a profound effect on all genres of literature including letters. A knowledge of ancient rhetorical theory, therefore, can contribute to understanding letters written by ancients (like Paul and Ignatius) who had more than a basic education.' Malherbe 1988: 2 also notes, 'That century also saw the work of Cicero, who occupies pride of place among Roman letter writers, most of whom were orators. By the time of Cicero Greek grammar and rhetoric had already left their imprint on Rome. The Greek private letter had assumed a definite form and presumably had attracted the attention of the rhetor-

lary handbooks on the other hand do, in fact, make explicit the connection (Stowers 1992: 291). Paul, *pace* Deissmann, was not writing private letters, but letters to communities to be read as though he himself were present and speaking.[23]

But again, we have to be careful not to impose a rigid form[24] or a rigid rhetorical classification (Anderson 1996: 109). Nevertheless, Duane Watson writes perceptively and gives a balanced statement of the situation when everything is considered:

> If Paul's epistles were to be read in the churches, a logical assumption is that they were fashioned in a way closely akin to a speech. It is conceded that since the body of the ancient letter was dictated by the needs of the author, one cannot rule out the use of rhetorical theory here. Paul, needing to communicate over vast distances has a rhetorical need to be persuasive and has used rhetorical theory in his letter body (Watson and Hauser 1994: 125).

Paul's letters reflect particular situations, but are not limited to that.[25] Occasionally, we see Paul using material in a letter which must have featured, perhaps in some other form, in his preaching; an example would be 1 Corinthians 15. Paul must often have had to speak of Resurrection to all sorts of groups, both believing and unbelieving. A frequent oral rehearsal of such arguments, in different settings, would help account for the fluent and structured argument detectable in 1 Corinthians 15 (Bünker 1984; Mitchell 1991). For our purposes, in dealing

icians. In any case, what is significant is that Greek and Latin epistolography are of a piece, and that the latter bears testimony to the development of epistolary theory.'

23. 'Having overcome Deissmann's restriction of the Pauline letters to private letters, we must not, of course, simply revert to the previous position which treated them primarily as dogmatic essays. Subsequent scholarship has reached something of a balance between treating Paul's letters as purely occasional, contextual writings, directed only to specific situations, and as attempts to express a Christian understanding of life which had ramifications for theological expression beyond the particular historical situation' (Doty 1973: 26). 'The letter is therefore a substitute for oral communication and could function in almost as many ways as speech' (Aune 1988: 158).

24. Likewise observed by Classen 1991: 23. 'Offensichtlich sieht Melanchthon die Möglichkeiten ebenso wie die Grenzen der Regeln und Vorschriften der Theorie. Sie können nützlich sein, sind aber auf ihre Brauchbarkeit zu überprüfen und flexibel anzuwenden'.

25. The large topic of Paul's contingency and coherence, a debate outside the concerns of this study, is touched on here.

with 2 Corinthians 8–9, it helps to remember that the collection was a major project of Paul's career and it is not difficult to imagine that, again in this case, he must have frequently stood before Christian communities and argued the case for subscribing to this project. Again, this would account for the general arguments from the example of Christ and from the promise of future reward. Undoubtedly his careful avoidance of handling the money himself was regularly part of his appeal, as he is elsewhere keen to keep clear of money issues. Such a *Sitz im Leben* for our text in the ministry of Paul before he writes at all would help account for the force and clarity of so succinct an argument as 2 Corinthians 8–9. The challenge remains, however, to show that Paul uses not only figures of speech and thought,[26] which occur in all literary cultures, but also the arrangement (*dispositio*[27]) and genre[28] of ancient rhetorical theory and, furthermore, to go on to show that these help us in our study of his texts. Beyond the ambitions of this thesis, one could go on to show that rhetoric accounts for sustained arguments over entire letters and this has been attempted, notably in regard to 1 Thessalonians (Johanson 1987), 1 Corinthians (Mitchell 1991; Pascuzzi 1997), Galatians (Betz 1979; Pitta 1992), and Romans (Aletti 1991; Elliott 1990).

## 1.2. *Intention and Rhetoric*

The document of the Pontifical Biblical Commission, entitled 'The Interpretation of the Bible in the Church', undertakes a wide-ranging review of exegetical methods. In the section on rhetoric, it points out that the risk of such analysis is a concern for mere style or aesthetics. Such a purely formal or aesthetic analysis would prescind from the controverted issues, theological or practical, which constitute the purpose and substance of the text.[29] The point is clear: a literary analysis may be

---

26.　The figures are such phenomena as metaphor and antithesis.

27.　*Dispositio* refers to the arrangement of the stages of a speech. Classically, these were: the Introduction (or *exordium*), the Statement of Facts (or *narratio*), the Proof (*probatio*) and the Conclusion (or *peroratio*).

28.　Classical rhetorical theory considered three kinds of speeches: forensic or legal, epideictic or celebratory and deliberative or political.

29.　*The Interpretation of the Bible in the Church* (Québec: Editions Paulines, 1994). See Part I, subsection B, subsection 1 (pp. 41-44). Classen 1991: 22 makes a similar observation when discussing Melanchthon: 'Es ist müßig darüber zu spekulieren, wie weit Melanchthon auch die voraufgehenden Kapitel als Teile eines Briefes oder einer Rede verstanden und gedeutet wissen will; fraglos interessiert ihn

accurate in so far as it goes, but may overlook or fail to deal with the subject matter of the text. The warning is an invitation to spell out the consequences of a rhetorical reading for understanding the text, both ʿ historically and theologically. The intention in this thesis is to consider those consequences after the completion of the rhetorical analysis.[30]

The document also stresses the importance of asking 'are the texts rhetorical in intention?', a question not remote from the concerns of this book.[31] What is meant by this question? It touches on the very controverted issue of authorial intention. In the course of the twentieth century, the New Criticism reacted sharply against the concern of the literary criticism of the day with discovering the author's intention or his/her psychological state at the time of writing (Freund 1987: 23-65; Cuddon 1991: 452). This 'unease' is synthesized by R. Wellek and A. Warren, when they write:

> The whole idea that the 'intention' of the author is the proper subject of literary history seems, however, quite mistaken. The meaning of a work of art is not exhausted by, or even equivalent to, its intention. As a system of values, it leads an independent life. The total meaning of a work of art cannot be defined merely in terms of its meaning for the author and his contemporaries. It is rather the result of a process of accretion, i.e. the history of its criticism by its many readers in many ages... It is simply not possible to stop being men of the twentieth century while we engage in a judgement of the past: we cannot forget the associations of our own language, the newly acquired attitudes, the impact and import of the last centuries (Wellek and Warren 1986: 41).[32]

nicht, ob Paulus seinem Brief eine *narratio* einfügt oder wo die *confirmatio* beginnt; ihm sind die Argumente wichtig, die der Apostel vorträgt, deren Anordnung, deren Ausgestaltung und die ergänzenden Überlegungen, vor allem die dadurch begründete Lehre'.

30. Cf. Chapters 5 and 6 in the present volume.

31. Anderson 1996: 125 is against the conscious use of rhetoric—a position which is consistent with his admission of possible influence but rejection of analysis by *dispositio* and genus. He writes: 'The application of rhetorical terminology to what Paul does in this letter (*scil.* Galatians) should *not necessarily* be taken to mean that Paul himself thought in these terms' (Emphasis mine).

32. Even when the author is available to give or has made known his 'intention' regarding a text, the same text may and inevitably does go on to generate more meaning, beyond the author's intention. The objectivity of the text has become an enduring legacy of the New Criticism—as may be seen in Palmer 1969: 146.

From the point of view of hermeneutics, it is not possible to reconstruct *completely* the meaning of a text at the time of its production. The obverse is also true: neither is it possible to limit the interpretation of a text to the meaning(s), for both author and readers, it bore at the time of production. Even when the author's intention is explicitly available, that intention cannot circumscribe or even freeze the meaning for evermore. Such considerations are especially pertinent for a text regarded as Scripture by believers because confining the reading to the concerns, questions and answers of the past is the equivalent of saying that the text can bear only the meaning it had at a particular historical moment. This is to exclude a contemporary relevance. Bearing all that in mind, however, the accretion of meanings which a text may bear cannot exclude the early reconstructed meaning(s) of the text. What a text meant in its original context, in so far as this can be reconstructed, remains an important moment in the capacity of the text to generate meaning and may act negatively as a control to exclude some interpretations as erroneous. In the interpretation of texts, one can distinguish the text, the author and the interpreter. Literary theory has, at different times, emphasized one of these, sometimes to the exclusion of the other. In particular, literary theory has relegated as irrelevant the author's intention. But, all data are significant, if not dominant, and the original intended import, is, in so far it can be retrieved, one moment in the discovery and recovery of the meaning of a text. To say that it is significant is not to say it is the dominant, still less the only possible meaning.

The question posed here ('are the texts rhetorical in intention?') is a variation on the theme of authorial intention. We are not yet asking what did the author mean by the text, but rather did the writer mean the text rhetorically, in other words, make conscious use of rhetoric?[33] The question 'are the texts rhetorical in intention?' can be answered if we show (a) that that it is possible, historically and culturally; (b) that the author shows second-level awareness of the power of words and (c) that the text may be investigated fruitfully using the techniques of rhetoric. We have to leave (c) to Chapters 4 and 5, that being the object of the study.

---

33. Even Anderson (1996: 109), so circumspect, allows the *influence* of rhetoric: 'But this does not mean that Paul's letters may not have been influenced by rhetorical methods of style and argumentation more generally. We have indicated above several factors that suggest this to be likely.'

In the case of Paul, the argument is somewhat circular. The texts can be rhetorical *in intention* only if Paul trained in rhetoric. We may think it likely Paul was trained in rhetoric only if the texts are evidence of that, and the texts are evidence of that if it can be shown that rhetoric, in the sense used in the manuals, helps to illuminate the text, by unveiling the persuasive stratagems and structures. We have increased probability the texts are *intended* rhetorically when a sufficient number of them yield to analysis using ancient rhetorical theory. Much current New Testament analysis seems to support this. But there is a specific problem here which arises in the case of Paul: he apparently rejects 'powerful speech'.

### 1.3. *Paul's Rejection of 'Fair Speech'*
Nobody denies that Paul is a powerful persuader—that is not yet to say he is a rhetor in the classical sense. He is aware of both the power and the limits of words (see 1 Thess. 1.5; 2.3-7; Gal. 1.10; 1 Cor. 1.17-25; 2.1, 4-5, 13; 3.1-2; 2 Cor. 1.17-18; 2.17; 4.2; 10.10; 11.6). In particular, three texts, singled out by Anderson (1996: 239) matter here:

*1 Cor. 1.17* οὐ γὰρ ἀπέστειλέν με Χριστὸς βαπτίζειν ἀλλὰ εὐαγγελίζεσθαι, οὐκ ἐν σοφίᾳ λόγου, ἵνα μὴ κενωθῇ ὁ σταυρὸς τοῦ Χριστοῦ.

*1 Cor. 1.17* For Christ did not send me to baptize but to proclaim the gospel, and not with eloquent wisdom, so that the cross of Christ might not be emptied of its power.

*1 Cor. 2.4* καὶ ὁ λόγος μου καὶ τὸ κήρυγμά μου οὐκ ἐν πειθοῖ[ς] σοφίας [λόγοις] ἀλλ᾽ ἐν ἀποδείξει πνεύματος καὶ δυνάμεως, 5 ἵνα ἡ πίστις ὑμῶν μὴ ᾖ ἐν σοφίᾳ ἀνθρώπων ἀλλ᾽ ἐν δυνάμει θεοῦ.

*1 Cor. 2.4* My speech and my proclamation were not with plausible words of wisdom, but with a demonstration of the Spirit and of power 5 so that your faith might rest not on human wisdom but on the power of God.

*1 Cor. 2.13* ἃ καὶ λαλοῦμεν οὐκ ἐν διδακτοῖς ἀνθρωπίνης σοφίας λόγοις ἀλλ᾽ ἐν διδακτοῖς πνεύματος, πνευματικοῖς πνευματικὰ συγκρίνοντες.

*1 Cor. 2.13* And we speak of these things in words not taught by human wisdom but taught by the Spirit, interpreting spiritual things to those who are spiritual.

Two other texts from 2 Corinthians are also relevant:

*2 Cor. 10.10* ὅτι αἱ ἐπιστολαὶ μέν, φησίν, βαρεῖαι καὶ ἰσχυραί, ἡ δὲ παρουσία τοῦ σώματος ἀσθενὴς καὶ ὁ λόγος ἐξουθενημένος.

*2 Cor. 10.10* For they say, 'His letters are weighty and strong, but his bodily presence is weak, and his speech contemptible'.

*2 Cor. 11.6* εἰ δὲ καὶ ἰδιώτης τῷ λόγῳ, ἀλλ᾽ οὐ τῇ γνώσει, ἀλλ᾽ ἐν παντὶ φανερώσαντες ἐν πᾶσιν εἰς ὑμᾶς.

*2 Cor. 11.6* I may be untrained in speech, but not in knowledge; certainly in every way and in all things we have made this evident to you.

These texts are sometimes taken to mean that Paul utterly rejected rhetoric. At the very least, we may say Paul is concerned with words and their use, showing an awareness of their capacity to persuade a reader or listener. But Paul shows not only an awareness of the power of words, but also considerable ability in wielding words as may be seen in 1 Corinthians 13 or 2 Corinthians 10–13. The apparent denial of rhetorical techniques could reflect the convention of modesty (*excusatio propter infirmitatem*) for the purposes of *captatio benevolentiae*. It could also simply mean that when it came to presenting a speech physically he was not excellent because he failed in the delivery (itself a focus of study in the manuals) and this may account for the contrast between his presence and his letters. It could reflect a desire to avoid debased rhetoric, the kind which can persuade you of anything, a kind of unprincipled manipulation by words. In all of this he is not so much rejecting rhetoric as rejecting a particular rhetoric, or rather an abuse of rhetoric. Against a total rejection of rhetoric as such we see not only his second-level (theoretical) awareness of the power of words but also his practical skills of persuasion. More, however, needs to be said.

In chapters 10–13 of 2 Corinthians, Paul is opposing a small group within the Corinthian community. He uses two techniques to meet the objections against him. In effect, he concedes that his presence as a speaker leaves much to be desired (2 Cor. 10.10), but he goes on to say that this does not matter when he makes a distinction between 'speech' and 'knowledge'. A certain *excusatio propter infirmitatem* is used disarmingly in order precisely to undermine the significance his opponents attribute to flowing eloquence. In this case his distinction between the medium and the message resembles the distinction available in *stasis* theory between the fact at issue and its '*qualitas*' (Kennedy 1994: 98-99). He makes use, in this case, of the kind of distinction which would have made particular sense to those who prize rhetoric. He uses rhetoric when facing rhetoricians much as he uses boasting when facing boasters, that is, while using both rhetoric and boasting at the same time he denies them any power or special significance. The power of his persuasion lies elsewhere.

The texts taken from 1 Corinthians are more substantial and need to be dealt with more carefully. There are three possibilities. Firstly, it is possible that he should be taken at his word and that here Paul simply and plainly rejects rhetoric outright. Many would say this is taking the obvious, unadorned meaning of the text. However, given that he uses rhetoric skilfully elsewhere as well as in those very chapters of 1 Corinthians 1–4, it is possible that the objection to rhetoric is not to skilful use of language as such, but rather a denial of *dependence* on the *power* of speech—his dependence lies elsewhere, in the powerlessness of the crucified Christ and in the spiritual conviction brought about by the spiritual gifts. Thirdly, it is possible that *at the time of his preaching* to the Corinthians he distinctly did not use techniques of rhetoric, for whatever reason, and it is this to which he now refers.

The first possibility is the traditional one. Plummer's great commentary at the beginning of the twentieth century may be taken as representative (Plummer 1911). His comments on our three texts here are instructive. On 1 Cor. 1.17 he tells us that 'preaching was St Paul's great work, but his aim was not that of the professional rhetorician'. (Plummer 1911: 15) Paul's words are directed against the conventional rhetorical standards by which a speaker was judged. The σοφία of 2.4 is understood to be 'the cleverness of the rhetorician' (Plummer 1911: 32) while in 2.13 it is taken to refer simply to 'man's wisdom' (46).[34]

In a similar tradition, Gordon Fee wonders whether Paul, in 1 Cor. 1.17 is rejecting both content (wisdom) and form (words) and, in his judgment, he thinks certainly the first and probably the second (Fee 1987: 63-66).

In his popular commentary on 1 Corinthians, Jerome Murphy-O'Connor (1979: 12, 22) reconstructs the contexts of Paul's first evangelization of the Corinthians as follows. Paul arrived in Corinth depressed; it is possible that his chronic illness, whatever it may have been, flared up again (2 Cor. 12.7), and he is aware that as a speaker he is not

---

34. Here Plummer notes that the construction with the genitive is found elsewhere in the New Testament. However, in classical Greek, the construction is found only among the poets, interestingly enough.

an impressive figure (2 Cor. 10.10). Rhetoric is rejected, not as such, but as a source or ground of persuasion. *At that time* Paul did not use the techniques and artifice of rhetoric to persuade the Corinthians, in order to let it be clearly seen that the basis for the conviction is not the form of words, but inner experience. All this would mean that the techniques of rhetoric were markedly absent during Paul's evangelization of the Corinthians. None of this would necessarily exclude the use of rhetoric in writing, especially when writing to those who are impressed by rhetoric. To show that you can use the same techniques without counting on them is a powerful way of relativizing the apparent oratorical success of your opponents. Effectively, it is a way of matching the verbal pyrotechnics, while emphatically denying a dependence on verbal manipulation.

In his 1990 doctoral thesis on the rhetorical situation of 1 Corinthians, Stephen Pogoloff discusses the relationship between the use of rhetoric (οὐκ ἐν σοφίᾳ λογου) and social status. He uses this to confront the paradox of Paul's artful use of rhetoric in those very passages where he rejects rhetoric. What is being rejected here is not only a dependence on rhetorical technique, but also the higher social status implied in such elevated language. He writes as follows:

> In Paul's narrative world, the normal cultural narratives of eloquence and status are radically reversed. What persuades is speech about what is ordinarily unfit for contemplation: not a life which is cultured, wise, and powerful, but one marked by the worst shame and the lowest possible status. Paul's rhetoric of the cross thus opposes the cultural values surrounding eloquence.
>
> This explains how Paul can at once attack rhetoric and yet employ it in that very attack. Traditionally, as we have seen, his interpreters have concluded that he rejected rhetorical devices of all kinds. Yet today we must take account of the relative sophistication of Paul's rhetoric …Paul's rhetoric is at least as artful in the very sections in which he 'rejects' rhetoric as elsewhere …Paul rejects not rhetoric, but the cultural values wedded to it. (Pogoloff 1992: 120-21)

The 'artful' use of rhetoric in these very chs. 1–4 of 1 Corinthians has been successfully analysed by Margaret Mitchell in her magisterial account of 1 Corinthians (1991: 65-110 and 184-294) confirming Pogoloff's observations just made.

## 1.4. *Paul's Education*

This takes us to the next question of the origin of such rhetorical skill: was it possible, historically, and culturally, that a Jew should have received in effect a classical education?

In his study of Paul before his conversion, a *tour de force* of historical reconstruction, Hengel touches most lightly on Paul's Greek education as a citizen of Tarsus (1991: ch. 2). This is disappointing, but there is a good reason for it: the paucity of direct evidence to go on. There are two sources which assist us in making a balanced evaluation of Paul's schooling: the texts of his letters and what we know of classical education as such. This is a controverted issue and it is necessary to quote at length from Anderson, Murphy-O'Connor and Betz. We look first at a typically forthright statement of Anderson:

> I do not believe that much can be made of the question of Paul's upbringing. It would seem rather unlikely that Paul enjoyed a formal rhetorical training. Even if *Act. Ap.* 22.3 is interpreted to allow for a grammatical education in Tarsus (a city well known for its high standard of education, both philosophical and rhetorical, cf. Str. 14.5.13-15), Paul probably attended a strict Jewish school (cf. *Act. Ap.* 23.6; *Ep. Phil* 3.5). Even then, *if* such a Jewish school maintained a typical Greek form of grammatical education, Paul, *at the most*, will have become acquainted with certain *progymnasmata*. His Pharisaical upbringing in Jerusalem under Gamaliel *may* also have had Greek influences. We do not know. But even then it seems highly unlikely that Paul received any formal training in rhetorical theory (cf. 2 *Ep. Cor.* 11.6 cited below). Where Paul speaks of his upbringing, he stresses its strict Jewish/Pharisaical character (cf. *Act. Ap.* 22.3; 23.6; 26.4-5; *Ep. Phil.* 3.5). We ought also to remember that at some point Paul learnt the *trade* of tent-making (Anderson 1996: 249).

This is a very revealing comment. Although confessing the lack of data, Anderson seems sure of what may be excluded. He seems unaware of Hengel's work on the pre-Christian Paul. According to Anderson, a full classical and rhetorical training may be excluded (while permitting, at most, familiarity with the *progymnasmata*). Paul's Greek shows itself 'very possible' to be a second language, according to Anderson.[35] Elsewhere he writes that Paul's Greek is that of the educated masses of his day.[36] Perhaps this is not as inconsistent as it appears at first—it would

---

35. Hengel thinks of Paul as fully bilingual, very much at home in the LXX (Hengel 1991: 35). See also Anderson 1996: 250.

36. 'How do the letters of Paul fit into all this? Given that Paul's letters do not

still allow for a general Hellenistic education. As a supplementary argument, he thinks the training for tent-making would have precluded an ordinary schooling. But is it necessary to think of tent-making as Paul's *first* trade? Murphy-O'Connor makes an interesting speculation that the need for a trade arose *after* Paul's conversion (1996: 85-89). These issues are difficult to decide but Paul does evince what could be read as an upper-class attitude to manual labour when he describes it as demeaning (Horrell 1996: 203).

For the purposes of this study, it is sufficient, given the paucity of evidence, to show that a familiarity with rhetoric is a *possibility* and secondly that using such rhetoric helps interpret the text. That possibility would have to await confirmation by analysis of the texts. If it were to be shown that texts of Paul were reasonably consistently patient of rhetorical analysis beyond the general sense that any text will tend to have a beginning, middle and end, then it would be possible to argue for a familiarity with the techniques of text production, as outlined in the rhetorical manuals. Whence the familiarity is a disputed question—possibly formal education, possibly informal absorption through Hellenistic culture. I bring two studies to bear on this issue, which support my case.

In his recent life of Paul, Jerome Murphy-O'Connor investigates the educational background of his subject (1996: chs. 2 and 3). He reviews Jewish, Hellenistic and Hellenistic Jewish educational practices (which included training in rhetoric) and then asks:

> Was Paul formed in such techniques? His social position argues in the affirmative, but he himself appears to deny it. He was not sent, he claims, to preach the gospel 'with eloquent words of wisdom' (1 Cor. 1.17). He asserts 'my speech and my proclamation were not in persuasive words of wisdom' (1 Cor. 2.4), and concedes that 'I am unskilled in speaking' (2 Cor. 11.6). The truth of such self-assessment appears to be confirmed by the Corinthians who said, 'his speech is beneath contempt' (2 Cor. 10.10). Neither Paul's protestations, however, nor the criticism of the Corinthians should be taken at face value. The latter admitted that his

reflect an "Atticising" or "Asianising" literary style, nevertheless their style and language is still a far cry from the vulgar language of many of the papyrus examples Deissmann himself provides. Further, whilst the basic structure of Paul's letters is in conformity with Greek tradition as shown by Koskenniemi, and whilst traces of various epistolary formulae are also to be found, Paul has frequently expanded and varied them. His expansions, at least on a stylistic level, often show some degree of rhetorical flourish' (Anderson 1996: 96).

letters were *bareiai kai ischyrai* (2 Cor. 10.10). While these adjectives could be rendered negatively as 'oppressive and severe', the consensus of scholars and translations is that they should be translated positively, e.g. 'weighty and strong' (RSV), 'impressive and moving'. In other words, his vigorous style was reinforced by the careful presentation expected of a well-trained writer. G.A. Kennedy's assertion that Paul was 'thoroughly at home in the Greek idiom of his time and in the conventions of Greek epistles' is borne out by the evidence of rhetorical arrangement, not only in the organisation of whole letters, but also in the parts of 1 Corinthians when he is dealing with different subjects. Manifestly he was so well trained that his skill was no longer conscious but instinctive (1996: 50).

In a general article on Paul, H.D. Betz cautions against reading Acts too trustingly, on account of a tendency to emphasize Paul's Jewish heritage and his links with Jerusalem, thus underrating his Hellenistic inheritance.[37] He then goes on to say:

> The fact that Paul acted as an international envoy, first on behalf of Jewish authorities (Acts 8.3; 9.1-2, 21; 22.4, 5, 19; 26.10-11; Gal. 1.13, 23; 1 Cor. 15.9; Phil 3.6), then as a Christian missionary, means that he must have received a good Hellenistic education. He gave speeches, taught, wrote long letters, and was involved in highly specialised theological debates. His abilities as a founder of churches, working with many collaborators on an international level, make it impossible to conceive of him as an uneducated and culture-bound Jew from the East. Comparative figures of the time, especially Josephus and Philo show that being well-educated and Jewish did not exclude one another.

> Objections to Paul's education as having been Hellenistic include recourse to his confession of being a layman in rhetoric (2 Cor. 11.6); cf. 1 Cor. 2.1-5) and his use of a secretary (Tertius, Rom. 16.22). Such arguments, however, miss the fact that 2 Cor. 11.6 is itself a rhetorical *topos*...and fail to explain how his letters became literary masterpieces. These letters—with their skillful rhetoric, careful composition and elaborate theological argumentation—reflect an author who was in every way uniquely equipped to become the 'apostle of the gentiles' (Rom. 11.13; cf. Gal. 2.8, 9; Rom. 1.5). This much is clear also from a comparison with his sometime mentor and associate Barnabas, whose abilities fell short of what was needed. Similarly, Luke regards Paul as well-equipped to defend himself in court, while the Jewish priests must have a professional orator (Acts 24.1) (Betz 1992: 187).

37. Gnilka 1996: 9-17 provides a brief summary of how scholarship has at different times emphasized the Greek and the Jewish inheritance of Paul.

It is usually conceded that Paul's shows consummate rhetorical skill in at least four places in his writings: Romans 1–4, 1 Corinthians 1–4 and 13; 2 Corinthians 10–13 (the 'Fool's Speech').[38] That is not yet to say that rhetoric is *omnipresent*, but it is sufficient to establish that Paul can use rhetoric in a very expert way indeed. That it was possible for a Jew to be thoroughly at home in both cultures can be seen from the Book of Wisdom and from the work of Philo of Alexandria. From that it is possible to argue backwards to a familiarity with rhetoric which goes beyond a layman's skill. This expertise of Paul was recognized even before Muilenberg's 'rediscovery' of rhetorical reading. In a book published in 1942, Nils W. Lund wrote as follows:

> Another extensive and penetrating study of form in the Pauline epistles is that of Johannes Weiss. He discusses a variety of the most common Greek and Roman rhetorical forms and in many of his results agrees with Bultmann. Both writers assume that the epistles of Paul have their present form because they represent speech rather than writing. Bultmann concludes that we may safely argue from the nature of Paul's writings to the nature of his sermons. Weiss thinks that Paul in dictating his letters developed a kind of spoken prose and that the Pauline epistles were written largely for the *ear*. Paul does not possess a good prose style; he uses short coördinated sentences paired off by some kind of a copula. Yet, Weiss goes on to say, '*What Paul is lacking in prose style he makes up for somewhat in his carefully written letters by a sure rhetorical movement, which is definite, stirring, frequent, and because of symmetry, rhythmic swing, and fullness of sound does appear artful*' (Lund 1942: 13).

Many letters in antiquity have survived—the very ones which were copied because they were valued as literature—for example, the letters of Plato, Isocrates, Demosthenes and Libanius, as well as Cicero, Pliny, Seneca and Fronto. The same phenomenon is found within the Christian tradition: the letters of the New Testament, of the Apostolic Fathers, Basil, Gregory of Nazianzus, Augustine and Jerome are still extant. Stowers notes that such letters tended 'to be more consciously literary' than other letters and 'are often highly shaped by Greek or Latin rhetoric' (1992: 291).

---

38. 'In short a cursory look at scholarship on 1 Corinthians indicates that Paul is a skilled rhetorician, who, throughout the centuries, has reached his goal of persuading his audience that he is right and the "others" are wrong' (Schüssler Fiorenza 1987: 390).

## 1.5. *The Redaction History of 2 Corinthians 8–9*

Turning to the text of 2 Corinthians 8–9, but still on the historical plane, we have to look at division theories of 2 Corinthians and specifically at the problems with chapters 8 and 9. Although the division theories of 2 Corinthians are not a major problem when we deal only with the unit or units of argument in 2 Corinthians 8 and 9, still, the theories belong to the history of the investigation of the text. The exegesis of 2 Corinthians has been dominated by theories of different letters, anywhere from three to ten or more. More recently, there is a growing consensus that 2 Corinthians 1–9 and 10–13 are the two basic units. Again, the history of the discussion has been well presented elsewhere and will not be repeated here.[39] The influence of redaction criticism may be seen in a chart which Doty offers of the letters of Paul, in which 2 Corinthians 8 and 9 are simply omitted![40] However, because rhetorical analysis presumes that the text is, at least in its major units, to be read as a whole, and is, therefore, intended as a rhetorical unit, the question of the redaction history of 2 Corinthians 8–9 cannot be avoided. However, treatment of this serious issue is postponed until Chapter 6, when we will present the arguments for and against the unity of these two chapters. The issue is less serious when we look only at 2 Corinthians 8 and 9 and later there will be an opportunity to outline the potential consequences of our rhetorical reading for the unity of the whole letter.

## 2. *Proposed Methodology*

### 2.1. *Texts*

Encyclopaedic works such as Quintilian or modern counterparts like Lausberg or Mortara Garavelli are exhaustive but also unwieldy in that you will almost always find some figure or other to correspond to the text before you; they also tend to be ahistorical. Rather than ransack all of the available texts, it seemed to me to be better to lay special emphasis on the manuals of Graeco-Roman rhetoric which have come down to us and which reflect that tradition out of which Paul might, conceivably, have written (Kennedy 1994: 82).

---

39. There is a very complete history of the discussion in Bieringer and Lambrecht 1994. See epecially Part One, section 2. 'Teilungshypothesen zum 2. Korintherbrief. Ein Forschungsüberblick' (pp. 67-105).

40. Doty 1973: 43. Admittedly he wrote the book before the use of classical rhetoric became popular.

Rhetorical theory developed in the Hellenistic period and these developments, both in theory and in practice, serve to distinguish this later rhetoric from its classical forebears (Kennedy 1994: 82). While Aristotle's *Ars Rhetorica* was not available for much of the period, the number of systematic studies increased and these studies went into greater detail regarding the planning, writing and delivery of a speech (Kennedy 1994: 82). Two areas in particular which saw special advance were the theory of figures (Kennedy 1994: 86) and stasis theory (97).[41] Finally, rhetoric came to inform the educational system, becoming largely identical with it.[42]

Who were the great names? In his extensive treatment of Hellenistic rhetoric, G.A. Kennedy (1963: ch. 5; 1994: ch. 5) reviews the personalities and schools of the period, while at the same time taking note of the accumulation of insights which came to constitute Hellenistic rhetoric. The work of Theophrastus (c. 370–285 BCE; successor to Aristotle as head of the Peripatetic school) is lost and has to be recovered from later citations. Theophrastus developed a theory of style, distinguishing four of its 'virtues': purity, clarity, appropriateness (τὸ πρέπον) and ornamentation. In the same tradition came the Later Peripatetics, represented by Demetrius of Phaleron; his work does not survive. In the middle of the second century BCE, Critolaus was head of the Peritatetic school, and what little is known of him comes through the discussion of definitions of rhetoric in Quintilian. At this time direct knowledge of Aristotle's works was lacking until their publication in the first century BCE. Demetrius' *De Elocutione* is judged by both Kennedy and Anderson to be useful for understanding Hellenistic rhetoric because of his discussion of the four styles and the figures.[43] As regard the philosophical schools, the contribution of the Stoics may be represented by

41. Hermagoras of Temnos was the first to work out a detailed theory of stasis. This is to do with the determination of the question at issue in a speech. His original work is lost but may be in part recovered from Cicero and later writings.

42. As we see from Quintilian, who prefaces his *Institutio Oratoria* with a (very humane) theory of education. Kennedy 1994: 83 writes, 'coincidentally a Greek boy had athletic training, perhaps geometry lessons, and often music lessons, but none of these was a concern of the school itself, which was exclusively devoted to literary studies'.

43. 'Despite the fact that this tract appears to have been little used by later rhetorical theorists…it shows much in common with traditional rhetorical theory… For this reason the treatise may be considered quite useful for rhetorical analysis of Paul' (Anderson 1996: 47). Cf. Kennedy 1996: 88-90.

Panaetius of Rhodes who thought that voice production had been neglected by rhetorical theory. On the other hand, the Academicians were somewhat hostile to the claims of rhetoric, thinking it should be limited to the law courts and assemblies. As regards taste in style, there were two movements: Asianism and Atticism. The latter tended to austerity; ostentation marked the former (Clarke 1996: 80).

The recovery of Hellenistic rhetoric depends to a large extent on Latin texts, with the exception of the anonymous *Rhetorica ad Alexandrum* and Demetrius' *De Elocutione*. For the rest, we depend especially on texts from the hand of Cicero. Several of his works merit attention. While still a teenager, Cicero planned an ambitious Latin rhetorical treatise, now known as *De Inventione*. This book was written as a textbook, with full and systematic discussion of the various issues. Like the anonymous *Rhetorica ad Herennium*, the *De Inventione* preserves Hellenistic theory (Anderson 1996: 59; Kennedy 1994: 118-21). The discussion of style in *Rhetorica ad Herennium* is of particular significance, being the earliest account of that peculiarly Hellenistic contribution to rhetoric (Kennedy 1994: 121-27; Anderson 1996: 59-61). In the same didactic vein, Cicero's *Partitiones Oratoriae* offers a simple account of invention and arrangement; in particular the discussion of the *quaestio finita* and the *quaestio infinita* has potential for studying St Paul (Anderson 1996: 48-50; Kennedy 1994: 146-47; Clarke 1996: 51). Cicero wrote further treatises on rhetoric, *De Oratore*, *Orator*, *De Optimo Genere Oratorum*,[44] *Brutus*[45] and *Topica*.[46] The much earlier *Rhetorica ad Alexandrum* was still used and consulted in the first century, as we see from citations taken from it (Anderson 1996: 33). Anderson does not regard it as especially useful for Paul, but does not exclude it, on account of its continued currency.

Following, therefore, the cautious advice of R. Dean Anderson and J. Smit, I propose to use the following texts: *Rhetorica ad Alexandrum* (350–300 BCE), *Rhetorica ad Herennium* (86–82 BCE), Cicero's *De Inventione* (80 BCE) and his *De Partitione Oratoria* (45 BCE). To these we may add Demetrius' *De Elocutione* (uncertain date, probably

---

44. These three works are considered to be quite unlike traditional rhetorical treatises, and may be a result of Cicero's embarrassment with his youthful work. Cf. Anderson 1996: 74.

45. This work is a history of Roman oratory, and judged by Anderson to be less than useful for our purposes.

46. The narrow study of the *loci* limits the usefulness of this text for Paul.

between the second century BCE and the first century CE). As occasion
demands, reference will be made to other handbooks and classical texts.

## 2.2. *Procedure*
*Delimitation.* Misuse of rhetorical schemata has been justly criticized.[47]
It is important to be able to identify the units of a text, great and small,
*before* beginning the task of assigning rhetorical categories such as
*exordium* (the introduction), *narratio* (the statement of facts) and so
forth, and *a fortiori* before thinking of rhetorical genre. The tools for
this task of delimitation[48] are chiefly these: semantic fields, inclusions,
chiastic and concentric structures, indicators of time, place and protago-
nists.[49] These permit us to identify tentatively the larger and smaller

47.  'Refusal to acknowledge the truth of what Quintilian said…has led to the
use of the rhetorical schema for an end for which it was never intended, namely, to
demonstrate the limits of a literary unity with a view to establishing its original
independence' (Murphy-O'Connor 1995: 79). (I thoroughly agree with this critique,
while maintaining the confirmatory role of the rhetorical categories.) Classen 1991:
14: 'Mir ist kein antikes Handbuch bekannt, das ein solches Schema oder Muster
für einen Brief empfiehlt; es handelt sich weitgehend um die übliche Gliederung
eines *logos* in fünf Teile (durch die lateinischen Bezeichnungen leicht erkennbar,
hier mit *propositio*, nicht geteilter *probatio* und—unüblich—*exhortatio* statt *peroratio*), ergänzt durch Vorspann und Schluß. Ob es Briefe gibt, die nach diesem
Schema angeordnet sind, vermag ich nicht zu sagen; ich möchte es bezweifeln und
kann jedenfalls kein Beispiel nennen.' Classen lays great store by Melanchthon's
use of rhetoric (Classen 1991: 19). 'Selbst diese knappe Skizze kann Methode und
Anliegen des jungen Melanchthon erkennbar werden lassen. Er ist bemüht, seinen
Schülern den Inhalt des Briefes, den Gang der Argumentation und die Struktur der
Schlüsse zu verdeutlichen, und zwar mit Hilfe einiger antiker Kategorien; soweit sie
ihm nicht ausreichend erscheinen, ergänzt er sie. Den Aufbau des Ganzen deutet er
nicht mit Hilfe eines vorgegebenen Schemas der Theorie).' It does not seem to me
especially significant that Melanchthon did not stress the *dispositio.*
48.  My ideas on delimitation of large and small units are derived from: Egger
1987: 56-59; Ska 1990: 1-2; it seems to me essential to establish the extent of units
by objective criteria before 'applying' or 'discovering' rhetorical categories.
49.  'Pour qui part de la *dispositio*, le plus sûr moyen de procéder n'est donc pas
de chercher d'abord les correspondances existant entre le texte de Paul et le modèle
qu'il est supposé suivre fidèlement, mais de déterminer les micro-unités argu-
mentives et les thèses ou *propositiones* qui les regissent et que les faits, puis les
preuves ont pour fonction de soutenir. Ce faisant, on évite d'imposer à une épître un
modèle auquel elle n'obeit pas nécessairement en toutes ses parties et l'on garde la
souplesse qui est l'une des caractéristiques du discours paulinien' (Aletti 1990: 7).
A concrete example of how this works may be seen in Elliott 1990: 235-36. 'Any

units—an identification to be confirmed or not when we come to look at the rhetorical arrangement and the content of the text.[50] Only when such a 'control' identification has been proposed, may one proceed to assign rhetorical categories to particular units and show them to be justified. However pedestrian a task this may appear to be, it is necessary. Not only does it afford assurance that the units are intended or deliberate units before reconstructing the *dispositio*, but also, it lays the ground for insights into the rhetoric itself. An example of this below is the presence of an *inclusio* in the opening and closing verses of 2 Corinthians 8–9, which in rhetorical terms establishes the necessary relationship between the *exordium* and the *peroratio*. The method being proposed here both agrees with and differs from the methodology of Kennedy and Watson. The methodologies agree in that text units ought to be identified prior to the assigning of rhetorical categories. They differ in that here the proposal is to use the advice of the handbooks strictly in reverse, that is, starting with the last moment of production (*elocutio*) and working 'backwards' through *dispositio* to *inventio*. The reasons for choosing this procedure are theoretical and practical; *theoretical* in that the stages used for the construction of a speech are not necessarily

segmentation of a text as cohesive as Romans must of course be somewhat provisional and artificial. There are nevertheless formal, thematic, and functional grounds for identifying Rom. 6.1–8.13 as a rhetorical unit. Although the rhetorical question in 6.1 clearly looks back to what precedes (cf. τί οὖν), the terse christological formulations of Romans 5 have given way now to a discussion of "the theological basis of the Christian's moral obligation" in 6.1-12, which requires further explication in 7.1-6, 7.7-25, and 8.1-13. The section is bracketed by contrasts in ch. 6 of the old and new life (6.1-13) and of service to sin or to righteousness (6.15-23), and the contrast of life (and obligation) "according to the flesh" and "according to the Spirit" (8.1-13). Punctuated with rhetorical questions (6.1-3, 15, 16, 21; 7.1, 7, 13, 24) and dense with logical connectives (γάρ, οὖν, ἄρα, οὖν), this passage is an extensive argumentative progression, the coherence of which is obscured when the passage is broken up into discrete dogmatic topics (e.g., "freedom from sin", "freedom from Law", "freedom from death"). The sustained deliberative tone and syllogistic progression evident here were characteristics attributed by the rhetorical handbooks to the figure of conversational reasoning, *ratiocinatio*, which by simulating dialectical reasoning lends to the speaker's handling of a controversial subject the appearance of the self-evident.'

50. 'The compositional macro-structure of a text is in all instances hierarchical in nature, that is, the text can be delimited into a hierarchy of sub-texts on different levels, which to a certain extent discloses the deep-structure of the text as a whole' (Hellholm 1993: 124).

the stages for the analytical 'de-construction' of a speech; *practical* in that it is more cautious to work first with the surface phenomena of the text and only then to look more deeply at the nature of the argument.

## 2.3. *Rhetorical Analysis*

The presentation of an epitome of classical rhetoric and its recent resurgence in New Testament scholarship are both beyond the limits of this book. Both of these tasks have already been undertaken and the reader is referred to such studies (Kennedy 1963, 1972, 1984; Clarke 1996).[51] Nevertheless, some *brief* account of rhetorical theory may be useful and may serve here as an illustration of the proposed method.

Theoretical rhetoric arose as the need for training in speech-making became apparent. Classically, there were three kinds of speech, divided according to setting, purpose and time: forensic (in the courts, for judgment about the past); celebratory (in public, for praising the present), and deliberative (in political debate, regarding the future). In abstract theory, the stages of production of a speech were fivefold: Invention, Disposition, Elocution, Memory and Delivery. The latter two (concerned with the public performance), do not concern us here, beyond noting that Paul's delivery may have been faulty, as he himself concedes. However, Invention, Disposition and Elocution are patient of investigation. A speaker began by deciding what was the nub of the issue (*constitutio* or στάσις), i.e. the core of the dispute (in the case of forensic or deliberative rhetoric), and then finding appropriate arguments of various kinds (*inventio* or εὕρεσις). Because there were stronger and weaker ways of presenting material, the next step was choosing the optimal ordering of the ideas (*dispositio* or τάξις), according to a suggested pattern (see below). The final stage of composition consisted of selecting figures of thought and figures of speech to embellish and fortify the speech, thus adding to the colour and emotion of the text (*elocutio* or λέξις). A metaphor, for example, would be one such figure.

Having established such units,[52] the order of analysis is to begin with the end product and dismantle the construction by beginning with the

51. The first chapter of Garuti 1995 gives an excellent account of the usual training in rhetoric in the Graeco-Roman school. See also under 'Rhetoric and Rhetorical Criticism', in *ABD*, V. See also Weiss: 1897.

52. This is grasped from the start of the present 'wave' of rhetorical studies, although not always observed (Muilenburg 1969: 8-9). Smit 1989: 12 n. 1 com-

outer layer (*elocutio*) and working back through *dispositio* and *inventio* to the *constitutio*. The importance of this independently made segment-ation of the text is well expressed by Muilenberg in his seminal essay.

It would be more cautious and less arbitrary to establish tentatively such segments and then to work backwards from the *elocutio*, through *dispositio* and *inventio* to the *constitutio* and *genus*. The method resembles archaeology. At first you see only the surface of the text, but, gradually, more and more of the underlying structure is revealed. Why proceed 'in reverse'? Because the rhetorical handbooks, followed in this by modern counterparts such as Lausberg and Mortara Garavelli, were manuals for the *creation* of speeches, not tools for analysing texts already produced. They thus follow the order of production. The order of analysis is to begin with the end product and dismantle the con-struction in reverse. It will help to be aware that the discrete moments of production are a theoretical abstraction; likewise, when we use these tools to 'uncreate' a speech, a certain artificiality attends the method. Nevertheless, the goal here is to avoid the risk of arbitrariness.

To clarify the method proposed, I wish to give a very brief explana-tory overview of the *elocutio*, *dispositio* and *inventio*.[53] As it is not the intention of this book to attempt yet another synthesis of classical rhetoric, the comments will of necessity be brief and selective, a fore-taste of what is to come in Chapter 4.

2.3.1. *Elocutio. Elocutio* could be conveniently rendered 'style' in English. It is that part of composition which concerns itself with the manner of expression—how the speaker or writer wants to express things. As rhetoric developed later, ornamentation became increasingly the primary object, to the point where, in ordinary speech, rhetoric has

ments, 'The division in episodes is mainly determined by topographical and semantic data. Gal. 1.13-14; place: Judaism; opposition: Jews vs. Gentiles. Gal. 1.15-24; place: not-Jerusalem; opposition: God vs. men. Gal. 2.1-10, place: Jeru-salem; opposition: Jews vs. Gentiles viz. the circumcised vs. the uncircumcised. Gal. 2.11-21, place: Antioch; opposition: Jews vs. Gentiles viz. the righteous observing the torah vs. the lawless sinners.' Further (Smit 1991: 195): 'Before we start to compare the *genus demonstrativum* of the rhetorical handbooks and 1 Cor. 13 regarding style, it is necessary to define, by means of text-linguistic criteria, the exact ambit of Paul's text which will be discussed. It is also expedient to examine which parts the delimited fragment in its turn consists of'.

53. For general, theoretical reference the reader is directed to Lausberg 1990, Barthes 1988 and Mortara Garavelli 1994.

come to mean that part of rhetoric known as the *elocutio* or the λέξις.[54]
Initially, however, it was not dominant and *elocutio* concerned itself
simply with the choice (*electio*) of words and images. Likewise, the
choice of style (grand, middle or low), the length of sentences, the use
of parataxis or hypotaxis, and especially the figures of speech and
thought were all the concern of *elocutio*.

The rhetorical manuals distinguish figures into two broad categories,
figures of speech and figures of thought.[55] The word 'figure' comes
from the Latin, *fingere*, meaning to mould or to shape. Figures of
speech are concerned with words at a very material level—their position in relation to each other and their sound. A common example in
Paul would be alliteration[56] using π or πᾶς. Figures of thought are techniques of expression, not on the material level of position or sound, but
on the level of ideas, and an example in Paul would be the seed metaphor used in various places. The figures have as their goal the embellishment of the presentation, so that the attention and interest of the
hearer is caught and focused according to the wishes of the speaker.
The function of the figures then is to escape the inevitable banalization
of the familiar, either in terms of words or in terms of thoughts expressed[57] and, classically, it was thought a great advantage to achieve the
impression of saying something new and unheard of.

54. 'Il binomio "retorica e poetica", ancor oggi praticato, esibisce nel primo dei
suoi costituenti una vera e propria sineddoche, nominado il tutto (*retorica*) per
significare una parte (*teoria dell'elocuzione*). Ma è la parte che ha finito per preva-
lere identificandosi, nell'uso e nella conscienza comuni, con la disciplina tutta
intera; se si vuole, è un esempio di antonomasia: ciò che è / era materia dell'*elecutio*
è, per eccellenza, materia della retorica' (Mortara Garavelli 1994: 60).

55. Both are treated in greater detail in Chapter 4.

56. Present even though it was considered vulgar and there was no special term
for it.

57. Again, Anderson 1996: 92 is helpful: 'A general *caveat* needs to be
sounded, however, in discussing style. In isolating forms of argumentation and
figures, rhetorical theory attempted to cover every possible form of expression. This
fact makes it a rather simple process to analyse and label an extant speech or letter
by these various terms. Such labelling, however, does not really help us much
unless we can say something about the *use* and *function* of such arguments or
figures. But it is precisely at this point that the extant treatises are weakest. Discussions of style and figures often seem divorced from considerations of persuasive
effect. This is not to say, however, that the treatises never make any suggestions in
this area and it is important that we not neglect those suggestions which are indeed
made.'

Figures of speech work on the material level of words—the actual sounds and physical position of words. According to the ancient rhetoricians, you have three possibilities with the physical reality of words: you can repeat a word, you can omit one or you can vary their order (*adiectio, detractio, ordo*). Given the scholastic leanings of the rhetoricians, these are then further subdivided and refined (a chart is given in the appendix). An example of *adiectio* (i.e. repetition) would be *epiphora*, which is repetition at a distance, as in 2 Cor. 8.2:

> 8.2    ὅτι ἐν πολλῇ δοκιμῇ θλίψεως
> ἡ περισσεία τῆς χαρᾶς **αὐτῶν**
> καὶ ἡ κατὰ βάθους πτωχεία **αὐτῶν**
> ἐπερίσσευσεν εἰς τὸ πλοῦτος τῆς ἁπλότητος **αὐτῶν·**

> 8.2    for during a severe ordeal of affliction,
> *their* abundant joy and
> *their* extreme poverty have overflowed
> in a wealth of generosity on *their* part.

The various kinds of figure of speech will be studied in their proper place.

It is somewhat strange that figures of thought were categorized under *elocutio* because, properly speaking, they belong with the *inventio*, having to do with the ideas. An example of a figure of thought would be *correctio*, a technique by which the speaker appears to correct himself, thereby adding both spontaneity and emphasis. There is a nice example at the start of 2 Cor. 8.3.

> 8.3    ὅτι κατὰ δύναμιν, μαρτυρῶ,
> καὶ παρὰ δύναμιν, αὐθαίρετοι

> 8.3    For, as I can testify, they voluntarily gave according to their means, and even beyond their means...

This example also serves to show why, perhaps, figures of thought and figures of speech are categorized together: the wording and the thought seem to go so well together—here with a play on κατὰ and παρὰ and the repetition of δύναμιν. Again, these figures of thought abound and have been classified in great detail under the headings of addition, suppression, order and replacement (*adiectio, detractio, transmutatio* and *immutatio*).[58]

---

58. Anderson (1996: 254) thinks Paul's use of the figures is a general cultural phenomenon and links him with no stylistic school.

2.3.2. *Dispositio.* An important part of the effectiveness of a speech was its arrangement or *dispositio*. This moment of the composition concerned itself with both the sequence of ideas and the function of the various parts of a speech. The terms used for the *dispositio* vary somewhat, and the following schema is offered as a guide:[59]

| Greek | | Latin[60] | | English |
|---|---|---|---|---|
| 1. προοίμιον | 1. | *exordium*/ *prooemium*/ *principium* | 1. | exordium/ opening |
| 2. (διήγησις)[61] | 2. | *narratio* | 2. | narration/ exposition |
| 2a. παρέκβασις | 2a. | *digressio*/ *egressus* | 2a. | digression |
| 2b. πρόθεσις | 2b. | *propositio*/ *expositio* | 2b. | proposition |
| | 2c. | *partitio*/ *enumeratio* | 2c. | partition |
| 3. πίστις | 3. | *probatio* | 3. | argumentation |
| 3a. κατασκευή | 3a. | *argumentatio*/ *confirmatio* | 3a. | confirmation/ demonstration/ proof |
| 3b. ἀνασκευή | 3b. | *refutatio*/ *confutatio*/ *reprehensio* | 3b. | refutation |
| 4. ἐπίλογος | 4. | *epilogus*/ *peroratio*/ *conclusio* | 4. | epilogue/ peroration/ conclusion |

59. Taken and slightly adapted from Mortara Garavelli 1994: 63. There is a more detailed schema in Lausberg 1990: 148-49. It is used here for general information. The terms used by the selected authors for this thesis may be found in Chapter 4 in a similar chart. Anderson 1996: 252 argues against finding a real rhetorical *dispositio* in Paul. He writes: 'The fact that we have been able to make some remarks drawn from the rhetorical theory connected with the *partes orationis* has more to do with the fact that most literary productions have a beginning, middle and an end, than that Paul was thinking in terms of a specifically rhetorical προοίμιον, πίστις and ἐπίλογος.'

60. This is a generalized chart covering all Greek and Latin terms. Because the sources for Hellenistic rhetoric have come down to us chiefly in Latin, the terms used in this thesis in Chapter 4 are likewise taken from the Latin. I will be using those terms emphasized in **bold**.

61. As noted by Bice Mortara Garavelli, there is a small inversion in the terminology. In Greek, πρόθεσις is the general name of the section which follows immediately on the *exordium*, while διήγησις is the name of a section within it. Cf. Aristotle, *Rhet.* 3.13. Footnote a. on p. 424 of the Loeb edition echoes the same idea: 'The generally accepted divisions are προοίμιον (*exordium*), διήγησις (narrative), πίστις (proof), ἐπίλογος (peroration). (διήγησις is a species of πρόθεσις, which is used instead of it just before.)'

2.3.3. *Exordium.* The *exordium* is the opening portion of the speech. As such, its goal is to draw the attention of the hearer, to render the hearer well disposed, attentive and docile.[62] There are two kinds of *exordium*—*principium* and *insinuatio*, the former being usual, the latter to be used when there was some obstacle to be surmounted. Usually, then, the *principium* is used and within it there are four ways of making hearers well disposed: 'by discussing own person, the person of our adversaries, that of our hearers, and the facts themselves' (*Herennium* 1.4.8). *Insinuatio* is used, at least in forensic rhetoric, or when the matter is difficult, when the hearers are already won over or are simply tired, when the matter is discreditable. *Insinuatio*[63] is a kind of subterfuge, because the speaker/writer approaches his real object obliquely. The manuals also discussed the strengths and weaknesses of the *exordium*. The strengths are: the use of ordinary vocabulary, so that it appears natural; a natural link with the *narratio*. Weaknesses are: an *exordium* which is too general, which could equally well be used by the opponent or even used against you; too great a length. The *Rhetorica ad Alexandrum* turns its attention specifically to the case when the hearers are against the person of the speaker or the subject matter (29.143b.35 and 29.1437b.15). The advice given there in the case of prejudice against a speaker will be useful for 2 Corinthians 8–9.

> If someone is under suspicion of some misconduct in the past, he must first employ anticipation to the audience, and say 'Even I myself am not unaware that there is a prejudice against me, but I will prove that the charges against me are false' (*Rhet. ad Alex.* 29.1437a1).

2.3.4. *Narratio.* In forensic rhetoric, the *narratio* is the simple statement of agreed facts,[64] the evidence before it is interpreted. It has three goals: to inform, to move and to please; likewise a 'strong' *narratio* would be brief, clear and probable.[65] To assist the speaker, the manuals suggest

---

62. *Rhet. ad Alex.* 29; *Herennium* 1.4.6; Cicero, *Inv.* 1.15.20. Cicero, *Part. Or.* 7.28.
63. *Herennium* 1.7.11: 'the Subtle Approach should be such that we effect all these results covertly, through dissimulation, and so can arrive at the same vantage-point in the task of speaking'.
64. Cicero, *Inv.* 1.19.27. Cicero, *Part. Or.* 9.31.
65. 'In making a speech of our own, when we are narrating something that happened in the past, or describing the present situation, or forecasting the future, we must do each of these things clearly, briefly and convincingly' (*Rhet. ad Alex.*

the following pigeon holes for material: *quis? quid? cur? ubi? quando? quemadmodum? quibus adminiculis?* (Who? What? Why? Where? When? How? With what?'[66] The later manuals made many minute categorizations,[67] which need not concern us here. Even in forensic rhetoric, and certainly in deliberative rhetoric, the *narratio* may be omitted, as Cicero says:

> In addition to observing these precepts, one must also be on guard not to insert a narrative when it will be a hindrance or of no advantage, and also not to have it out of place or in a manner other than that which the case requires.[68]

The writers vary as to the position of the *propositio*—some think it closes the *narratio*,[69] others think it opens the *confirmatio*, others still think that the *exordium*[70] may have a *propositio*.

Aristotle, with brevity and incisiveness, when speaking of arrangement (τάξις) says: 'A speech has two parts. It is necessary to state the subject and then to prove it'.[71] In itself, the *propositio* should be brief and clear.[72] However, in Hellenistic rhetorical theory, the *propositio* as

---

30.1438a.20). 'Clearness of exposition will be obtained from the language or from the facts', (30.1438a.27). Cf. *Herennium* 1.9.14; Cicero, *Inv.* 1.20.28.

66. Quintilian 4.2.55, cf. Lausberg 1990: 183.

67. For example, the quantity, the quality, the relation and the mode of the *narratio*.

68. This is Cicero's advice on what to do when too detailed a 'case history' would put the audience off: 'A narrative can be a hindrance when a presentation of the events alone and by themselves gives great offence, which it will be necessary to mitigate in arguing and pleading the case. When this situation arises, it will be necessary to distribute the narrative piecemeal throughout the speech and to add an explanation directly after each section so that the remedy may heal the wound and the defence may immediately lessen the animosity' (Cicero, *Inv.* 1.21.30). (In reality, Paul tells us why he doesn't go into detail regarding the collection—2 Cor. 9.1.) Further on, Cicero continues (1.21.30): 'The narrative is also useless when the audience has grasped the facts so thoroughly that it is of no advantage to us to instruct them in a different fashion. In such a case one must dispense with narrative altogether.'

69. E.g. 'When the Statement of Facts has been brought to an end, we ought first to make clear what we and our opponents agree upon...' (*Herennium* 1.10.17).

70. Quintilian 3.9.5 reporting the opinion of Aristotle in Aristotle, *Rhet.* 3.13.

71. Aristotle, *Rhet.* 3.13. He goes on to say that 'narrative' has a place only in forensic rhetoric.

72. 'The most complete and perfect argument, then, is that which is comprised of five parts: the Proposition, the Reason, the Proof of the Reason, the Embellish-

such did not receive the same extensive attention as other parts of the speech. If we can show where the proof in any argument begins, then we should be in a position to identify, with other indicators, the *propositio*, in the technical sense, i.e. the thesis to be proved. To keep the argument clear, the author may use subsequent propositions to mark the stages of proof; still, the *propositio* is to govern the entire argument and each step in the argument derives its place and sequence from the *propositio*.

2.3.5. *Probationes*. The proofs (*probationes*) to be adduced are distinguished into various categories, depending on whether they were based on evidence[73] (non-technical, i.e. non-*constructed* proofs) or on deduction[74] (technical proofs). After that there is a wide range of techniques available—syllogism, example, maxim and so forth.

2.3.6. *Peroratio*. The *peroratio* is related to the *exordium* and shares some of its functions. Psychologically, it is meant to trigger a recapitulation of the entire speech by recalling the beginning. At the same time it is meant to touch the feelings of the audience, to incline them to agreement. Her. 2.30.47 gives the following functions to the *peroratio*:

ment, and the Résumé. Through the Proposition we set forth summarily what we intend to prove' (*Herennium* 2.18.28).

73. 'The next section will be confirmation. This will be based on proofs if the facts are denied by the opposite party, but on considerations of justice and expediency and the like if they are admitted. First among the proofs must be placed the evidence of witnesses and confessions that we have obtained by torture, if any be available. Next this evidence must be confirmed by means of maxims and general considerations, if it be convincing, or if not entirely convincing, by probability, and then, by examples, tokens, signs and refutations, and by considerations and the enunciation of maxims to finish with. If the facts are admitted, proofs may be passed over, and legal arguments employed, as in the earlier passages' (*Rhet. ad Alex.* 37.1442b.35).

74. 'Of proofs there are two modes: some proofs are drawn from words and actions and persons themselves, other are supplementary to what the persons say and do. Probabilities, examples, tokens, enthymemes, maxims, signs and refutations are proofs drawn from actual words and persons and actions; the opinion of the speaker, the evidence of witnesses, evidence given under torture, oaths are supplementary. We ought, then, to understand the exact nature of each of these, and the sources that will supply us with arguments for each, and the differences between them' (*Rhet. ad Alex.* 18.1428a.16).

summing up (*enumeratio*), amplification and appeal to pity (*commiseratio*).

2.3.7. *Inventio*. *Inventio* is the discovery of what you want to say.[75] It means both discovery of the chief point of the argument and at the same time all the stages of presentation and proof. It takes us back to precisely how the speaker/writer understood what was at stake. Within the discussion of what one wanted to say, a distinction is made between the *quaestio finita* and the *quaestio infinita*. The latter was a question of principle (is marriage good?) while the *quaestio finita* was a concrete case (should Gaius marry?).

## 3. *Conclusion*

In this opening Chapter, the intention was to do two things. The first was to review the possibility of using ancient rhetoric to read Paul; the second was to propose and illustrate (briefly) a proposed methodology. Specifically, this methodology proposes (a) the use of a limited number of Hellenistic handbooks; and (b) the use in reverse order of the stages of composition of a speech. Before we begin the delimitation, however, it is necessary to see what other rhetorical analyses have made of this text. Chapter 2 presents an overview of rhetorical readings of 2 Corinthians 8–9. Chapter 3 will put into practice the rhetorical methodology, starting with the delimitation. Chapter 4 will consist of a rhetorical reading of 2 Corinthians 8–9. Chapter Five will synthesize the results and Chapter 6 will attempt to be a dialogue with H.D. Betz and concludes with some observations on Paul's education.

---

75. *Herennium* 1.2.3; 1.3.4-5; Cicero, *Part. Or.* 1.2.5; 20.68; 31.109; Cicero, *Inv.* 1.7.9.

Chapter 2

A HISTORY OF RHETORICAL READINGS OF 2 CORINTHIANS 8–9

Your orators never make you either bad men or good, but you make
them whichever you choose; for it is not you that aim at what they wish
for, but they who aim at whatever they think you desire. You therefore
must start with a noble ambition and all will be well, for then no orator
will give you base counsel, or else he will gain nothing by it, having no
one to take him at his word.

Demosthenes, *On Organization* §36

The purpose of this Chapter is to report on the main *rhetorical* analyses
of 2 Corinthians 8–9 in the exegetical tradition. There are two reasons
for undertaking this task. First, it is necessary to respect the observation
that rhetorical criticism appears to ignore a rich inheritance from the
past, as if it were something completely without antecedent; a subsidiary purpose will be to learn from that tradition and find corroboration of the method and insights. Second, a study purporting to offer a
new reading of a well studied text is always in both dialogue and dispute with preceding readings. It is, accordingly, necessary to review
such partners in dialogue. Throughout, the question of method remains
to the forefront in the following review.

There is a certain inequality among the different writers presented.
Thus, although we begin chronologically with John Chrysostom, he can
hardly be said to use rhetorical *method* in his reading of the text. He is
interesting because he stands within the still living rhetorical tradition
and because his rhetorical observations are both spontaneous and acute.
The outstanding figures in this historical review are Heinrici and Betz,
whose discussions of rhetoric and Paul constitute high points in the
modern use of rhetoric. They, therefore, receive relatively greater attention. Names of lesser significance are included for completeness (for
example Ben Witherington III) or because they shed light not only on
the rhetoric but on related issues (for example Danker on benefaction
and the work of Young and Ford on the integrity of 2 Corinthians). In

the contemporary discussion, pride of place is given to Betz, to whom the other contemporary writers all make reference. Egagement with his proposed rhetorical reading is, however, postponed until the penultimate Chapter of this book.

The use of rhetoric as a distinct methodology is relatively recent. That is not to say that aspects of rhetoric were not noticed or used in preceding centuries—on the contrary, as we shall see in this chapter. Even in recent times, however, few have undertaken a rhetorical analysis of 2 Corinthians 8–9.[1] We begin rather further back: in the patristic period with John Chrysostom.

## 1. *John Chrysostom (c. 400)*

J.N.D. Kelly describes the sermon-commentaries of John Chrysostom as among the most impressive and readable from the patristic period, notable not only for their method, but also for their content (Kelly 1995: 94). All the more surprising, then, is the relative neglect of John Chrysostom in modern studies of method and the history of exegesis.[2]

Chrysostom is a representative of the Antiochene school of exegesis, a school consciously opposed to the allegorical readings of the Alexandrian school. The reading is based on a logical, grammatical-historical reading of the text.[3] That portion of his work which makes up his homiletic commentary on the Corinthian letters cannot be dated with certainty, although a reference to Constantinople at the end of Homily 26 on 2 Corinthians seems to imply that the place was not Constantinople itself. If that is so, then the homilies may have been delivered within that period before his consecration as bishop (26 February 398).[4] His later expulsion from Constantinople, a sign of fear,

---

1.    It is instructive for instance that Crafton 1991 makes no attempt to extend his dramatistic and rhetorical reading to include 2 Cor. 8–9, although that might well have suited his purposes. Very little material on 2 Cor. 8–9 is reported in Watson and Hauser 1994.

2.    Both Augustine and Origen receive detailed treatment in the *New Jerome Biblical Commentary*. There is only one entry for Chrysostom. He is likewise neglected in *A Dictionary of Biblical Interpretation*. Keegan 1985 simply ignores the Antiochean school. An exception is B. de Margerie 1993, who devotes an entire chapter to John Chrysostom.

3.    See Jeanrond 1992: 434; Grant and Tracy 1984: ch. 7, pp. 63-72; Baur 1959: 321.

4.    Kelly 1995: 91 dates the homilies to 392/3.

confirms his reputation as a speaker of great eloquence and power. He was a trained rhetor and it is possible that his early education in the art of speaking was under Libanius (see Pollastri 1882), a rhetor who himself had taught successively at Athens, at Nicomedia and at Antioch in Syria, the birthplace of John Chrysostom. The teacher was a great admirer of the pupil.[5] As a preacher and exegete, he was a student of Diodore of Tarsus, but one prepared to admit a spiritual sense in Scripture, as long as the literal sense was safeguarded.

The 30 homilies on 2 Corinthians take the form of a *lectio cursiva* commentary, combining exposition with exhortation. Each homily begins with commentary on the next few verses, mingled with exhortation, and ends with a longer passage of pure exhortation. Our text of 2 Corinthians 8–9 is commented on from the middle of Homily 16 until the end of Homily 20. It is useful to read John Chrysostom because he is within the still living tradition of rhetoric and provides what is, in effect, a sensitive rhetorical reading of the text.[6] According to recent critical study, the disjunctions in 2 Corinthians are best explained by denying the unity of the text. It will be interesting to see whether a classically trained rhetor feels the same disjunctions to be inappropriate from a rhetorical point of view. Chrysostom does not suspect that 2 Corinthians might be a collection of several letters: he simply assumes the unity of the text. His few remarks on the coherence of the text cannot, therefore, be taken to be in dialogue with the division theories. Nevertheless, we may say that he sees 8–9 as a distinct topic within the letter, different from what precedes and from what follows. Furthermore, his rhetor's feeling for the overall coherence of the text leads him occasionally to comment on the coherence of these two chapters. Apart from the integrity of 2 Corinthians, the observations Chrysostom makes about specific rhetorical strategies will be of interest.

Starting at 8.1, Chrysostom feels no disjunction—on the contrary, he thinks the preceding material in ch. 7 has prepared the hearer for 8–9.

---

5.    The continued role of rhetoric in education and in particular the Christian adoption of the ideals and methods are described in Di Berardino and Studer 1996: 283-96. Both Chrysostom and Augustine are treated there.

6.    Of course his purpose is primarily pastoral and he is not offering a *technical* analysis—however, he cannot help himself noticing the shrewd strategies of Paul in his persuasion.

> Having encouraged them with these encomiums, he again tries exhortation. For on this account he mingled these praises with his rebuke, that he might not by proceeding from rebuke to exhortation make what he had to say ill received; but having soothed their ears might by this means pave the way for his exhortation.[7]

In the same way, at the beginning of his comment on 10.1, there is no indication that Chrysostom felt the change to be unduly abrupt. On the contrary, he thinks the change of subject opportune (εὐκαίρως). At the same time he thinks the content of 10–13 is of a piece with the entire epistle.

> Having completed, in such sort as behoved his discourse of almsgiving, and having shown that he loves them more than he is loved, and having recounted the circumstances of his patience and trials, he now opportunely (εὐκαίρως) enters upon points involving more of reproof, making allusion to the false apostles, and concluding his discourse with more disagreeable matter, and with commendations of himself.[8]

Again, there is no sense in Chrysostom that the break at 9.1 presents an insurmountable difficulty or indeed that there is any incoherence or duplication between 8 and 9. He seems positively to enjoy the style of Paul at that point, as we shall see below. The other structural question, that of the arrangement (*dispositio* or τάξις) of the discourse, is not a formal question raised by Chrysostom. However, he does recognize that 8.1-6 constitutes an introduction to the main point. Thus he indicates the purpose of the praises in 8.1-6 by saying of v. 7 that:

> Seest thou that for this reason it was that he began by those praises, that advancing forward he might draw them on to the same diligence in these things also.[9]

---

7.   Homily 16 [2] at 8.1: Ἐπάρας αὐτοὺς τοῖς ἐγκωμίοις, παραίνεσιν πάλιν καθίησι. Διὰ γὰρ τοῦτο τῇ ἐπιπλήξει παρέμιξε τοὺς ἐπαίνους, ἵνα μὴ ἀπὸ ἐπιπλήξεως εἰς παραίνεσιν κατελθὼν δυσπαράδεκτον ποιήσῃ τὸν λόγον, ἀλλὰ λεάνας αὐτῶν τήν ἀκοήν, οὕτω προοδοποιήσῃ τῇ παραινέσει.

8.   Homily 21 [1] at 10.1: Ἀπαρτίσας τὸν περὶ ἐλεημοσύνης λόγον, ὡς ἔδει, καὶ δείξας ὅτι πλεῖον αὐτοὺς ἀγαπᾷ, ἢ ἀγαπᾶται, καὶ τὰ περὶ τῆς ὑπομονῆς αὐτοῦ καὶ τῶν πειρασμῶν διηγησάμενος, εὐκαίρως λοιπὸν τῶν ἐπιτιμητικωτέρων ἅπτεται λόγων, τοὺς ψευδαποστόλους αἰνιττόμενος, καὶ εἰς τὰ φορτικώτερα κατακλείων τὸν λόγον, καὶ ἑαυτὸν συνιστῶν.

9.   Homily 17 [1] at 8.7. Εἶδες ὅτι διὰ τοῦτο ἐκεῖθεν ἤρξατο ἀπὸ τῶν ἐπαίνων ἐκείνων, ἵνα ὁδῷ προθαίνων, εἰς τὴν αὐτὴν αὐτοὺς καὶ ἐν τούτοις ἐκλύσῃ σπουδήν.

He also notices the moment when persuasion proper begins, i.e. at v. 9.

> Then he proceeds afterwards to the head and crown of his persuasion
> (*scil.* v. 9).[10]

Finally, he is aware that towards the end of ch. 9 we are dealing with
the end of a block of argument, the purpose of which has been virtue or
ἀρετή.

> For this avails very greatly in inciting unto all virtue; and therefore he
> concluded his discourse with it.[11]

### 1.1. *Rhetorical Strategies Used by Paul*
Chrysostom draws his listeners' attention to the brilliance (σύνεσις) of
Paul at several points. He notes first the oblique way Paul approaches
his awkward subject (Homily 16 [2] at 8.1). Paul even avoids saying
immediately what it is he wants to say (Homily 16 [2] at 8.2) and he is
very careful to obviate offence, humouring his hearers (Homily 17 [1]
at 8.7; at 8.10). Chrysostom does not speak directly of Paul's anxious
state as he writes these two chapters, but he does notice the great care,
the constant softening of expression,

> For the word 'is accepted,' here implies 'is required'. And he softens it
> greatly, in confident reliance upon this example, and as winning them
> more surely by leaving them at liberty. Wherefore also he added, Verse
> 13. 'For I say not this, that others may be eased, and ye distressed'.[12]

In the same way Paul knows how to manipulate feelings: the Corinthians desire the higher graces and so in these two chapters Paul calls
the whole matter a 'grace'. Likewise, Paul is capable when necessary of
manipulation, as in:

> Then he even heightens the anxiety, saying etc.[13]

---

10. Homily 17 [1] at 8.8. Εἶτα λοιπὸν ἐπὶ τὸ κεφάλαιον καὶ τὴν κορωνίδα τῆς
συμβουλῆς ἵεται.
11. Homily 20 [2] at 9.15: Καὶ γὰρ μέγιστον τοῦτο εἰς προτροπὴν ἀρετῆς
ἁπάσης· διὸ καὶ ἐνταῦθα τὸν λόγον κατέκλεισεν.
12. Homily 17 [1] at 8.12: Τὸ γὰρ, Εὐπρόσδεκτος, ἐνταῦθα τὸ, ἀπαιτεῖται,
δηλοῖ. Καὶ σφόδρα λιπαίνει, τούτῳ θαρρῶν τῷ ὑποδείγματι, καὶ τούτῳ δοῦναι
ἐξουσίαν μᾶλλον ἐφελκόμενος· διὸ καὶ ἐπήγαγεν, Οὐ γὰρ ἵνα ἄλλοις ἄνεσις,
ὑμῖν δὲ θλῖψις.
13. Homily 19 [1] at 9.4: Εἶτα καὶ αὔξει τὴν ἀγωνίαν, λέγων κτλ.

Apart from these general observations, Chrysostom observes the following rhetorical strategies, which we report in sequence.

*Homily 16 (2 Cor. 7.13–8.6).* Chrysostom notices the change from encomiums (τοῖς ἐγκωμίοις) to exhortation (παραίνεσιν), the former preparing for the latter. Paul begins obliquely, praising the Macedonians in *three* ways; Chrysostom counts *seven* arguments, showing thereby that Paul is really insistent. Likewise the careful use of the word grace is noted: it attracts in a double way; the Macedonians received a gift and the Corinthians are known to be people desiring the gifts. Furthermore, vv. 1-6 are all of a piece—Chrysostom counts the praise and insistence of Paul (three praises, seven testimonials of their freedom/ abounding generosity).[14] Verse 6 connects with what precedes it:

> And what connexion is there here? Much; and closely bearing on what went before.[15]

*Homily 17 (2 Cor. 8.7-15).* Chrysostom is aware also of covert preparation (κατεσκεύασε λανθανόντως).[16] At v. 14 he notices that the hearers are left to work things out for themselves (καταλείπει δὲ αὐτὸ τῷ λογισμῷ τῶν ἀκοατῶν),[17] perhaps a mild example of enthymeme or incomplete syllogism.[18] The enthymeme is powerful because of two effects: it flatters the hearer and the intended insight comes from within. He notices at v. 15, the use of an 'ancient story' (παλαιὰν ἱστορίαν) to bring forward the persuasion and he explains it extremely well: everybody received the same manna and hence insatiability was punished by God.

---

14. Homily 17 [2] at 8.1-4.

15. Homily 16 [4] at 8.6: Καὶ ποία ἀκολουθία αὐτὴ; Πολλὴ καὶ σφόδρα τῶν ἔπροσθεν ἐχομενη. The translator uses an alternative English spelling.

16. Homily 17 [2] at 8.13: 'Consider, for instance, how even in what follows he is covertly preparing the way for this' and at 8.14: 'See how he hath covertly prepared for their giving beyond their power and of their want'.

17. I.e. a form of enthymeme, always very effective because the insight is triggered internally and hence is 'mine', so to speak, from the start.

18. The enthymeme or rhetorical syllogism has been much studied. It is a syllogism, but an incomplete one. The effect is highly manipulative in that insight is triggered within the hearer by the involuntary completing of the syllogism. The insight, thereby occurs 'internally' and is immediately more convincing.

*Homily 18 (2 Cor. 8.16-24)*. The example of Titus is presented to underscore his freedom from compulsion. Chrysostom asks why 'the brother' is not named, but he does not pursue the question rhetorically, being interested rather in simply discovering who the brother is.[19] In fact, later in the chapter, he seems to think that v. 22 presents yet another figure[20] who is also introduced with an encomium. As regards Paul's careful avoidance of the suspicion of blame, Chrysostom called it evidence of his tender care and condescension—he suspects, apparently, no tension in the relationship.[21]

*Homily 19 (2 Cor. 9.1-9)*. At 9.1 Chrysostom mentions the rhetorical figure of omission (παράλειψις):

> And he does this often in accusation also, using the rhetorical figure, omission, for this is very effective. For the judge seeing the magnanimity of the accuser entertains no suspicions even.[22]

It may be no more than a manner of speaking, but here Chrysostom seems to recognize that Paul is, in some sense, on trial and that his persuasion presumes that the Corinthians are, in some sense, judges. It may mean no more than 'arbiter' and so we need not think immediately of forensic rhetoric.

Continuing on 9.1, he observes the use of 'ethos', using the very term ἔθος:

> And he gives occasion to suspect even more than he says, and invests himself with the presumption of a good disposition.[23]

At 9.2c he notes a very clever combination of emulation:

> Seest thou how he rouses them each by the other, these by those, and those by these, and, along with the emulation, has intermingled also a very high encomium.[24]

---

19. He decides it was Barnabas, but goes no further with the question as to why he is not named. One effect is that the emphasis is shifted (in the text) from the identity of 'the brother' to the approval of the churches.

20. Homily 18 [2] at 8.22.

21. Homily 18 [1] at 8.20.

22. Homily 19 [1] at 9.1: Οὕτω καὶ ἐπὶ τῆς κατηγορίας ποιεῖ πολλάκις, κατὰ παράλειψιν λέγων· καὶ γὰρ μεγάλην ἔχει τὴν ἰσχύν. Ὁ γὰρ δικαστὴς ὁρῶν τὴν μεγαλοψυχίαν τοῦ κατηγόρου, οὐδὲ ὑποπτεύει λοιπόν.

23. Homily 19 [1] at 9.1: καὶ δίδωσι καὶ μεῖζον ὑποπτεύειν, ἢ εἰπεῖν, καὶ ἤθους χρηστοῦ ὑπόνοιαν περιτίθησιν ἑαυτῷ.

24. Homily 19 [1] at 9.2: Εἶδες πῶς δι᾿ ἀλλήλων αὐτοὺς διεγείρει, τούτους μὲν

Paul implies that his reputation and that of the Corinthians belong together and the rhetorical effect of this is noted:

> And see how, whilst stirring up and inflaming them still more, he feigns to be standing by them, as if espousing their party in some rivalry and contention.[25]

This same identification is noted for v. 3, and then the heightening of anxiety is observed in v. 4:

> Then he even heightens the anxiety, saying etc.[26]

The energy behind his use of anxiety is the theme of shame

> The shame is greater when the spectators he has arrayed against them are many, even those same persons who had heard [his boasting].[27]

He notes and greatly approves of the 'if' clause in v. 4:

> For thus he also made what he said unsuspected, but had he expressed himself in that other way, he would have even made them the more contentious.[28]

Chrysostom thinks Paul is aware of a mild contradiction between claiming discourse is unnecessary (9.1) and then discoursing at length:

> Again, he resumed the subject in a different manner: and that he may not seem to be saying these things without object, he asserts that the sole reason for this journey was, that they might not be put to shame. Seest thou how his words, 'It is superfluous for me to write,' were the beginning of advising.[29]

δι᾽ἐκείνων, ἐκείνους δὲ διὰ τούτων, καὶ τῷ ζήλῳ καὶ ἐγκόμιον ἀνέμιξε μέγιστον.

25. Homily 19 [1] at 9.2: Καὶ ὅρα πῶς διεγείρων αὐτοὺς καὶ ἀνάπτων μειζόνως, ὑποκρίνεται μετ᾽ αὐτῶν ἑστάναι, καθάπερ ἐν φιλονεικίᾳ τινὶ καὶ ἀμίλλῃ τὸ μέρος αὐτῶν ἐπιλεγόμενος.

26. Homily 19 [1] at 9.4: Εἶτα καὶ αὔξει τὴν ἀγωνίαν, λέγων κτλ.

27. Homily 19 [1] at 9.4: Μείζων ἡ ἐντροπή, ὅταν πολλοὺς ἐπιστήσῃ τοὺς θεατάς, αὐτοὺς τοὺς ἀκηκοότας.

28. Homily 19 [1] at 9.4: Οὕτω γὰρ καὶ ἀνύποπτον ἐποίει τὸν λόγον· εἰ δὲ ἐκείνως εἶπε, καὶ φιλονεικοτέρους ἐποίησεν ἄν.

29. Homily 19 [2] at 9.5: Πάλιν αὐτὸ ἀνέλαβεν ἑτέρως· καὶ ἵνα μὴ δόξῃ ἁπλῶς ταῦτα λέγειν, καὶ τὴν αἰτίαν τῆς ὁδοῦ οὐκ ἄλλην εἶναί φησιν, ἀλλ᾽ ὥστε μὴ καταισχυνθῆναι αὐτούς· Ὁρᾷς ὅτι τὸ, Περιττόν μοί ἐστι τὸ γράφειν ὑμῖν, ἀρχὴ συμβουλῆς ἦν;

He adds a very telling comment to v. 5:

> And neither was he content with this, but he adds a testimony from Scripture also, saying 'For God loveth a cheerful giver...' In this passage I am of opinion that a large [giver] is intended; the Apostle however has taken it as giving with readiness. For because the example of the Macedonians and all those other things were enough to produce sumptuousness, he does not say many things on that head, but upon giving without reluctance. For if it is a work of virtue, and yet all that is done of necessity is shorne of its reward, with reason also he labors at this point.[30]

*Homily 20 (2 Cor. 9.10-15)*. In Homily 20, Chrysostom notes how Paul gives variety to his discourse (ποικίλλει τὸν λόγον)[31] by adducing different kinds of argument and example (ἀπὸ τοῦ παραδείγματος). Paul is capable of using praise/flattery to persuade, as in:

> For that he may not represent them as giving thanks on this account solely, (I mean, because they received somewhat) see how highly-minded he makes them...[32]

## 1.2. *Concluding Summary on the Homilies*

The following rhetorical terms are used by Chrysostom: encomium, paranesis, paralepsis,[33] ethos,[34] paradigm (= *exemplum*), witness (of Scripture) and history. Paul can use flattery and praise; he appeals to their very own desires; he can conceal his purpose; he can use the

---

30. Homily 19 [2] at 9.5: Καὶ οὐδὲ τούτῳ ἠρκέσθη, ἀλλά καὶ ἀπὸ Γραφῆς μαρτυρίαν ἐπάγει, λεγων· Ἱλαρὸν γὰρ δότην ἀγαπᾷ ὁ Θεός· ...Ἐνταῦθα οἶμαι τὸ, ἱλαρὸν, δαψιλῆ λέγεσθαι· πλὴν αὐτὸς εἰς τὸ μετὰ προθυμίας διδόναι αὐτὸ παρέλαβεν. Ἐπειδή γὰρ τὸ παράδειγμα Μακεδόνων, καὶ τὰ ἄλλα ἅπαντα ἱκανὰ ἦν ἐργάσασθαι τὴν πολυτέλειαν· οὐ πολλὰ περὶ αὐτῆς φθέγγεται, ἀλλὰ περὶ τοῦ μὴ ἄκοντας διδόναι. Εἰ γὰρ ἔργον ἐστὶν ἀρετῆς, πᾶν δὲ τὸ ἐξ ἀνάγκης ὑποτέμνεται τὸν μισθὸν, εἰκότως τοῦτο ἐργάζεται.

31. Homily 20 [1] at 9.10: 'This he does, and gives variety by it to his discourse, tearing up by the roots those their (*sic*) unmanly and faint-hearted reasonings, and using many arguments to dissipate their fear of poverty, as also the example which he now brings.'

32. Homily 20 [2] at 9.12-14: ἵνα γὰρ μὴ δείξῃ αὐτοὺς διὰ τοῦτο εὐχαριστοῦντας μόνον, διὰ τὸ λαβεῖν λέγω, ὅρα πῶς ὑψηλοὺς αὐτοὺς ποιεῖ·

33. The figure by which one pretends to pass over something.

34. The figure by which one asserts the good/bad name of the speaker, hearer, protagonist or city.

language of benefaction and shame as well as honour. Finally, he can both leave them to draw their own conclusions (enthymeme[35]) and elsewhere give the impression of being 'on their side'. Both of these latter techniques are covert and therefore even more powerful. He sees the persuasion sometimes in forensic terms (the judge), sometimes in athletic terms (the ὁ ἀγών). Paul puns ('grace', as we shall see, has many meanings). Finally, as we saw at the start, without drawing attention to it explicitly, he has a certain grasp of the overall structure of chs. 8–9. Chrysostom is constantly in admiration of Paul's ability to marshal arguments for his case in a manner which will least offend and most persuade.

One needs to ask as this point: is the recovery of material from John Chrysostom significant for this work? As regards the psychological switch from intimate collaboration to virulent condemnation, i.e. the change in mood from 2 Corinthians 8–9 to 2 Corinthians 10–13, it is not without interest that a sensitive rhetor such as John Chrysostom finds nothing strange in this change of mood, bearing in mind that moods, both of speaker and hearer, are the very stuff of rhetoric. The important aspect of Chrysostom is that he stands within the still-living tradition of rhetoric and was a trained rhetor himself. All this adds considerable weight to his almost inadvertent rhetorical remarks. Finally, as regards his technical appreciation of the rhetoric, the single observations will be taken up in Chapter 5 and compared with the analysis achieved in Chapter 4.

### 2. *Carl Friedrich Georg Heinrici (1900)*

As far as I am aware the next writer to use rhetoric in exegesis, after John Chrysostom, is Johannes Piscator. Johannes Piscator (= Fischer 1546–1628) brought to fullest expression the typical Reformation genre of the *analysis logica* of the sacred text (cf. Classen 1995). His *Analysis logica utriusque epistolae Pauli ad Corinthios* is unfortunately unavailable for the present study. Apparently, he was especially interested in the relationship between the various propositions in a given book and so the text would be interesting from a rhetorical point of view. However, rhetoric as such was not, apparently, *central* to his work (Backus 1996).

---

35. The enthymeme is an abbreviated syllogism which the hearer is meant to complete.

A somewhat shorter gap separates the work of Johannes Piscator and that of C.F. Georg Heinrici, who was professor of theology at Leipzig. He had a special interest in the Corinthian correspondence and provided a commentary on each letter in the Meyer's Kommentar series (Heinrici 1896, 1900). Both volumes enjoyed several editions. These are expository commentaries and so Heinrici is not doing a rigorous rhetorical analysis in the modern sense. However, he consciously credits Paul with rhetorical ability in the course of a sharp scholarly exchange between himself and E. Norden (author of the famous *Die antike Kunstprosa vom VI. Jahrhundert V. Chr. bis in die Zeit der Renaissance*[36]). The discussion is interesting because it provoked Heinrici to add an appendix to a later edition of his commentary on 2 Cor, entitled *Zum Hellenismus des Paulus*. This is a defence of the rhetorical reading of Paul.

Before looking into Norden's comments and Heinrici's response, a brief résumé of Heinrici's rhetorical insights into 2 Corinthians 8–9 is in order. He thinks of the entire letter as a unity, and *a fortiori* thinks of 8 and 9 as belonging together. The tone has changed in these two chapters—he accurately notes that Paul here is 'zurückhaltender, vorsichtiger' (Heinrici 1900: 265). The two chapters also have in common a certain vocabulary underlined by repetition.[37] Following his own sectioning of the text, he makes the following observations.

*8.1-6.* In v. 1 δέ indicates a change of subject.[38] He notes, without emphasis and without the technical term, the *inclusio* formed between 8.1 and 9.14 by χάρις and θεός. The repetition of αὐτῶν is judged to have made the writing heavy. The train of thought in v. 2 is paradox. Heinrici calls ἡ κατὰ βάθους πτωχεία 'eigentümlicher, poetisch gefärbter Ausdruck' and notes that it is a metaphor. Parenthesis is found in

---

36. Norden 1915. The work enjoyed two previous editions—1898 and 1909. The fact that Norden left his attack on Heinrici unchanged needs some comment. Heinrici had countered the 'aphoristic' assertions of Norden, but apparently Norden did not think his arguments sufficient to warrant changing his opinion.

37. 'Die Wiederholung gewisser Stichworte (προθυμία, προενάρχεσθαι, ἐπιτελεῖν, παρακαλεῖν, παράκλησις, αὐθαίρετος, ἰσότης, περισσεύειν zum Theil gewählte Ausdrücke, s. die Einzelerklärung) macht den Eindruck mühevollen, schwerfälligen Fortschreitens, ähnlich wie 1:3-11' (Heinrici 1900: 265).

38. Called by Heinrici μεταβατικόν (1900: 267). This is regular elsewhere in Paul.

v. 3 at καὶ οὐ καθὼς ἠλπίσαμεν just as at μαρτυρῶ.[39] There is a certain build-up from κατὰ δύναμιν and παρὰ δύναμιν.

*8.7-15.* The comment on ἀλλ᾽ of v. 7 is instructive:

> Ἀλλ᾽ is neither οὖν (*Beza*), nor *agedum (Emmerl.)* but *at*, breaking off the discourse thus far, something like our *doch*.

He denies the presence of *epanalepsis* in the repetition of ἐν.[40] Verse 9 is not in parenthesis (= in rhetorical sense?), but rather the founding presupposition for his suggestion. The somewhat anaphoric effect in the repeated substantivized infinitives in v. 10 is accompanied by the climactic effect of 'not only...but also'. Heinrici classifies v. 12 as Gnome (= our '*sententia*'), here used to support the immediately preceding ἐκ τοῦ ἔχειν. It is likewise an example of personification. In v. 13, ἄλλοις ἄνεσις, ὑμῖν θλῖψις is asyndeton. Verse 14 shows antithesis. Verse 17 begins the evidence for Titus' σπουδὴ. He denies that v. 19 is in parenthesis—it depends syntactically on v. 18. The participle in v. 19 is a case of anacoluthon. The well-known Gorgian figure of speech is to be found in v. 22: ἐν πολλοῖς πολλάκις. Verse 23 is described as 'eine elliptische Oratio variata' (Heinrici 1900: 292). The expression 'oratio variata' I have not been able to find, even in Lausberg; however, the meaning is plain enough. Verse 24 contains the *figura etymologica* in τὴν ἔδειξιν ἐνδείκνυσθαι.

*9.1-5.* Heinrici thinks of ch. 9 as a continuation of ch. 8, evidence being the linking γὰρ. Furthermore, when Paul wants to start a new argument, he uses περὶ δέ and not, as here, περὶ μέν. Later on, v. 4 is parenthetical and the phrase ἵνα μὴ λέγω ὑμεῖς as an example of paralepsis.[41] The repeated προ- in v. 5 is noted without being named.

*9.6-15.* Verse 6: antithetical parallelism. The repeated ἐπ᾽ εὐλογίαις is used in two senses, forming antanaklasis. The πs of v. 8 are a case of

---

39. 'parentetische Betheuerung affectvoller Rede' (Heinrici 1900: 270).

40. 'Die Wiederholung des ἐν (64) ist nicht zur Klarheit erforderlich, da es sich hier eben um eine Veranschaulichung des Allgemeinbegriffs (ἐν παντί), nicht aber um eine epanaleptische Näherbestimmung (I 1:5) handelt' (Heinrici 1900: 274). We have to see later if epanalepsis is present.

41. Heinrici 1900: 298. This figure, also known as *praeteritio*, is one by which one draws attention to something by apparently denying it.

*paronomasia*, with a certain effect of climax. An argument *a minori ad maius* may be found in v. 10. He denies that v. 13 should be treated as parenthetical.

In general, Heinrici is a very close reader of the arguments, even when he is not always using explicit rhetorical categories to name the figures and stages. A further engagement with the comments of Heinrici will be undertaken in the rhetorical synthesis of Chapter 5. It is appropriate at this point to turn to a discussion on Pauline rhetoric sparked by Heinrici's work.

Norden's reaction to Heinrici's work comes in the second volume of his encyclopaedic work, *Die antike Kunstprosa* (beginning on p. 451). Like some present-day classical scholars, he regards as baleful the influence of Christianity on classical culture, not troubling to conceal his prejudice.[42] He disarmingly (*captatio benevolentiae*?) confesses his own difficulty in reading St Paul.[43]

It is logical, then, that he finds the use of rhetoric to expound Paul impossible. He thoroughly objects to Heinrici, not hesitating to disparage the latter's familiarity with ancient rhetoric.[44]

42. Norden 1915: 452-60: 'Lest we misunderstand, he sets out four mighty antitheses between the new religion and the old culture. In contrast to classical culture, Christian literature lacks freedom.'

43. 'Paulus ist ein Schriftsteller, den wenigstens ich nur sehr schwer verstehe; das erklärt sich mir aus zwei Gründen: einmal ist seine Art zu argumentieren fremdartig, und zweitens ist auch sein Stil, als Ganzes betrachtet, unhellenisch' (Norden: 1915: 499). (He is probably not alone in this, although the grounds are more sophisticated.)

44. 'Unter den Neueren hat wohl keiner das hellenische Element der Briefe des Apostels maßloser übertrieben als G. Heinrici, Erklärung der Korinthierbriefe II, Berlin 1887. Gegen die Methode, mit der in diesem Werk die hellenische Literatur, vor allem die Redner und Philosophen, herangezogen werden, muß ich laut Protest erheben. Ich bitte denjenigen, der etwas von antiker Rhetorik versteht—der Verfasser scheint seine wesentliche Kenntnis aus Volkmann zu schöpfen—die Kapitel 10–12 des zweiten Korinthierbriefs zu lesen und sich zu fragen, ob er darin "die bewährten Mittel der antiken Verteidigungsrede" ' (Norden 1915: 493-94). 'Erkennt: gewiß, insofern jeder Mensch, der sich zu verantworten hat, verwandte Töne anschlägt, aber muß er die von anderen erlernen' (p. 403). He raises the pertinent question of Paul's education. Further studies of chs. 10–13 have really overtaken Norden's criticism.

This 'lauter Protest' ('loud protest') provoked a response in which Heinrici defends (somewhat testily[45]) himself and his method.[46] Heinrici shows that, contrary to Norden's claim, he himself has carefully used comparisons with contemporary literature (439–40). As an example of Paul's familiarity with Hellenistic speech, he cites the use of diatribe (440). He thinks Norden greatly overlooks the effect of living in a Hellenistic city such as Tarsus. Norden apparently depends on the impression Renan formed of Paul's style,[47] a rather extreme position. The distinction between the style of Paul and the style of other early letters (Hebrews, *1 Clement*, *Barnabas*) seems sufficient *proof* that Paul's style and argument are 'ungreek'. Likewise Norden's impression that Paul is 'rabbinic' rather than 'Hellenistic' can be shown to be based on a few mistaken interpretations, such as overestimating his (rare) use of Hebrew/Aramaic.[48] Again, Heinrici thinks Paul's style is not at all like midrash, although here Heinrici himself presents something of a caricature of midrash. However, as he points out, it is not the case that what is *not* Greek in Paul *must* be rabbinic. It could also be simply Paul (Heinrici 1900: 447). Augustine is drawn into the argument: in *De doctrina Christiana* 4.7.11.17 he praises Paul's use of rhetoric. For Norden, this is merely 'interesting'. Heinrici cleverly takes us back to Paul's own citation of his enemies and contemporaries: αἱ ἐπιστολαὶ βαρεῖαι καὶ ἰσχυραί, while pointing out that both adjectives are technical terms in rhetoric (Heinrici 1900: 448). As a final indication of *his own* conviction that Paul uses rhetoric, Heinrici says that being so much part of the culture accounts historically for the success of Paul as apostle to the Gentiles.

45. Heinrici describes Norden's New Testament comments as 'aphoristic'.

46. Heinrici 1900: 436-58: 'Anhang—Zum Hellenismus des Paulus.' See p. 438: 'Die Art, wie er in seinen Briefen sich äussert, bewährt seinen schöpferischen, originalen Geist, der frei von den Fesseln bestimmter Schulung die Mittel der Überzeugungskunst beherrscht, welche die Voraussetzung seiner Erfolge als Heidenmissionar waren. Ist es befremdlich, dass diese Mittel sich berühren mit der bewährten Redetechnik, welche in der Kaiserzeit mehr als früher Bestandtheil der allgemeinen Bildung geworden war? dass Paulus anknüpfte an das Gemeinsame, um für das Neue, das er brachte, empfänglich zu stimmen.'

47. Heinrici 1900: 445 cites Norden citing Renan as follows: 'Il est impossible de violer plus audacieusement...le génie de la langue grecque...; on dirait une rapide conversation stenographiée et reproduite sans correction.'

48. The categories 'rabbinic' and 'Hellenistic' have been show in modern scholarship to be unwieldy.

Heinrici is able to turn the tables somewhat on Norden by using Norden to support his case[49] and he can show that many instances of rhetorical usage can be detailed in Paul's writing.

None of this means that Paul does not have an individual style; on the contrary! His style, according to Heinrici, is very individual and compressed, unlike other writers, from whatever period, classical, Hellenistic or Byzantine (Heinrici 1900: 453).

Heinrici makes a comment which he does not fully explain, but which would go against the present thesis, when he observes that 2 Corinthians 8–9 would not serve as examples of trained writing, but is rather 'liturgical' in tone.[50]

He does not mean that rhetoric cannot be used, but simply that the special marks of Paul's style are not present, such as personification, diatribe etc. The reference to 'liturgical' is interesting because, as we shall see, there is something ecclesiastical about the vocabulary in at least part of 2 Corinthians 8–9. In Chapter 3, it will be investigated whether or not 2 Corinthians 8–9 constitute a dense passage of subtle

49. 'Als Beispiele für die Thatsache, dass Paulus "oft genug von den geläufigen Mitteln zierlicher griechischer Rhetorik Gebrauch gemacht hat", werden auch von *Norden* hervorgehoben die Homoioteleuta, Paronomasien "und dergleichen sehr viel" (503), die Antithesen (507), deren Eindruck mit den Worten fixirt wird: "das ist der Ton, der wie eine παλίντονος ἁρμονία aus Paulus Schriften zu uns hinüberklingt" (508)—also doch ein Grundton echt hellenischen Klangs. Auch betreffs der Periodisirung wird zutreffend hervorgehoben, dass der atl. Parallelismus der Glieder mit nichten die Sprachfarbe kennzeichnet, wie dies bei den synoptischen Reden Jesu und im Johannesevangelium meist der Fall ist, sonder vielmehr die Eurythmie der Parataxen, wie der Grieche sie in gehobener Rede gebraucht. Auch einzelne gute Perioden werden markirt und die vielfachen Unregelmässigkeiten des Satzbaus daraus erklärt, dass der Apostel "den Mangel an Kunst des Periodisirens mit griechischen Schrifstellern jener Zeit theile" (506 A.3). Doch auf diese richtigen Bemerkungen fällt wider ein ganz schiefes Licht, wenn schliesslich des Paulus Briefstil mit den leistungen der "asianischen Sophistik" verglichen wird' (Heinrici 1900: 449).

50. 'Der Sprachcharakter der referierenden Stücke wie 1Th 1-3. Röm 18-16. II Kor 8-9 zeigt diese Stileigentümlichkeiten nicht. Hier herrscht die *Tendenz* auf die möglichst feierliche, umständliche und volle Vergegenwärtigung der religiösen Beziehungen vor, die in den ständigen Hinweisen auf Gott und Christus (das formelhaft angewandte ἐν Χριστῷ, διὰ Χριστοῦ u. a.) und in der Häufung von schildernden Adjectiven, von synonymen Substantiven, von Subordinationen in Genitiven, in Folge- und Zwecksätzen sich zeigt. Man möchte hier den Stil liturgisch nennen' (Heinrici 1990: 455).

argumentation, which rhetoric helps to unfold. It should already be clear that Heinrici is not at all concerned with the rhetorical structure (τάξις), but rather with the figures of speech and thought. Again, his comments will be compared with the results arrived at here in Chapters 4 and 5.

### 3. *Hans Dieter Betz (1985)*

Although Betz's commentary on 2 Corinthians 8–9 stands firmly within the historical critical tradition (he cites widely his predecessors), he does bring to bear on the text a deep appreciation of epistolary and rhetorical conventions, not to speak of his knowledge of the cultural background, both in general and in particular. He provides a useful history of the critical tradition from Semler onwards, and continues that tradition by opting for two distinct letters in chapters 8 and 9 and sees his work as a confirmation of that of Semler (Betz 1985: 35-36). In his commentary, he accordingly deals with 2 Corinthians 8 in ch. 2 and 2 Corinthians 9 in ch. 3. In both cases the commentary is *preceded* by a full rhetorical outline.

Betz presents no theory of rhetorical methodology in regard to the *dispositio*. However, it would be unfair to say that he simply asserts this outline because in the commentary he shows why such moments as the *exordium* and the *peroratio* are to be found in the verses he indicates. There are fundamental differences in method and results between Betz's work and this thesis and detailed comparison will be presented later in our Chapter Six. For the moment, however, we continue the exposé of his work.[51]

In the commentary, Betz *begins* with the rhetorical outline and in the comment he mingles rhetorical, epistolary and historical questions. The interest here focuses on the use of rhetoric, and for the sake of clarity, it seems useful to place side by side his rhetorical outline and a summary of his discussion of the *dispositio*. The rhetorical figures, more fully described and explained later, are separately presented in summary fashion.

---

51. The reader is referred to the appropriate verse of the commentary for these detailed observations.

## 3.1. *Letter A 8.1-24*

*Dispositio*

| | | | |
|---|---|---|---|
| omitted | [I. Epistolary prescript] | | |
| 1-24 | II. Body of the letter | | |
| | 1-5 | *Exordium* | |
| | 6 | *Narratio* | |
| | 7-8 | *Propositio* | |
| | 9-15 | *Probatio* | |
| | | 9 | *First Proof* |
| | | *10-12* | *Second Proof* |
| | | *13-15* | *Third Proof* |
| | 16-22 | Commendation of the delegates | |
| | 23 | Authorization of the delegates | |
| | 24 | *Peroratio* | |
| omitted | [Epistolary postcript] | | |

*8.1-5. The* Exordium *(Introduction).* This is the *exordium* because its purpose is to gain the reader's attention. Its function is to provoke comparison between the Macedonians and the Corinthians.

*8.6. The* Narratio *(Statement of Facts).* This is the *narratio* because it is distinct from the *exemplum* of the *exordium* and tells of something which happened just before writing. Betz makes reference without further explanation to the works on rhetoric by Volkmann (1885), Lausberg (1990) and Martin (1974) and to his own commentary on Galatians (Betz 1979).

*8.7-8. The* Propositio *(Proposition).* The thesis, or issue at stake, normally follows the *narratio*. Verse 7 is in two parts: 7a reflects the Corinthians' self-understanding while 7b contains Paul's hopes for them. Thus the points of agreement and disagreement are set forth. At this point, Betz distinguishes the two triads of characteristics. The second triad contains the issues under dispute.

*8.9-15. The* Probatio *(Proofs).* Betz reviews Cicero and Quintilian on the number of proofs in a deliberative argument, Cicero counting four: *res expetendae* ('things to be sought'), *honesta* ('things honourable'), *utilia* ('things advantageous'), *honestas* ('honesty'), and Quintilian counting three: *honestum* ('honourable'), *utile* ('useful'), τὸ δυνατόν ('possible'). Paul likewise has three points: the honourable (8.9), the expedient (10-12) and the fair (13-15). Paul actually names the latter two, but the first has no title and Betz takes some trouble to show that the first proof fits the triad. Betz does not deal with the authorization of the envoys under the rubric of rhetoric.

*8.24. The* Peroratio *(Peroration).* According to Betz, οὖν signals the start of the peroration which should normally contain a summary of what preceded.[52] Further evidence that we are dealing with the *peroratio* would be the summary nature and the future orientation of the content.

*Rhetorical Figures.*
*Exemplum*[53]—the churches in Macedonia (8.1-2) Specifically, an encomium.
*Synkrisis*[54]—rivalry between the Corinthians and the Macedonians (agonistic motif).
Oxymoron—8.2.
Oath—8.3.
Ellipsis—8.5 (which is also the climax of the *exordium*).
*Anacoluthon*—8.7b, in the ἵνα clause.
*Correctio*[55]—8.8, an epistolary *topos* or common place.
Chiasm 8.9—which is also an *exemplum*.
*Sententia*[56]—8.10, a *topos* of expediency.
*Sententia*—8.12, a proof text.
Proof text—8.15.
Proverb—8.21.
*Figura etymologica*[57]—v. 24 with ἔνδειξιν ἐνδεκύομαι, which Betz claims is unique.

52. Betz appeals again, without further precision, to Volkmann, Lausberg, Martin, and lastly to his own work on Galatians.
53. *Exemplum* is a figure which uses an event or story to illustrate a point.
54. *Synkrisis* is a technique of comparison.
55. *Correctio* is the figure by which one improves upon an expression.
56. *Sententia* is a proverb or maxim.
57. Betz provides a broad reference to Greek literature, ignoring the manuals of rhetoric.

## 3.2. *Letter B 9.1-16*

*Dispositio*

| | | | |
|---|---|---|---|
| omitted | [I. Epistolary prescript] | | |
| 1-15 | II. Body of the letter | | |
| | 1-2 | *Exordium* | |
| | 3-5a | *Narratio* | |
| | 5bc | *Propositio* | |
| | 6-14 | *Probatio* | |
| | | 6 | *Thesis* |
| | | 7 | *First Proof* |
| | | 8 | *Second Proof* |
| | | 9-11 | *Third Proof* |
| | | 12 | *Fourth Proof* |
| | | 13-14 | *Fifth Proof* |
| | 15 | *Peroratio* | |
| omitted | [Epistolary postcript] | | |

Here, again, is a summary of his reasoning.

*9.1-2. The* Exordium *(Introduction).* The tone is introductory, according to Betz, as evidenced by the use of περί at the start. The editor, according to Betz, has chosen to follow the same technique as in ch. 8, that is, the epistolary prescript and postscript have been omitted, while the *exordium* is matched at the end by a *peroratio*. The rhetorical situation was that of *taedium* and so Paul begins by saying there is no need to write at all. Verse 2 is an example of *captatio benevolentiae*.[58]

*9.3-5b. The* Narratio *(Statement of Facts).* As regards showing that here we are dealing with a *narratio*, Betz refers us back to the previous references to Volkmann, Lausberg and Martin. He notes a similarity with the sending of the brothers in 8.20-22, which is found, however, not in the *narratio*, but in the *probatio* of the Letter A.

*9.5b-c. The* Propositio *(Proposition).* The *propositio* follows the *narratio*, and its purpose is like the earlier *propositio*, to set forth areas of agreement and disagreement. The remaining tasks were twofold. First,

---

58. *Captatio benevolentiae* may be used at any point, but is especially suited to the *exordium*.

the Achaians were responsible for successful completion of the collection in Corinth as well. Second, the manner of the participation, its spiritual dimension, should not be lost sight of.

*9.6-14. The* Probatio *(Proof).* Paul begins an elaborate interpretation of εὐλογία, consisting of an initial thesis (v. 6) and five consecutive proofs (7-14). Hence the passage may be termed a *probatio*. The type of rhetoric involved here is rhetoric *a finitione*, which Quintilian explains as 'Arguments, then, may be drawn from definition, sometimes called *finitio* and sometimes *finis*'. (Quintilian 5.10.54). The five proofs may be classified as follows:

> Proof 1 (v. 7) [category not made explicit];
> Proof 2 (v. 8) from the nature of God;
> Proof 3 (vv. 9-11) by Scripture, allegorical reading, ethical conclusions;
> Proof 4 (v. 12) by comparison;
> Proof 5 (v. 13-14) [category not made explicit].

*9.15. The* Peroratio *(Peroration).* This is classified firstly as a brief prayer. Could it also be the *peroratio*? Betz thinks that this verse is probably the first example of an early Christian prayer of thanksgiving and presumably the congregation would continue the prayer. It summarizes the content of Letter B, dealing as it did with various aspects of gift of blessing. By this thanksgiving, Paul wishes to motivate his hearers to complete the task.

*Rhetorical Figures.*
*Sententia*—9.6a
Antithesis—9.6b (with the entire verse exhibiting *parallelismus membrorum*)
Proverb—9.7
Proof from Scripture—9.9
Allegory—9.10
Epithets[59]—9.10

Finally, Betz classifies these two letters as administrative letters and provides abundant evidence to show that the language is 'administrative'. The two parts of Letter A belong to deliberative and juridical

---

59. *Epitheton* is the figure of adding descriptive phrases to expand and add emphasis.

rhetoric respectively; while Letter B is one piece and belongs to deliberative rhetoric.[60]

Betz brings a dazzling familiarity with Greek literature as well as epistolary and administrative conventions to enrich our grasp of these chapters. It is not so clear, however, that his use of rhetoric is well grounded, both as regards method and application.[61] Betz remains, however, the major partner in dialogue for this thesis and a detailed refutation of his *dispositio* is undertaken in our conclusions in Chapter Six.

## 4. *F. Young and P. Ford (1987)*

*Meaning and Truth in 2 Corinthians* is an attempt at a fresh reading of the letter.[62] It belongs to a series (Biblical Foundations in Theology), the explicit aim of which is 'to bridge the gap between biblical scholarship and the larger enterprise of Christian theology' (Editors' Foreword). It attempts a large theological reading of the entire letter, within its Jewish and Hellenistic context, using, in particular, the methods of modern hermeneutics and sociology. The authors are convinced that the letter can be read as a unity, this conviction is based, in part, on a reading of some classical and modern rhetoric and on a comparison sketched between this letter and the Second Epistle of Demosthenes. The discussion is organized in a way different to other users of rhetoric because Young and Ford are more concerned with a general overview than with a detailed rhetorical analysis.[63] As a result, they do not engage in questions of rhetorical methodology.

The discussion begins with the question of the genre of 2 Corinthians. They hold there is a striking comparison between 2 Corinthians and the Second Epistle of Demosthenes. On p. 37, they write:

> Superficially there is a striking resemblance to 2 Corinthians. Both are epistles, both are from men appealing to have their case reviewed, for both their case revolves around their relationship with and services to the community addressees—that is, they are apologetic appeals, in the ancient and proper sense of apology. Both begin by focusing on common

60. This administrative vocabulary is discussed below.

61. Betz offers the same analysis, much abbreviated, in his article on 2 Corinthians in *ABD*, I: 1148-54.

62. Although published in 1987, i.e. two years after Betz's commentary on 2 Cor. 8–9, there is no reference to the latter work in Young and Ford.

63. Young and Ford (1987: 37-44) contains the major discussion of rhetoric.

ground, respect, mutual recognition assumed as the basis from which to make the case, both go over points for and against the pleader, reminiscing about services rendered, answering charges; and, assuming that 2 Corinthians is a unity, each ends with a passionate review of the material covered, in which tact and politeness gives way to hard-hitting emotion.

They note that the Second Epistle is a very fine example of the standard form of forensic speech in epistolary form. The structural outline (i.e. *dispositio*) they take from a variety of sources, namely, Aristotle's *Rhetoric*, Dionysius of Halicarnassus' *Lysias* and Quintilian's *Institutio Oratoria*. This is outlined on p. 38 using the following terms:

(a) Introduction or *exordium* (προοίμιον)
(b) The narrative (διήγησις)
(c) The proof(s) (πίστις, πίστεις)
(d) The peroration (ἐπίλογος).

A closer identification of rhetorical units is not attempted, although chs. 10–13 are identified with the peroration of the whole letter. Young and Ford are more interested in the genre, which they identify as apologetic letter, using the 21 categories of Demetrius.

These are extensive claims and proving them would call for an entirely different book to the one which Young and Ford wrote. They are, however, aware of the general objections to the use of classical rhetoric.

Young and Ford think that Paul's letter writing, at least, was impressive. His speech may have been less impressive, but even there our authors offer an interpretation of 11.6, in which ἰδιώτης is taken to mean 'idiosyncratic', peculiar to myself, rather than 'a layman'. They notice too the language of apology in 12.19 and the approving commentary of John Chrysostom, who 'at least up to a point seems to have recognised in Paul a fellow-rhetorician' (Young and Ford 1987: 40).

What of Paul's education? Here Young and Ford are very cautious. They follow Quintilian and Kennedy in noting that a certain rhetorical arrangement is 'inevitable' or 'universal'. But they go beyond that to claim that Paul would have had some considerable grasp of Greek culture—especially if he had been sent to Jerusalem, where 'the pupils of Gamaliel received instruction in the wisdom of the Greeks' (Young and Ford 1987: 41). Finally, rhetoric pervaded all aspects of life and would have filtered down to other levels of society to a greater or lesser extent. All in all, it is not to be unexpected that Paul would have used the culturally available conventions. That general point is then supported by specific examples, such as diatribe in Romans, the use of the topos of Socratic tradition and his audacious adaptations of epistolary conventions.

> Paul's language, though not striving for the stylistic polish of con-
> temporary rhetoric, with its cadences, rhythms, figures of speech, etc., is
> nevertheless the language of someone trying to create an effect, full of
> antitheses, repetitions, the language typical of public address, whether
> political or evangelistic. (Young and Ford 1987: 40).

Young and Ford avoid exaggerated rhetorical claims for Paul and modestly claim merely that 2 Corinthians was self-consciously conceived as an apology according to the norms of the day. Read linearly, as recommended by Kennedy, the rhetorical shape may be observed.

> The fact that it opens with a tone of approval, in spite of underlying ten-
> sions which progressively emerge, fits with this fundamental purpose; so
> does the emotional ending. The spiralling arguments of the body of the
> letter can very easily be analysed into a series of apologetic proofs which
> conform to Quintilian's view that they should be presented in a flexible
> sequence not according to some rigid enumeration. (Young and Ford
> 1987: 41).

The understanding of the use of rhetoric is nuanced by the following comment:

> Our conclusion is not that Paul was a Jewish Demosthenes, but that
> 2 Corinthians was self-consciously conceived as an apology according to
> the norms of the day. This theory accounts for the changes in emotional
> tone within the epistle, for it was written with a view to producing cer-
> tain effects on the reader/listener. It was aimed at persuading, and uses
> the arts of persuasion. Read in a linear way (Kennedy stresses the impor-
> tance of reading ancient texts as speeches, and thus being able to appre-
> ciate their linear quality), the rhetorical shape of the whole epistle can be
> observed (Young and Ford 1987: 43-44).

Young and Ford have a very useful account of the cultural background of economy. For them it is a metaphor which helps to under-gird the unity of the letter and in this respect chs. 8 and 9 have a special place (Young and Ford 1987: 176-80). Although apparently unaware of the work of F.W. Danker, they are aware of the potential of semantic fields in interpreting these chapters. The issue of the collection is of great importance, not only on a practical level, but also symbolically. This project functions almost 'sacramentally' (Young and Ford 1987: 180), that is, it brings together three essential themes: the unity between Jews and Gentiles, the validity of Paul's apostolate and a reflection of the gracious economy of God, by which ordinary things are given extraordinary value.

It would be possible to criticise the rhetorical aspects of this study: there is no methodology, no discrimination regarding sources used, and the comparison with Demosthenes is less than complete. However, Young and Ford were not attempting a *rhetorical* study of Paul, but a theological reading which incorporates some new approaches and is specifically concerned with the integrity of the entire letter. From those points of view, their study has much to offer. At the end of this work, the question will be asked whether this rhetorical analysis of chapters 8 and 9 has anything to offer regarding the question of the unity of the epistle. Then, some of the insights of Young and Ford will be taken up again.

### 5. *Frederick W. Danker (1989)*

F.W. Danker is the author not only of a commentary on 2 Corinthians, but also of *Benefactor: Epigraphic Study of a Graeco-Roman and New Testament Semantic Field*. Written in 1982, this latter book was used by Betz in his Hermeneia commentary on 2 Corinthians 8–9. In turn, Danker graciously acknowledges his debt to Betz, while proposing to continue the discussion. Like Betz, Danker is dealing with 2 Corinthians from an explicitly rhetorical point of view. Given, however, that his commentary is in a general series and covers all of 2 Corinthians, it was not really feasible for him to undertake a complete rhetorical analysis. His rhetorical concerns are threefold: figures of speech, similarities in the rhetorical tradition and the general persuasive strategies of Paul. This means that he leaves out explicit discussion of *dispositio* and *inventio*. Given the earlier book, it is no surprise to find that he makes consistent reference to the benefactor semantic field. The task here is to record the rhetorical observations of Danker. At the end, I will discuss Danker's position on the unity of chapters 8 and 9, and their place in 2 Corinthians as a whole.

### 5.1. *Rhetorical Figures*
In the course of his commentary, Danker notes the following 'figures of speech'. As these are not especially numerous, it is convenient to view them in verse sequence.

*8.2.* Amplification on the word περισσεία (Danker 1989: 118).

*8.7.* Verse 7 is in effect an amplification of the ἵνα clause in v. 6 (Danker 1989: 123). There is likewise a chiasm formed by the words faith/earnestness and utterance/knowledge. *Paronomasia* (Danker 1989: 125) is found in v. 7 in a play on the word χάρις.

*8.9. Exemplum* of Christ (Danker 1989: 126).

*8.11.* Failure to match words and deeds is a commonplace of Roman and Hellenistic literature (Danker 1989: 127).

*8.12-15.* Paul echoes, in his own language, a common cultural maxim (Danker 1989: 128) about equity.

*8.21.* Balanced structure was especially pleasing to the Greeks (Danker 1989: 132).

*9.5.* Wordplay using the prefix προ and on the words εὐλογία and πλεονεξία (Danker 1989: 137).

*9.6.* A maxim, much enjoyed by the Greeks because the form echoed the orderliness of the thought (Danker 1989: 138).

*9.10.* A metaphor (growth) which was common in the culture (Danker 1989: 142).

*5.2. Persuasive Strategies*
Paul's relationship with the Corinthians was often fragile, and asking such people for money presented a difficulty. Paul circumvents the difficulty by couching his request in language redolent of the cultural phenomenon of benefaction (Danker 1989: 121); this flattering language offers status to people who might otherwise never hope to attain it. Likewise, in 8.7, the unexpected reference to his own love for the Corinthians has a cultural explanation. He is following the example of the Lord, as they should. Virtue was cultivated by calling attention to the heroic exploits of national heroes (Danker 1989: 125).

5.3. *Integrity*

Danker holds that the affliction–joy contrast which opens ch. 8 is in continuity with 2 Cor. 4.17-18 and with the polarities of grief–repentance and anxiety–joy expressed in ch. 7. He also thinks that the term joy echoes the cognate verb rejoice in 7.7, 9, 13, 16 and the noun in 7.4 and 13. The notion of 'increase' in 7.15 is likewise continued in the beginning of ch. 8 (Danker 1989: 118). A further link between 7 and 8 is formed by the semantic field of zeal, present in these chapters seven times, against 11 occurrences in all of Paul (Danker 1989: 124).

When it comes to 9.1, Danker notes putative redactors have joined the chapters with the 'minimum of seam work' (Danker 1989: 134). Apparently, he thinks the supposed break here is not an insurmountable obstacle. He supports the change of vocabulary by noting that the rhetors avoided boredom by changing topic somewhat. This parallels a similar tactic in Demosthenes' 'On the crown' 50. The phrase in 9.1 which gives so much trouble (Περὶ μὲν γὰρ) bridges the transition to the theme of shame, already implicit in 8.24 (Danker 1989: 134-36).

Finally, Danker finds the use of similar vocabulary in the opening sentences of ch. 8 and the closing sentences of ch. 9 'a powerful piece of evidence for the unity of chaps. 8 and 9' (Danker 1989: 143).

Danker provides no argumentative structure for 8 and 9. The importance of Danker for this study will be more evident in Chapter 3, when his work on the vocabulary of benefaction will help in the delimitation of the text and its units. This in turn will be of greater significance for assessing the underlying cultural background to the persuasiveness of 2 Corinthians 8–9. His identification of figures of speech will be taken up in Chapters 4 and 5.

## 6. *Ben Witherington III (1995)*

Witherington's socio-rhetorical commentary[64] on 2 Corinthians is excellent on background information and sources. He provides a wealth of material which helps to recuperate the resonance of this ancient text in its historical and cultural setting. It is also well written, but, at the same time, it can be frustrating from a methodological point of view. Witherington is aware of the sources for rhetorical analysis and makes passing use of them. However, he establishes no special method for

---

64. He deals with chs. 8–9 on pp. 411-28.

identifying units and the accusation could be levelled that he simply asserts rather than demonstrates the identifications.

His rhetorical analysis covers the entire letter, which he structures rhetorically as follows:

1. The epistolary prescript (1.1-2).
2. The epistolary thanksgiving and *exordium* (1.3-7).
3. The *narratio* (1.8–2.14), which explains some of the facts that occasioned the letter and climaxes with a further thanksgiving and transition (2.15f.).
4. The *propositio* (2.17), which states the basic fact under dispute.
5. The *probatio* and *refutatio* (3.1–13.4), which includes:
   a. Paul's characterization of his ministry and of his anti-Sophistic rhetorical approach (3.1–6.13);
   b. a deliberative digression (6.14–7.1), in which Paul put his audience on the defensive, urging them to stop attending temple feasts with pagan friends;
   c. Paul's defence of the severe letter (7.2-16);
   d. a largely deliberative argument concerning the collection (chs. 8 and 9); and
   e. a rhetorical *synkrisis* (comparison) of Paul and his competitors in Corinth, the false *apostoloi*, with a strong emotional appeal.
6. The *peroratio* (13.5-10).
7. The closing epistolary greetings and remarks (Witherington 1995: 335-36).

Because he is reading the entire letter, he begins by situating chs. 8–9 within the whole argument. When Paul comes to ch. 8, he assumes that he has achieved two things: that his good character (the ethos of Paul) has been established with the audience and secondly he thinks them well disposed towards himself (the ethos of the Corinthians).[65] It is this confidence which allows him to move from defending himself to putting them on the defensive. Witherington classifies the arguments as deliberative/forensic (1995: 412).

The commentary on the letter is informative and stimulating on the background of *amicitia* and benefactors. Similarly, Witherington is aware that these chapters function within the broader question of keeping the Jewish and Gentile missions in communion and he furthermore engages in possible historical reconstructions of the sequence of events.

---

65. I am not so sure about this because in 2 Corinthians 8–9 Paul effectively effaces himself and is extremely cautious towards the Corinthians as the careful rhetorical strategy shows.

However, for a precisely rhetorical reading Witherington contents himself with occasional references to the manuals, in the course of a broader exposition of 8–9. Apparently 8.1-6 is a unit, with a new section starting at v. 7. Verse 7 to the end of ch. 8 seem to be a unit. A new section within the same argument begins in 9.1 and Witherington comes down on the side of those who do not think a new letter starts here. He treats ch. 9 as a unit, noticing at the end that the shift in tenses from the future to the present between chs. 9 and 10 also marks a shift from deliberative mode to forensic mode.[66] Witherington has been included 'for completeness' sake' and because he is the most recent writer who expressly deals with the rhetoric of 2 Corinthians. The sparseness of his rhetorical observations reduces the significance of his commentary for this study.

## 7. Conclusion

While there is a vast exegetical literature on 2 Corinthians, it may be said that this letter as such has been somewhat neglected in terms of rhetorical analysis. It is hard to know why people do *not* write, but this may well be on account of the complicated theories of several letters and editors.

From the review undertaken in this chapter of the *status questionis*, it is clear that the most substantial and scientific study comes from H.D. Betz. There is more, of course, to Betz's commentary than the rhetorical observations and much of what he says is not in contradiction with what is proposed here. However, the *dispositio* of 2 Corinthians 8–9 offered in Chapter 4 below is in significant disagreement with the one proposed by Betz. It will be necessary, therefore, to compare both and weigh the claims of both proposals. It seems sensible to delay such a detailed comparison until the alternative has been fully described, and, therefore, this comparison is presented in the concluding Chapter of the present work.

In the meantime, it may suffice to notice the lack of an explicit methodology. The issue of delimitation does not arise, except in so far as he wants to justify the choice of 2 Corinthians 8–9. Within the chapters, no attempt is made to establish discrete units previous to the establishment of the *dispositio*. Neither does Betz show any concern for which rhetorical manuals are used.

66. Note his earlier description of these two chapters as deliberative/forensic.

Given the significance and indeed dominance of Betz, the contributions by the other writers in establishing the *status questionis* are of relatively lesser importance. The wider review, however, was undertaken because no biblical investigation ever starts at an absolute beginning and the insights of others are of value. The work of Chrysostom is valuable because he is the only representative of the living rhetorical classical tradition who makes rhetorical remarks about the selected chapters. Mainly, this is concerned with figures of speech, although his overall admiration for the subtlety of Paul's persuasion is a notable feature of his commentary. It seems to go beyond respect for the saint. In a similar way, Heinrici serves to confirm the discovery of figures of speech which will be undertaken in Chapter 4. Beyond that, his argument with Norden and his replies form an important part of the discussion entered into in Chapter 1 on the influence and use of rhetoric in Paul. Paul's place, as a Hellenistic Jew, in the society of his time is discussed further as part of the conclusions in Chapter 6.

The other contemporary figures we have dealt with, Young and Ford, Danker and Witherington, are generally concerned with the integrity of 2 Corinthians. Their contribution to the specifically rhetorical observations is strictly limited, as none of them presents a disposition for 2 Corinthians 8–9 or indeed a methodology for using rhetoric. Nevertheless, apart from completeness, they are significant because the question of the integrity both of 2 Corinthians 1–13 and 2 Corinthians 8–9 was touched on in Chapter 1 and will be taken up again from an expressly rhetorical viewpoint in our conclusions in Chapter 6. Also Young and Ford emphasize economy both as reality and as metaphor, both of which are significant for 2 Corinthians 8–9.

The review of the *status questionis* leaves us then, with the following tasks. First, the figures of speech and thought (Chrysostom, Heinrici, Betz and Danker) need to be verified and the investigation of such figures place approached in a methodical way; this is undertaken in the first part of Chapter 4. Second, the *dispositio* of 2 Corinthians 8–9 needs to be established and then compared with the work of Betz (Chapters 4 and 6).

The first step in our uncovering of the rhetoric of 2 Corinthians 8–9 consists of a delimitation of the unit 2 Corinthians 8–9 and of the smaller units within that, as explained in Chapter 1. To this task we now turn.

Chapter 3

DELIMITATION OF 2 CORINTHIANS 8–9

The purpose of this chapter is to lay the foundations for a rhetorical analysis by a detailed delimitation of 2 Corinthians 8–9 both in terms of its place within the entire letter and in terms of the units within the two chapters. One of the goals of such a delimitation is to ground the selection of these two chapters for the purposes of this study in the vocabulary used. The content of the chapter consists largely of statistical observations and, in order to facilitate the discussion, use has been made of visual representations of the statistics. The data are first presented verbally and then visually, in figures 1-7. After a brief Introduction, Part I deals with the delimitation of chs. 8 and 9 in terms of the entire letter and Part II deals with the delimitation of subsections within those two chapters. In the course of the presentation, attention is drawn to the various semantic fields to be found here which form a very considerable portion of the persuasion in 2 Corinthians 8–9. A conclusion will bring the results together. Comment on the significance of the units discovered is reserved until Chapter 5.

In Chapter 2, we saw how different authors deal with the issue of the *dispositio*. This is not the only issue at stake in a rhetorical analysis, but at a time when structural analyses of various kinds are popular, it has enjoyed a high profile. The purpose of this chapter is to delimit and segment chs. 8 and 9. The approach here is 'superficial' or 'material': we look at the material on the surface of the text—repeated words, semantic fields, indicators of a subunit such as *inclusio* or chiasm. Probabilities in exegesis are strengthened by convergence of indicators, and indicators taken chiefly from narrative analysis will be used as well: time, place, persons, action. These are used to establish probable or likely units. The identification of such units awaits corroboration in the rhetorical analysis proper.

It is important neither to understate nor to overstate what is at stake here. Not to overstate: *alone* these material indicators tell us the *probable* units of discussion; a certain artificiality attends the placing of the content in parentheses, even temporarily. Not to understate: *without* these indicators, the identification of units and especially units of argument can be quite arbitrary and people using a rhetorical method have come up with different accounts of the divisions and subsections of chs. 8 and 9. There is a need, therefore, to establish the segments of the text independently of, and previous to, the identification of rhetorical stages in the argument. Such segmentation is provisional and must be confirmed later in terms of the content and in terms of rhetoric.

## 1. *Delimitation of 2 Corinthians 8–9*

Three steps are taken to show that chs. 8–9 form a unit of discussion: (1) They share a vocabulary distinct from what appears before in chs. 1–7 and after in chs. 10–13; (2) the vocabulary in chs. 8–9 is substantially characteristic of the chapters and serves to isolate them; and (3) finally there is an *inclusio* to indicate that these chapters should be read as a single unit.

### 1.1. *Distinct from the Text Before and After*
It is widely conceded that chs. 8–9 may be distinguished from chs. 1–7 and chs. 10–13. The subject matter of chs. 8–9 is not hinted at in chs. 1–7, although many writers reckon that in ch. 7 a preparation is made in terms of praise and flattery. That a new *subject* is to be broached is indicated in the opening words of 8.1: Γνωρίζομεν δὲ ὑμῖν, ἀδελφοί. Elsewhere in Paul, this and similar phrases function regularly as an indicator of the transition to a new subject. This is exceptionally clear in 1 Corinthians 15.

| | |
|---|---|
| *1 Cor. 15.1* | **Γνωρίζω δὲ ὑμῖν**, ἀδελφοί, |
| | τὸ εὐαγγέλιον ὃ εὐηγγελισάμην ὑμῖν, |
| | ὃ καὶ παρελάβετε, ἐν ᾧ καὶ ἑστήκατε, |
| *1 Cor. 15.1* | Now I would remind you, brothers and sisters, |
| | of the good news that I proclaimed to you, |
| | which you in turn received, in which also you stand, |

Here Paul is introducing a subject not yet treated in 1 Corinthians. Again in 1 Cor. 12.3, where the expression γνωρίζω ὑμίν is used in parallel with οὐ θέλω ὑμᾶς ἀγνοεῖν, which is itself accompanied by the renewal of the address ἀδελφοί.

*1 Cor. 12.3*      διὸ **γνωρίζω ὑμῖν** ὅτι
                   οὐδεὶς ἐν πνεύματι θεοῦ λαλῶν λέγει·
                   Ἀνάθεμα Ἰησοῦς,
                   καὶ οὐδεὶς δύναται εἰπεῖν· Κύριος Ἰησοῦς,
                   εἰ μὴ ἐν πνεύματι ἁγίῳ.

*1 Cor. 12.3*      Therefore I want you to understand
                   that no one speaking by the Spirit of God ever says
                   'Let Jesus be cursed!'
                   and no one can say 'Jesus is Lord' except by the Holy Spirit.

It is usually conceded that chs. 12–14 form a distinct unit in 1 Corinthians as does ch. 15.

Finally, the expression Γνωρίζομεν δὲ ὑμινν is not quite the same as the use in Gal. 1.11, where the form indicates a transition from the *exordium* to the *propositio*, γὰρ being slightly less adversative than δὲ.

*Gal. 1.11*        **Γνωρίζω γὰρ ὑμῖν**, ἀδελφοί,
                   τὸ εὐαγγέλιον τὸ εὐαγγελισθὲν ὑπ᾽ ἐμοῦ
                   ὅτι οὐκ ἔστιν κατὰ ἄνθρωπον·

*Gal. 1.11*        For I want you to know, brothers and sisters,
                   that the gospel that was proclaimed by me
                   is not of human origin;

The adversative conjunction δὲ is stronger than γὰρ and serves also to make the transition in 2 Cor. 8.1 to a new topic.

After ch. 9, the opening words of 2 Cor. 10.1 mark an especially solemn introduction to what follows: Αὐτὸς δὲ ἐγὼ Παῦλος παρακαλῶ ὑμᾶς. As a break between sections this forceful address is unique to 2 Cor. 10.1, although in its forcefulness, it resembles the opening of Gal. 1.6.

## 1.2. *Distinctive Semantic Fields of 2 Corinthians 8–9*
Within chs. 8–9, there are several significant semantic fields, which distinguish these chapters. They fall into the following categories: (a) words to do with gift, grace, giving, thanksgiving; (b) words to do with poverty, wealth, need and abundance; (c) words to do with planting, sowing, harvesting, seed, bread, food, increase; (d) words to do with honour and shame; (e) words to do with attitudes and emotions; (f) words to do with benefactor. These are taken in sequence.

a. *Words to do with gift, grace, giving, thanksgiving.* ἁπλότης,[1] χάρις,[2] δίδωμι,[3] δότης,[4] δωρεά,[5] εὐχαριστία,[6] χορηγέω,[7] ἐπιχορηγέω,[8] σκορπίζω.[9]

The *Greek–English Lexicon of the New Testament based on Semantic Domains (GELNTSD*[10]) lists these words in two places, under 'Give' (57.71-124) and under 'Thanks' (33.349-53). They can be treated, however, as a single semantic field (a) because χάρις occurs in both listings and both meanings are used by Paul, thus bridging the two semantic fields; (b) because of the root χάρις in εὐχαριστέω. I include, as well, in this semantic field the following verbs (a) σκορπίζω (57.95) because in context it means to give generously; (b) χορηγέω (35.31) and ἐπι-χορηγέω (35.31) because in context they both mean to 'offer, make available or simply give',[11] and thus belong to the same semantic field. Σκορπίζω, διασκορπίζω and διασπείρω (διασπορά) are related in the LXX,[12] thus laying the ground for a possible link with the semantic field of agriculture.

Of these words, only δότης is strictly unique, but the others occur in significant concentration, as may be seen from the following chart.

1.  ἁπλότης: 1.12; **8.2; 9.11, 13**; 11.3.
2.  χάρις: 1.2,12,15; 2.14; 4.15; 6.1; **8.1, 4, 6, 7, 9, 16, 19; 9.8, 14, 15**;12.9; 13.13.
3.  δίδωμι: 1.22; 5.5,12,18; 6.3; **8.1,5,10,16; 9.9**; 10.8; 12.7; 13.10.
4.  δότης· **9.7**.
5.  δωρεάν: **9.15**; 11.7 (as an adverb).
6.  εὐχαριστία: 4.15; **9.11, 12**.
7.  χορηγέω: **9.10**.
8.  ἐπιχορηγέω: **9.10**.
9.  σκορπίζω: **9.9**.
10. Published by Louw and Nida. It is a lexicon designed for translators of the Greek New Testament and it brings together words which constitute semantic fields, thus facilitating comparison and contrast of connotation and denotation. The numbers in brackets in the text refer to the appropriate sections of volume I of *GELNTSD*.
11. As pointed out in *EDNT*, III: 45.
12. *TDNT*, VII: 418.

Figure 1. *Words to do with gift, grace, giving, thanksgiving*

| A | B | C | D |
|---|---|---|---|
|  | *44* | *8.48* | *5187* |
| 1 | 5 | 9.12 | 548 |
| 2 | 1 | 3.08 | 325 |
| 3 | 0 | 0.00 | 331 |
| 4 | 2 | 5.49 | 364 |
| 5 | 3 | 7.73 | 388 |
| 6 | 2 | 6.13 | 326 |
| 7 | 0 | 0.00 | 385 |
| **8** | **12** | **25.64** | **468** |
| **9** | **13** | **41.01** | **317** |
| 10 | 1 | 2.83 | 353 |
| 11 | 1 | 1.64 | 609 |
| 12 | 2 | 4.03 | 496 |
| 13 | 2 | 7.22 | 277 |

In the following illustration of the frequencies, the horizontal axis represents the chapters in 2 Corinthians and the vertical axis represents the number of occurrences.

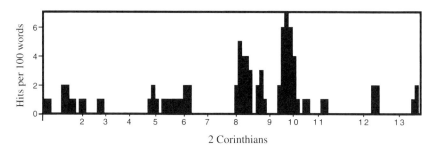

To explain the significance of these tables, in each figure:

column *A* on the left gives the chapter number;
column *B* gives the actual number of occurrences;
column *C* gives the proportion of occurrences per 1000 words (thus giving a kind of average);
column *D* gives the total number of words in each chapter.

The first row of figures, in italics, is to be read as follows: under *B* the actual number of occurrences; under *C* the average proportion per 1000 words; under *D* the total number of words in 2 Corinthians. As we are concerned with chs. 8 and 9, the data for these two chapters are in **bold.**

In the graph, the proportion of occurrences per 100[13] words is referred to as 'hits'; this informal terminology is part of the programme used and cannot be altered. The graph itself portrays the proportion of 'hits' in each chapter, using two axes, one horizontal and the other vertical. The horizontal axis gives the chapters in 2 Corinthians while the vertical axis gives the proportion of 'hits' per 100 words. The graph is too imprecise to be part of the argument; it serves simply as a visual representation of the detailed information contained in the preceding paragraph(s) and in the columns alongside. Finally, in this kind of detailed work, it is important to keep the larger picture in view and with that in mind headings and conclusions have been provided after each block of analysis.

The preponderance, in the graph, of the semantic field of 'giving' in chs. 8 and 9 is confirmed by the statistics. This semantic field is a first step in distinguishing these two chapters. These are key words because they deal with the subject matter of the argument—the collection for Jerusalem—a subject not otherwise alluded to in 2 Corinthians.

b. *Words to do with quantity and wealth.* Under 'Quantity', *GELNTSD* 59, we find the following words gathered: ἁδρότης[14] (59.60), αὐξάνω[15] (59.63), ὀλίγος[16] (59.13), περισσεία[17] (59.53), περισσεύω[18] (59.52), περίσσευμα[19] (59.53) πληθύνω[20] (59.68-69). The compilers allocate a different place to αὐτάρκεια[21], (at 75.6) under 'adequate, qualified', but place ἀρκέτος and ἀρκέω at 59.45 and 46 respectively, where the root means sufficient, adequate. In our context, αὐτάρκεια belongs to the same semantic field of quantity. Likewise ὑπερβάλλω[22] is allocated to

---

13. The discrepancy between the two modes of assessing proportion (i.e. per 1000 words in the list and per 100 words the graph) is a technical problem. The graph is more accurate using per 100 words, but the program permits in the list analysis per 1000 words only. The discrepancy does not affect the argument, merely the mode of presentation.

14. ἁδρότης: **8.20**.

15. αὐξάνω: **9.10**; 10.15.

16. ὀλίγος: **8.15**.

17. περισσεία: **8.2**; 10.15.

18. περισσεύω: 1.5 (×2); 3.9; 4.15; **8.2, 7** (×2)**; 9.8** (×2), **12**.

19. περίσσευμα: **8.14** (×2).

20. πληθύνω: **9.10**.

21. αὐτάρκεια: **9.8**.

22. ὑπερβάλλω: 3.10; **9.14**.

78.33 under 'degree'. However, the word field includes again περισ-σεία and περισσεύω (78.31), and in addition περισσότερος (78.31). There is, therefore, a bridge between domains 59 and 78, which allows us to use them together here. To these we can add the very common word πολύς[23] (59.1; 59.11; 67.77; 78.3).

Figure 2a. *Words to do with quantity*

| A | B | C | D |
|---|---|---|---|
| | 45 | 8.68 | 5187 |
| 1 | 4 | 7.30 | 548 |
| 2 | 4 | 12.31 | 325 |
| 3 | 4 | 12.08 | 331 |
| 4 | 2 | 5.49 | 364 |
| 5 | 0 | 0.00 | 388 |
| 6 | 2 | 6.13 | 326 |
| 7 | 2 | 5.19 | 385 |
| **8** | **14** | **29.91** | **468** |
| **9** | **8** | **25.24** | **317** |
| 10 | 2 | 5.67 | 353 |
| 11 | 1 | 1.64 | 609 |
| 12 | 2 | 4.03 | 496 |
| 13 | 0 | 0.00 | 277 |

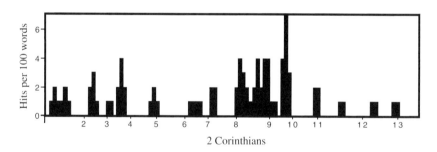

2 Corinthians

The chart is less than clear on account of the very common word πολύς (×24) and if that is omitted the dominance of this domain in 2 Corinthians 8–9 becomes clearer.

23. πολύς: 1.11 (×2); 2.4 (×2), 6, 17; 3.9, 11, 12; 4.15; 6.4, 10; 7.4 (×2); **8.2** (×2), **4, 15, 22** (×2); **9.2, 12**, 11.18; 12.9, 21.

Figure 2b. *Words to do with quantity excluding* πολύς

| A | B | C | D |
|---|---|---|---|
| | *21* | *4.05* | *5187* |
| 1 | 2 | 3.65 | 548 |
| 2 | 0 | 0.00 | 325 |
| 3 | 1 | 3.02 | 331 |
| 4 | 1 | 2.75 | 364 |
| 5–7 | 0 | 0.00 | 1099 |
| **8** | **8** | **17.09** | **468** |
| **9** | **6** | **18.93** | **317** |
| 10 | 2 | 5.67 | 353 |
| 11 | 0 | 0.00 | 609 |
| 12 | 1 | 2.02 | 496 |
| 13 | 0 | 0.00 | 277 |

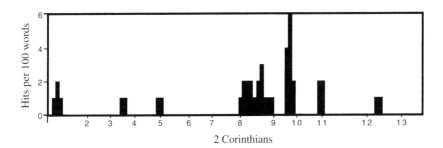

A related, contrasting semantic sub-domain of wealth and poverty is also to be found in *GELNTSD* 57, as follows: ἐλαττονέω[24] (57.41), ἔχω[25] (57.1), πένης[26] (57.50), πλεονάζω[27] (57.23), πλοῦτος[28] (57.30), πλουτέω[29] (57.25), πλουτίζω[30] (57.29), πλούσιος[31] (57.26), πτωχεύω[32]

24. ἐλαττονέω: **8.15** (hapax in New Testament).
25. ἔχω: 1.9, 15; 2.3, 4, 13; 3.4, 12; 4.1, 7, 13; 5.1, 12; 6.10; 7.1, 5; **8.11, 12** (×2); **9.8;** 10.6, 15; 12.14. This verb is hardly special to this section; however, in 8 it is used in the sense of possessions.
26. πένης: **9.9** (hapax in New Testament).
27. πλεονάζω: 4.15; **8.15.**
28. πλοῦτος: **8.2.**
29. πλουτέω: **8.9.**
30. πλουτίζω: 6.10; **9.11.**
31. πλούσιος: **8.9.**
32. πτωχεύω: **8.9** (hapax in New Testament).

(57.54), πτωχεία[33] (57.52), ὑστέρημα[34] (57.38). Here too we may include the verb προσαναπληρόω[35] (35.34), 'to supply what is lacking', which occurs in our texts only in conjunction with ὑστέρημα. The incidence of this semantic field is as follows:

Figure 3a. *Words to do with wealth and poverty*

| A | B | C | D |
|---|---|---|---|
| | *40* | *7.71* | *5187* |
| 1 | 2 | 3.65 | 548 |
| 2 | 3 | 9.23 | 325 |
| 3 | 2 | 6.04 | 331 |
| 4 | 4 | 10.99 | 364 |
| 5 | 2 | 5.15 | 388 |
| 6 | 2 | 6.13 | 326 |
| 7 | 2 | 5.19 | 385 |
| **8** | **13** | **27.78** | **468** |
| **9** | **5** | **15.77** | **317** |
| 10 | 2 | 5.67 | 353 |
| 11 | 2 | 3.28 | 609 |
| 12 | 1 | 2.02 | 496 |
| 13 | 0 | 0.00 | 277 |

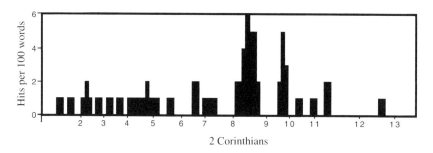

2 Corinthians

If you were to remove the very common ἔχω, which accounts for fully 22 of the 37 occurrences of the semantic field, a more indicative chart results:

33. πτωχεία: **8.2, 9**.
34. ὑστέρημα: **8.14** (×2); **9.12**; 11.9. Again, apart from the occasional word which is unique to here, the concentration of the vocabulary of poverty/wealth makes the units 8–9 distinct from 1–7 and 10–13.
35. προσαναπληρόω: **9.12**; 11.9.

Figure 3b. *Words to do with wealth and poverty omitting the very common 'to have'*

| A | B | C | D |
|---|---|---|---|
|  | *18* | *3.47* | *5187* |
| 1–3 | 0 | 0.00 | 1204 |
| 4 | 1 | 2.75 | 364 |
| 5 | 0 | 0.00 | 388 |
| 6 | 1 | 3.07 | 326 |
| 7 | 0 | 0.00 | 385 |
| **8** | **10** | **21.37** | **468** |
| **9** | **4** | **12.62** | **317** |
| 10 | 0 | 0.00 | 353 |
| 11 | 2 | 3.28 | 609 |
| 12–13 | 0 | 0.00 | 773 |

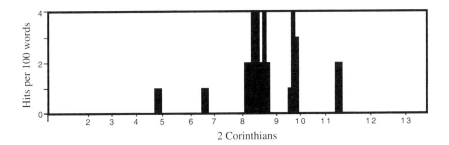

c. *Words to do with produce, harvesting, sowing, seed.* Γένημα[36] (13.49), θερίζω[37] (43.14), σπείρω[38] (43.6), σπόρος[39] (3.25). Even though these words are dispersed, somewhat, in *GELNTSD*, they clearly form a semantic field, that of agriculture. The occurrence of these words in all of 2 Corinthians is limited to two verses:

*2 Cor. 9.6*    Τοῦτο δέ, ὁ **σπείρων** φειδομένως φειδομένως καὶ **θερίσει**, καὶ ὁ **σπείρων** ἐπ᾽ εὐλογίαις ἐπ᾽ εὐλογίαις καὶ **θερίσει**.

*2 Cor. 9.10*    ὁ δὲ ἐπιχορηγῶν **σπόρον** τῷ **σπείροντι** καὶ ἄρτον εἰς βρ-ῶσιν χορηγήσει καὶ πληθυνεῖ τὸν **σπόρον** ὑμῶν καὶ αὐξήσει τα **γενήματα** τῆς δικαιοσύνης ὑμῶν.

36. γένημα: **9.10**.
37. θερίζω: **9.6** (×2).
38. σπείρω: **9.6** (×2); 10.1.
39. σπόρος: **9.10** (×2).

Figure 4. *Words to do with produce, harvesting, sowing, seed*

| A | B | C | D |
|---|---|---|---|
|  | 8 | 1.54 | 5187 |
| **1–8** | **0** | **0.00** | **3135** |
| **9** | **8** | **25.24** | **317** |
| 10–13 | 0 | 0.00 | 1735 |

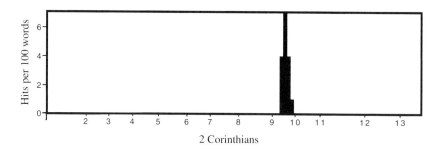

2 Corinthians

These words do not especially help us to isolate 8–9, but they do identify an important section within it. The semantic field of harvesting is a concrete metaphorical instance of the general semantic field of abundance, represented by the root περισσ-. A related semantic field, in terms of cause and effect, is that of 'bread, food': ἄρτος[40] (5.1, 8) βρῶσις[41] (5.1), confined in our text to one verse, but linked with the agriculture field in terms of produce.

2 Cor. 9.10 ὁ δὲ ἐπιχορηγῶν σπόρον τῷ σπείροντι καὶ **ἄρτον** εἰς **βρῶσιν** χορηγήσει καὶ πληθυνεῖ τὸν σπόρον ὑμῶν καὶ αὐξήσει τὰ γενήματα τῆς δικαιοσύνης ὑμῶν.

The vocabulary of sowing and harvesting has a special value in the subsequent argument because just as God causes nature to produce, likewise fecundity in human relationships is his gift. The presence of such a small semantic field does not affect the question of the integrity of these chapters and the letter.

d. *Words to do with honour and shame.* Δοκιμάζω,[42] δοκιμὴ,[43] ἐνδείκνυμι,[44] ἔνδειξις,[45] ἔπαινος,[46] καταισχύνω,[47] καυχάομαι,[48] καύχημα,[49]

40. ἄρτος: **9.10**.
41. βρῶσις: **9.10**.
42. δοκιμάζω: **8.8, 22**; 13.5.
43. δοκιμή: 2.9; **8.2; 9.13**; 13.3.
44. ἐνδείκνυμι: **8.24**.

καύχησις,[50] κενόω,[51] μωμάομαι.[52] Again, the language here is not necessarily unique to 8–9, as may be seen from this presentation.

Figure 5a. *Words to do with honour and shame*

| A | B | C | D |
|---|---|---|---|
|  | 44 | 8.48 | 5187 |
| 1 | 2 | 3.65 | 548 |
| 2 | 1 | 3.08 | 325 |
| 3–4 | 0 | 0.00 | 695 |
| 5 | 2 | 5.15 | 388 |
| 6 | 1 | 3.07 | 326 |
| 7 | 4 | 10.39 | 385 |
| **8** | **8** | **17.09** | **468** |
| **9** | **5** | **15.77** | **317** |
| 10 | 6 | 17.00 | 353 |
| 11 | 8 | 13.14 | 609 |
| 12 | 5 | 10.08 | 496 |
| 13 | 2 | 7.22 | 277 |

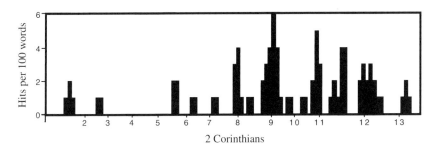

The inclusion of the καυχ- root results in a certain distortion, because it is so prevalent, especially in the last five chapters. Its exclusion permits clearer view of the presence of this semantic field. The root καυχ- is both prevalent and highly significant in 10–13. If one were permitted to

45. ἔνδειξις: **8.24**.

46. ἔπαινος: **8.18**.

47. καταισχύνω: 7.14; **9.4**.

48. καυχάομαι: 5.12; 7.14; **9.2**; 10.8, 13, 15, 16, 17 (×2); 11.12, 16, 18 (×2), 30 (×2); 12.1, 5 (×2), 6, 9.

49. καύχημα: 1.14; 5.12; **9.3**.

50. καύχησις: 1.12; 7.4, 14; **8.24**; 11.10, 17.

51. κενόω: **9.3**.

52. μωμάομαι: 6.3; **8.20**.

extrapolate from that root to allow the presence of the rest of the vocabulary, however small and unspecific, to stand out a somewhat clearer, if less adequate, picture emerges of the vocabulary of honour and shame in 8–9, as follows:

Figure 5b. *Words to do with honour and shame omitting the common root* καυχ-

| A | B | C | D |
|---|---|---|---|
|  | 15 | 2.89 | 5187 |
| 1 | 0 | 0.00 | 548 |
| 2 | 1 | 3.08 | 325 |
| 3–5 | 0 | 0.00 | 1083 |
| 6 | 1 | 3.07 | 326 |
| 7 | 1 | 2.60 | 385 |
| **8** | **7** | **14.96** | **468** |
| **9** | **3** | **9.46** | **317** |
| 10–12 | 0 | 0.00 | 1458 |
| 13 | 2 | 7.22 | 277 |

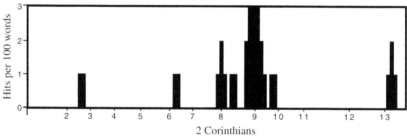

e. *Words to do with attitudes and emotions.* There is a substantial group of words in 2 Corinthians 8–9 which reflect attitudes and emotions. The ones in **bold** are unique to these chapters: ἀγαπάω[53] (25.43), ἀγάπη[54] (25.43), **αὐθαίρετος**[55] (25.66), ἐλπίζω[56] (25.59), ἐπιποθέω[57] (25.47), εὐπρόσδεκτος[58] (25.86), ζῆλος[59] (25.46), θέλω[60] (25.1), θέλημα[61]

---

53. ἀγαπάω: **9.7**; 11.11; 12.15 (×2).
54. ἀγάπη: 2.4, 8; 5.14; 6.6; **8.7, 8, 24**; 13.11, 13.
55. αὐθαίρετος: **8.3, 17**.
56. ἐλπίζω: 1.10, 13; 5.11; **8.5**; 13.6.
57. ἐπιποθέω: 5.2; **9.14**.
58. εὐπρόσδεκτος: 6.2; **8.12**.
59. ζῆλος: 7.7,11; **9.2**; 11.2; 12.20.
60. θέλω: 1.8; 5.4; **8.10, 11**; 11.12; 12.6, 20 (×2).
61. θέλημα: 1.1; **8.5**.

(25.2), καταισχύνω⁶² (25.194), καύχημα⁶³ (25.203), καύχησις⁶⁴ (25.204), καυχάομαι⁶⁵ (33.368), λύπη⁶⁶ (25.273), παρακαλέω⁶⁷ and παράκλησις⁶⁸ (25.150), **πλεονεξία**⁶⁹ (25.22), **προθυμία**⁷⁰ (25.68), **σπουδαῖος**⁷¹ (25.75), σπουδή⁷² (25.74), χάρα⁷³ (25.23, 24).

In chart form, the occurrence of this semantic field looks like this:

Figure 6. *Words to do with attitudes and emotions*

| A | B | C | D |
|---|---|---|---|
|   | 119 | 22.92 | 5187 |
| 1 | 16 | 29.20 | 548 |
| 2 | 8 | 24.62 | 325 |
| 3–4 | 0 | 0.00 | 695 |
| 5 | 7 | 18.04 | 388 |
| 6 | 3 | 9.20 | 326 |
| 7 | 18 | 46.75 | 385 |
| **8** | **23** | **48.94** | **468** |
| **9** | **9** | **28.39** | **317** |
| 10 | 7 | 19.83 | 353 |
| 11 | 11 | 18.06 | 609 |
| 12 | 13 | 26.21 | 496 |
| 13 | 4 | 14.44 | 277 |

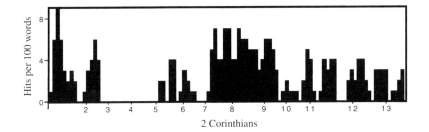

62. καταισχύνω: 7.14; **9.4**.
63. καύχημα: 1.14; 5.12; **9.3**.
64. καύχησις: 1.12; 7.4,14; **8.24**; 11.10, 17.
65. καυχάομαι: 5.12; 7.14; **9.2**; 10.8, 13, 15, 16, 17 (×2); 11.12, 16, 18 (×2), 30 (×2); 12.1, 5 (×2), 6, 9. Included here because of the presence of the root in two nouns as well.
66. λύπη: 2.1,3,7; 7.10 (×2); **9.7**.
67. παρακαλέω: 1.4, 6 (×3); 2.7, 8; 5.20; 6.1; 7.6 (×2), 7; **8.6; 9.5**; 10.1; 12.8, 18; 13.11.
68. παράκλησις: 1.3, 4, 5, 6 (×2), 7; 7.4, 7, 13; **8.4, 17**.
69. πλεονεξία: **9.5**.
70. προθυμία: **8.11, 12, 19; 9.2**.
71. σπουδαῖος: **8.17, 22** (×2).
72. σπουδή: 7.11, 12; **8.7, 8, 16**.

This is simply too undifferentiated a semantic field to help with de-limitation, but it does serve to show that presence of words to do with emotion and attitudes which are typical of 7–9, and may lay the ground for the suggestion that, rhetorically speaking, ch. 7 is a preparation for chs. 8–9, as claimed by many authors nowadays echoing John Chryso-stom's observations. The presence of so much vocabulary to do with emotions alerts us to the common rhetorical technique of appealing to feeling.

f. *Words to do with benefactor.* In his very useful work *Benefactor: Epigraphic Study of a Graeco-Roman and New Testament Semantic Field*, F.W. Danker (1982: 317-66) offers a profile of benefactors, that is, the associated semantic field as illustrated in epigraphs. 'Benefac-tion' was an important cultural phenomenon according to which suc-cessful people used their advantages for the public good, in the form of facilities such as fountains and monuments. There was mutual gain: the recipient gained either a monument or some facility such as a fountain and giver gained both fame and a good reputation.[74] Inscriptions recording the nature of the benefaction show a distinct vocabulary. The importance here is that Paul is echoing the language of a great cultural given in the Graeco-Roman world, and such language would have had an almost unconscious persuasive effect.[75] The words which recur in 2 Corinthians are the following: αὐθαίρετος,[76] βαρέω,[77] βάρος,[78] χορηγέω,[79] χρηστότης,[80] δικαιοσύνη,[81] δύναμις[82] δωρεά,[83] εἰλικ-

---

73. χάρα: 1.24; 2.3; 7.4, 13; **8.2**.

74. 'The social cement which bound the inhabitants of the Graeco-Roman world together was the reciprocity of benefactions. Seneca in a work devoted to the top, *De Beneficiis*, called it "the chief bond of human society" ' (Murphy-O'Connor 1995: 305).

75. Further consideration is given to this in Chapter 5 below.

76. αὐθαίρετος: **8.3, 17**.

77. βαρέω: 1.8; 5.4.

78. βάρος: 4.17.

79. χορηγέω: **9.10**.

80. χρηστότης: 6.6.

81. δικαιοσύνη: 3.9; 5.21; 6.7, 14; **9.9, 10**; 11.15.

82. δύναμις: 1.8; 6, 7; **8.3** (×2); **12.9** (×2), 12; 13.4 (×2).

83. δωρεά: **9.15** (Danker notes only the accusative i.e. adverbial form as part of the semantic field as attested).

ρίνεια,[84] ἐπιείκεια,[85] ἐπιταγή,[86] ἐπιτελέω,[87] ἔργον,[88] ἐπιχορηγέω,[89] φειδομένως,[90] ἰσότης,[91] λειτουργία,[92] λόγος,[93] προνοέω,[94] προθυμία,[95] σπουδαῖος,[96] θλῖψις,[97] ὑπομονή.[98]

For technical reasons, I omitted[99] three fixed expressions of the semantic domain, which are found only in ch. 8. **κατὰ δύναμιν** and **πάσῃ σπουδῇ**. The occurrence of **ἑαυτὸν δίδοναι** (in 2 Cor. 8.5) is also part of the semantic field.

Figure 7. *Words to do with benefaction*

| A | B | C | D |
|---|---|---|---|
|  | 71 | 13.69 | 5187 |
| 1 | 8 | 14.60 | 548 |
| 2 | 3 | 9.23 | 325 |
| 3 | 1 | 3.02 | 331 |
| 4 | 4 | 10.99 | 364 |
| 5 | 3 | 7.73 | 388 |
| 6 | 7 | 21.47 | 326 |
| 7 | 2 | 5.19 | 385 |
| **8** | **20** | **42.74** | **468** |
| **9** | **10** | **31.55** | **317** |
| 10 | 4 | 11.33 | 353 |
| 11 | 3 | 4.93 | 609 |
| 12 | 4 | 8.06 | 496 |
| 13 | 2 | 7.22 | 277 |

84. εἰλικρίνεια: 1.2; 2.17.
85. ἐπιείκεια: 10.1.
86. ἐπιταγή: **8.8**.
87. ἐπιτελέω: 7.1; **8.6, 11** (×2).
88. ἔργον: **9.8**; 10.11; 11.15.
89. ἐπιχορηγέω: **9.10**.
90. φειδομένως: **9.6** (×2).
91. ἰσότης: **8.13, 14**.
92. λειτουργία: **9.12**.
93. λόγος: 1.18; 2.17; 4.2; 5.19; 6.7; **8.7**; 10.10, 11; 11.6.
94. προνοέω: **8.21**.
95. προθυμία: **8.11, 12, 19; 9.2**.
96. σπουδαῖος: **8.17, 22** (×2).
97. θλῖψις: 1.4, 8; 2.4; 4.17; 6.4; 7.4; **8.2, 13**.
98. ὑπομονή: 1.6; 6.4; 12.12.
99.    It was difficult to get the program to look at these expressions at the same time as the others.

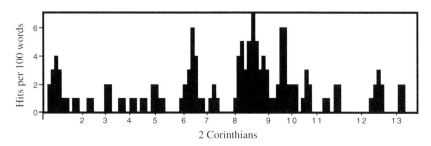

2 Corinthians

This semantic field occurs throughout the letter, but the actual incidence in chs. 8 and 9 is significantly higher than in the rest of the text (i.e. 25 out of 59). This vocabulary is distinctive in terms of its frequency and specific reference here.

*Inclusio.* There are two expressions here which function as an *inclusio*:

τὴν χάριν τοῦ θεοῦ (8.1) and
τὴν ὑπερβάλλουσαν χάριν τοῦ θεοῦ (9.14);

εἰς τὸ πλοῦτος τῆς ἁπλότητος αὐτῶν (8.2)
ἐν παντὶ πλουτιζόμενοι εἰς πᾶσαν ἁπλότητα (9.11)

the grace of God (8.1)
the surpassing grace of God (9.14)

in a wealth of generosity (8.2)
You will be enriched in every way for your great generosity (9.11)

In the text itself the elements of an inclusion recur in inverse order, forming a distant chiasm:

| | | |
|---|---|---|
| 2 Cor. 8.1 | τὴν χάριν τοῦ θεοῦ | A |
| 2 Cor. 8.2 | εἰς τὸ πλοῦτος τῆς ἁπλότητος αὐτῶν· | B |
| 2 Cor. 9.11 | ἐν παντὶ πλουτιζόμενοι εἰς πᾶσαν ἁπλότητα, | B′ |
| 2 Cor. 9.14 | διὰ τὴν ὑπερβάλλουσαν χάριν τοῦ θεοῦ ἐφ᾽ ὑμῖν. | A′ |

The presence of an *inclusio* is confirmed by some single words repeated here: δοκιμή (2 Cor. 8.2 and 9.13), κοινωνία (2 Cor. 8.4 and 9.13) and διακονία (2 Cor. 8.4 and 9.13). All these words are of considerable significance for the case that Paul wishes to make, as their concentration in 2 Cor. 9.13 illustrates.

In rhetorical terms, not only are repetitions significant[100] but omis-

---

100. As regards the *inclusio* itself, the second occurrence of each phrase is further distinguished by a qualification ('all' and 'overflowing').

sions are likewise potentially significant. Reference to the suffering of
the Macedonians may serve as an illustration. While in 2 Cor. 8.1-6
Paul names the Macedonians, they receive no explicit mention in 2 Cor.
9.11-15, but rather the qualities, values and desiderata they serve to
illustrate receive attention. It is noticeable, for instance, that their suffering, so markedly emphasized in 2 Cor. 8.1-6, has no place in 2 Cor.
9.11-15. This is because their deprivation was a foil to their generosity
and such a foil is no longer necessary. On the contrary, a further implied (and perhaps not so subtle) comparison between the rich Corinthians and the poor Macedonians could, at this point in the appeal for
money, be counter-productive. The rhetor has always to keep the *benevolentia* of his audience in mind.

The evidence for treating chs. 8 and 9 as distinct within 2 Corinthians
is threefold: (1) at 8 and 10 there are new beginnings; (2) the characteristic semantic fields of chs. 8 and 9 distinguish these chapters; and especially (3) the inclusions constitute sufficient evidence to say that 8–9
may reasonably be taken to form a unit for textual analysis within
2 Corinthians. Of course, this delimitation needs the confirmation of the
rhetorical structure of 2 Corinthians 8–9. Many critics at this point
would say that chs. 8 and 9 are distinguishable within all of 2 Corinthians and are related in subject matter, but constitute separate documents. However, given the force of the striking *inclusio* between 2 Cor.
8.1-6 and 2 Cor. 9.11-15, the burden of proof rests with those who
would say that a separate document begins with Περὶ μὲν γὰρ at 9.1.

Some considerable space has been devoted to the delimitation of
2 Corinthians 8–9. Although the special nature of these two chapters is
not hotly disputed, rehearsing the characteristics of 2 Corinthians 8–9 is
not without benefit from the point of view of appreciating the persuasion. The semantic field of benefaction, in particular, reveals a cultural
given which adds great force to the persuasion because Paul is appealing to what is already (unconsciously) believed. The much less focused
(from a cultural viewpoint) semantic fields of abundance, wealth and
poverty, and gift derive much of their force from this cultural datum of
benefaction. The rather smaller semantic field of seed and harvest has a
power which derives from both the culture and Christian tradition. The
cultural aspect is brought out by Betz in an excursus on Paul's agrarian
theology (1985: 98-100). The Christian force of this metaphor lies in its
presence in almost every layer of the tradition. It is language found in
Mark, Q, John, James, 1 and 2 Peter, 1 John and the Apocalypse. As

well as in 2 Corinthians 9, it is also found in 1 Corinthians 3 and 9 and 15, Galatians 6 and Philippians 1. Paul uses language which has a particular resonance for his Corinthian and Christian hearers.[101]

We now move to the second task of this Chapter, the delimitation of the subunits of 2 Corinthians 8–9.

### 2. *Delimitation of the Units within 2 Corinthians 8–9*

The delimitation of subsections within 2 Corinthians 8–9 is very pertinent to this study, because rhetorical critics do not agree on these smaller units. The identification is, of course, tentative and awaits corroboration, if that should be the case, from the rhetorical units. The convergence of indicators should, it is hoped, obviate any arbitrariness in selecting and entitling rhetorical units. Conversely, the rhetorical units will strengthen the probability of the delimitation. The means used have already been indicated at the start of this Chapter. These smaller subsections are also identified by a convergence of indicators.[102]

#### 2.1. *2 Corinthians 8.1-6(7)*
*Indicators*: people mentioned and *inclusio*.

The personalities mentioned help to delimit a passage. The Macedonians and Titus form the core 'story' of 2 Cor. 8.1-6, but are absent from the immediately following section, from 2 Cor. 8.7 onwards. Titus is next mentioned in 8.16 and the Macedonians recur at 2 Cor. 9.2. There is also an *inclusio* formed between 2 Cor. 8.1-2 (ὑμῖν, τὴν χάριν, περισσεία) and 2 Cor. 8.6-7 (ὑμᾶς, τὴν χάριν, περισσεύετε, ὑμῖν, τῇ χάριτι, περισσεύητε). A weaker indicator is the use of the personal pronoun, (second person plural) in 2 Cor. 8.1 and then not used again until 2 Cor. 8.6. This is supported by the omission of verbs in the second person plural until 2 Cor. 8.7.

If, however, we do have a unit at 2 Cor. 8.1-6(7) it is not clear whether v. 7 should be added to that or not. Precisely at v. 7 Paul introduces new vocabulary: πίστις, λόγος and γνῶσις being otherwise absent from the text. At this point the verbs change to the second person plural.

---

101. See below Chapter 5, which deals with the cultural persuasiveness of this language.

102. Use is made here of criteria described by Egger 1987: 56-59 and Ska 1990: 1-2.

### 2.2. *2 Corinthians 8.(7)8-15*

*Indicators*: people *not* mentioned; semantic field of possession; citation to close the argument; inclusion.

The Macedonians of 2 Cor. 8.1-6 and Titus of 2 Cor. 8.15-24 are missing by name from this section, where the verbs are in the second person plural. 2 Corinthians 8.8-15 is further marked by the vocabulary of ownership. Of course this is present over the entire 2 Corinthians 8–9, as we saw, but it is especially evident in 2 Cor. 8.8-15. The words are: πτωχεύω (v. 9 only), πλούσιος (v. 9 only), πτωχεία (vv. 2 and 9), πλουτέω (v. 9 only), ἔχω (vv. 11-12 [×2]; 9.8), περίσσευμα (v. 14 [×2] only), ὑστέρημα (v. 14 [×2]; 9.12) and the important word ἰσότης (vv. 13 and 14 only). The words in the citation in v. 15 are found only in that verse.

Paul regularly closes an argument with a citation from the unassailable authority of Scripture. Alone, however, a citation would not be an indicator of a unit. Nevertheless, in conjunction with the other indicators above, the closing citation in v. 15 indicates the end of a block. The same technique is evidenced in 9.6-10 where the large citation-allusion works as a close to the entire argument of 8–9.

Finally, there is an inclusion between the double use of περισσεύω in 8.7 and the double use of περίσσευμα in 8.14.

### 2.3. *2 Corinthians 8.16-24*

*Indicators*: people mentioned, a concentric structure, semantic fields.

Here there is special reference to Titus, who was absent from 2 Cor. 8.8-15. The mention of Titus works like a frame at the start and at the end. Similarly an unnamed individual—'the brother'—makes his appearance; both of these are quite fully described here, and although they are present under the rubric 'brothers' in the next section, there the emphasis will be not so much on them as on the reaction of the Corinthians to them.

Subject to further confirmation, the text falls into a pattern based on who is mentioned in it, thus:

| | | |
|---|---|---|
| vv. 16-17: | Thanks be to God | |
| | Titus | |
| vv. 18-19. | | The first brother (known to the church) |
| vv. 20-21: | | Paul's own probity |
| vv. 22: | | The second brother (our brother) |
| v. 23: | | Titus and the brothers |
| | Glory to Christ | |
| v. 24: | Appeal | |

Such a concentric presentation permits two things: it confirms that this unit is indeed a unit and secondly, it allows us to ask, as always, of a concentric pattern, is the physical centre (Paul's probity) the semantic centre? It tells us the topic of this section, which is apparently the appointment of emissaries, but really Paul's own transparency. Verse 23 summarizes and leads to the appeal in v. 24.

The vocabulary of testing and approval is distinct here, appropriate to the subject matter of commissioning and recommending: ἔπαινος (2 Cor. **8.18**), μωμάομαι (2 Cor. 6.3; **8.20**), καλός (2 Cor. **8.21** and 13.7—here in the sense of what is honourable), δοκίμαζω (2 Cor. **8.8, 22** and 13.5—the use in v. 22 refers to the testing of the brother, not the Corinthians as in v. 8), ἔνδειξις (2 Cor. **8.24**) and ἐνδείκνυημι (2 Cor. **8.24**). Linked with this vocabulary of testing you have the preposition ἐνώπιον (2 Cor. 4.2; 7.12; **8.21** [×2]) and πρόσωπον (a frequent word in 2 Corinthians but only in **8.24** in chs. 8–9).

There is also the semantic field of 'ecclesiastical' or apostolic terms: συμπέμπω (2 Cor. **8.18, 22**), ἀδελφός in the singular twice, in the plural once, referring to special companions of Titus (2 Cor. **8.18, 22**); ἐκκλησία (2 Cor. 8.1, 18, **19, 23, 24**); εὐαγγέλιον (2 Cor. **8.18** and 9.13 in these chapters); χειροτονέω (2 Cor. **8.19**); συνέκδημος (2 Cor. **8.19**), διακονέω (2 Cor. 3.3; **8.19, 20**), κοινωνός (2 Cor. 1.7 and **8.23**), συνέργος (2 Cor. 1.24 and **8.23**); ἀπόστολος (2 Cor. 1.1; **8.23**; 11.5, 13). Just how pervasive is this 'ecclesial' language of 8.16-25 may be seen from the following inventory:

18  συνεπέμψαμεν, ἀδελφὸν, εὐαγγελίω, ἐκκλησιῶν
19  χειροτονηθεὶς, ἐκκλησιῶν, συνέκδημος, διακονουμένη
20  διακονουμένη
22  συνεπέμψαμεν, ἀδελφὸν, ἐκδοκιμάσαμεν
23  κοινωνὸς, συνεργός, ἀδελφοι, ἀπόστολοι ἐκκλησιῶν
24  ἐκκλησιῶν.

When we look at these words, we see there are two semantic fields operating here: probity/testing and missionary/apostolic. Why does the 'ecclesiastical' language come to the fore here? Because Paul is illustrating that the collection is not his responsibility, but that of the wider church, thus lending even greater authority to the appeal. Having thus protected himself, he can make a strong appeal in v. 24, which in terms of its vocabulary takes us back to the proposition of the whole letter, that is 2 Cor. 1.12-14.

## 2.4. *2 Corinthians 9.1-5*

*Indicators*: vocabulary distinct from before and after; semantic field of honour and shame, and preparation.

The vocabulary of 2 Cor. 9.6-10 is quite different, being joined only by the word εὐλογία, which in vv. 6-10 has a somewhat different meaning.

The vocabulary of 2 Cor. 8.16-24 shares two important words with 2 Cor. 9.1-5: ἀδελφός and the root καυχ- (although not the actual forms). There is likewise a shared concern with practical arrangements, with this difference: in both sections Paul is concerned to protect himself from any suggestion of misappropriation, but in 2 Cor. 8.16-24 the emphasis is on the practical arrangements, while in 2 Cor. 9.1-5 on effect of the Macedonian emissaries on the Corinthians. This is reflected in the proper nouns in each section. In 2 Cor. 8.16-24 Titus and 'the brother' are mentioned; in 2 Cor. 9.1-5 they become 'the brothers' and 'the Macedonians', which is also where the actual words Achaia and Macedonians[103] occur.

The semantic field of preparation includes these words: παρασκευ-άζω,[104] ἀπαρασκεύαστος,[105] ἕτοιμος.[106] With these verbs goes a group of expressions in v. 5, which all express the idea of *something before-hand*: προέρχομαι,[107] προκαταρτίζω[108] and προεπαγγέλλομαι.[109] These words are all either uniquely here or in a special concentration.

There is also the semantic field of shame/honour: καυχάομαι,[110] καύχημα,[111] κενόω[112] and καταισχύνω.[113]

103. In this whole discussion, the proper nouns Achaia (9.2) and Macedonians (9.2, 4) occur only here.
104. παρασκευάζω: **9.2, 3**.
105. ἀπαρασκεύαστος: **9.4**.
106. ἕτοιμις: **9.5**; 10.6, 16.
107. προέρχομαι: **9.5**.
108. προκαταρτίζω: **9.5** (hapax in New Testament).
109. προεπαγγέλλομαι: **9.5**.
110. καυχάομαι: 5.12; 7.14; **9.2**; 10.8, 13, 15, 16, 17 (×2); 11.12, 16, 18 (×2), 30 (×2); 12.1, 5 (×2), 6, 9.
111. καύχημα: 1.14; 5.12; **9.3**.
112. κενόω: **9.3**.
113. καταισχύνω: 7.14; **9.4**.

## 2.5. *2 Corinthians 9.6-10*

*Indicators*: semantic fields of agriculture/righteousness; concentration of citations and allusions; inclusion.

The unit 9.6-10 is also marked off by similarity of vocabulary at the beginning and end.

2 Cor. 9.6 Τοῦτο δέ, ὁ **σπείρων** φει- | 2 Cor. 9.10 ὁ δὲ ἐπιχορηγῶν **σπόρον**
δομένως φειδομένως καὶ <u>θερίσει</u>, καὶ | τῷ **σπείροντι** καὶ ἄρτον εἰς βρῶσιν
ὁ **σπείρων** ἐπ᾽ εὐλογίαις ἐπ᾽ εὐλο- | χορηγήσει καὶ πληθυνεῖ τὸν σπόρον
γίαις καὶ <u>θερίσει</u>. | ὑμῶν καὶ <u>αὐξήσει</u> τὰ <u>γενήματα</u> τῆς
 | δικαιοσύνης ὑμῶν.

2 Cor. 9.6 The point is this: the one | 2 Cor. 9.10 He who supplies seed to
who sows sparingly will also reap spar- | the sower and bread for food will sup-
ingly, and the one who sows bounti- | ply and multiply your seed for sowing
fully will also reap bountifully. | and increase the harvest of your right-
 | eousness.

This is not exactly an *inclusio*, but strikingly enough this small semantic field occurs only in these two verses in chs. 8 and 9.

This section shows a very particular vocabulary—the semantic field of sowing/harvesting and supplying food: αὐξάνω,[114] ἄρτος,[115] βρῶ-σις,[116] χορηγέω,[117] ἐπιχορηγέω,[118] γένημα,[119] πληθύνω,[120] θερίζω,[121] σκορπίζω,[122] σπείρω,[123] σπόρος.[124]

There is a second semantic field—that of good deeds/righteousness, the presence of which alerts us to the main theme of the argument: ἔργον,[125] ἀγαθός[126] and δικαιοσύνη.[127] A related word is 'heart'[128]—

114. αὐξάνω: **9.10**; 10.15.
115. ἄρτος: **9.10**.
116. βρῶσις: **9.10**.
117. χορηγέω: **9.10**.
118. ἐπιχορηγέω: **9.10**.
119. γένημα: **9.10**.
120. πληθύνω: **9.10**.
121. θερίζω: **9.6**.
122. σκορπίζω: **9.9**.
123. σπείρω: **9.6** (×2); 10.1.
124. σπόρος: **9.10** (×2).
125. ἔργον: **9.8**; 10.11; 11.15.
126. ἀγαθός: 5.10; **9.8**.
127. δικαιοσύνη: 3.9; 5.21; 6.7, 14; **9.9, 10**; 11.15.
128. καρδία: 1.22; 2.4; 3.2, 3, 15; 4.6; 5.12; 6.11; 7.3; **8.16; 9.7**.

which speaks of the source of these deeds of righteousness—this is all to be freely done and not grudgingly[129] or under obligation.[130]

These semantic fields occupy different portions of the text, becoming an extended metaphor, which tends to allegory at the end.

The bridging of the two semantic fields—anticipated in the citation from Psalm 111 (LXX)—is effected in the last line of this section, 2 Cor. 9.10. From 2 Cor. 9.11 Paul returns to the original vocabulary of 2 Cor. 8.1-6.

This section is distinct on account of the number of citations—three—to be found in it. These are (all from LXX, with verbatim citation in **bold**, related words underlined):

| | |
|---|---|
| *Prov. 22.8* | ὁ σπείρων φαῦλα θερίσει κακά |
| | πληγὴν δὲ ἔργων αὐτοῦ συντελέσει |
| *[8α]* | ἄνδρα **ἱλαρὸν** καὶ **δότην** εὐλογεῖ ὁ **θεός** |
| | ματαιότητα δὲ ἔργων αὐτοῦ συντελέσει |
| | |
| *Ps. 111.9* | **ἐσκόρπισεν ἔδωκεν τοῖς πένησιν** |
| | **ἡ δικαιοσύνη αὐτοῦ μένει** |
| | **εἰς τὸν αἰῶνα τοῦ** αἰῶνος |
| | τὸ κέρας αὐτοῦ ὑψωθήσεται ἐν δόξῃ |
| | |
| *Isa. 55.10* | ὡς γὰρ ἐὰν καταβῇ ὑετὸς ἢ χιὼν ἐκ τοῦ οὐρανοῦ |
| | καὶ οὐ μὴ ἀποστραφῇ ἕως ἂν μεθύσῃ τὴν γῆν |
| | καὶ ἐκτέκῃ καὶ ἐκβλαστήσῃ |
| | καὶ δῷ σπέρμα **τῷ σπείροντι καὶ ἄρτον εἰς βρῶσιν** |

Furthermore there are allusions elsewhere in this section. Thus 2 Cor. 9.6 is possibly an echo of Prov. 11.24.

| | |
|---|---|
| *Prov. 11.24* | εἰσὶν οἳ τὰ ἴδια σπείροντες πλείονα ποιοῦσιν εἰσὶν καὶ οἳ |
| | συνάγοντες ἐλαττονοῦνται |

In 2 Cor. 9.7, there is an allusion to Deut. 15.10:

| | |
|---|---|
| *Deut. 15.10* | διδοὺς δώσεις αὐτῷ καὶ δάνειον δανιεῖς αὐτῷ ὅσον ἐπιδέεται |
| | καὶ οὐ λυπηθήσῃ τῇ καρδίᾳ σου διδόντος σου αὐτῷ ὅτι διὰ τὸ |
| | ῥῆμα τοῦτο εὐλογήσει σε κύριος ὁ θεός σου ἐν πᾶσιν τοῖς |
| | ἔργοις καὶ ἐν πᾶσιν οὗ ἂν ἐπιβάλῃς τὴν χεῖρά σου... |

Of course there are allusions elsewhere, too, but there seems to be a special concentration of citation and allusion here, marking the end of

---

129. λύπη: 2.1, 3, 6; 7.10 (×2); **9.7**.
130. ἀνάγκη: 6.4; **9.7**; 12.10.

the sequence of arguments from 2 Corinthians 8 to 9. As noted above, Paul frequently closes arguments with citations and here we have a wealth of them. We shall have to await the analysis of the *dispositio* before it can be said with certainty that at this point the argument has concluded.

### 2.6. 2 Corinthians 9.11-15

There is a definite unity of vocabulary—which, for want of a better term, could be entitled catechetical-liturgical thus: εὐχαριστία; διακονία; λειτουργία; δοξάζω; ὁμολογία; εὐαγγέλιον; κοινωνία; χάρις. These words are also found elsewhere, but here they form a coherent semantic field. There is a special concentration of the root χαρ-, and an *inclusio* (v. 11: εὐχαριστίαν τῷ θεω; v. 15: Χάρις τῷ θεῷ). Verse 11 shares some of the vocabulary typical of the unit just before it (9.6-9), thus forming a bridge. The anacoluthon between v. 10 and 11 supports placing the break at this point.

### 2.7. 2 Corinthians 8.1-6(7) and 9.11-15

8.1-6(7) and 9.11-15 have a shared vocabulary which is noteworthy. The words shared by these two sections only are: δοκιμή (8.2 and 9.13), ἁπλότης (8.2 and 9.11, 13), κοινωνία (8.4 and 9.13). A 'supporting' vocabulary would be: διακονία (8.4 and 9.1, 12, 13), ἅγιος (8.4 and 9.1, 12) and θεός (8.1, 5, 16 and 9.7, 8, 11, 12, 13, 14, 15); πλοῦτος and πλουτίζω (8.2 and 9.11, respectively, words sharing the same root); χάρις, used ten times in these chapters, appears four times in 8.1-7 and twice in 9.11-15.

| 2 Cor. 8.1-6(7) | 2 Cor. 9.11-15 |
|---|---|
| *2 Cor. 8.1* Γνωρίζομεν δὲ ὑμῖν, ἀδελφοί, τὴν χάριν τοῦ <u>θεου</u> τὴν δεδομένην ἐν ταῖς ἐκκλησίαις τῆς Μακεδονίας, 2 ὅτι ἐν πολλῇ **δοκιμῇ** θλίψεως ἡ περισσεία τῆς χαρᾶς αὐτῶν καὶ ἡ κατὰ βάθους πτωχεία αὐτῶν ἐπερίσσευσεν εἰς τὸ <u>πλοῦτος</u> τῆς ἁπλότητος αὐτῶν· 3 ὅτι κατὰ δύναμιν, μαρτυρῶ, καὶ παρὰ δύναμιν, αὐθαίρετοι 4 μετὰ πολλῆς παρακλήσεως δεόμενοι ἡμῶν τὴν χάριν καὶ τὴν **κοινωνίαν** τῆς **διακονίας** τῆς εἰς τοὺς **ἁγίους**, 5 καὶ οὐ | *2 Cor. 9.11* ἐν παντὶ <u>πλουτιζόμενοι</u> εἰς πᾶσαν **ἁπλότητα**, ἥτις κατεργάζεται δι᾿ ἡμῶν εὐχαριστίαν τῷ <u>θεῷ</u>· 12 ὅτι ἡ <u>διακονία</u> τῆς λειτουργίας ταύτης οὐ μόνον ἐστὶν προσαναπληροῦσα τὰ ὑστερήματα τῶν <u>ἁγίων</u>, ἀλλὰ καὶ περισσεύουσα διὰ πολλῶν εὐχαριστιῶν τῷ <u>θεῷ</u>. 13 διὰ τῆς **δοκιμῆς** τῆς <u>διακονίας</u> ταύτης δοξάζοντες τὸν <u>θεὸν</u> ἐπὶ τῇ ὑποταγῇ τῆς ὁμολογίας ὑμῶν εἰς τὸ εὐαγγέλιον τοῦ Χριστοῦ καὶ **ἁπλότητι** τῆς |

καθὼς ἠλπίσαμεν ἀλλα᾽ ἑαυτοὺς ἔδωκαν πρῶτον τῷ κυρίῳ καὶ ἡμῖν διὰ
θελήματος **θεοῦ** 6 εἰς τὸ παρακαλέσαι ἡμᾶς Τίτον, ἵνα καθὼς προενήρξατο οὕτως καὶ εηπιτελέση εἰς ὑμᾶς
καὶ τὴν χάριν ταύτην. 7 Ἀλλ᾽ ὥσπερ
ἐν παντὶ περισσεύετε, πίστει καὶ
λόγῳ καὶ γνώσει καὶ πάση σπουδῇ
καὶ τῇ ἐξ ἡμῶν ἐν ὑμῖν ἀγάπῃ, ἵνα
καὶ ἐν ταύτῃ τῇ χάριτι περισσεύητε.

**κοινωνίας** εἰς αὐτοὺς καὶ εἰς πάντας, 14 καὶ αὐτῶν δεήσει ὑπὲρ ὑμῶν
ἐπιποθούντων ὑμᾶς διὰ τὴν ὑπερβάλλουσαν χάριν τοῦ <u>θεου</u> ἐφ᾽ ὑμῖν.
15 Χάρις τῷ <u>θεῷ</u> ἐπὶ τῇ ἀνεκδιηγήτῳ
αὐτοῦ δωρεᾷ.

Given that there is a correspondence between the beginning of ch. 8 and the close of ch. 9, which we saw above, one could also ask whether there were links between the various sections identified.

## 3. *Conclusion*

With that we have come to the end of the delimitations of both chs. 8 and 9 and the subsections within them. The first part of the Chapter dealt with distinguishing chs. 8 and 9 from the rest of the letter. It does not follow that chs. 8 and 9 are therefore distinct *documents*, best ana-lysed independently of their context. For the purposes of this study, it is sufficient to see that these chapters form a distinct discussion within 2 Corinthians, which can be analysed using Hellenistic rhetoric. The second part of this Chapter looked at subdivisions within chs. 8–9, with a view to observing the material indicators of discrete units. Bearing in mind the various observations and considerations, plausible textual units would seem to be the following:

8.1-6(7)
8.8-15
8.16-24
9.1-5
9.6-10
9.11-15

It is occasionally not certain where exactly a verse belongs, such as 2 Cor. 8.7 and 2 Cor. 9.10/11. However, I hope to show that these are moments of transition which open and close the argument and bridge the text units. Paul is not a mechanical user of rhetoric nor a math-ematical organizer of vocabulary. As said at the start of the Chapter, it remains to be seen whether the analysis of the *dispositio* will support this proposed structure.

Finally, although these are discrete units, there are some verbal connections between the various sections. While these do not function quite as the *mots crochets* of Albert Vanhoye, in his analysis of the Letter to the Hebrews (1963), they do link together the stages in the arguments and they also serve to remind us that although discrete moments may be observed, they function nevertheless as part of the whole. An extreme atomization of textual units is counter-productive. In this case, χάριν at the end of 8.6 is taken up immediately in 8.7 and 8.9, where the argument begins, as we shall see. The close of 8.16-24, using the word καυχήσεως prepares us for the topic of honour and shame taken up in 9.1-5, where the term καύχημα is used. The link between 9.5 and 9.6 is effected by the word εὐλογία, which in the context of 9.5 suggests freedom, and in 9.6 denotes abundance. Finally, God who is the unnamed subject of 9.10 is explicitly named in v. 11, although the topic changes.

A comparison with some of the authors treated in Chapter 2 will make clear the differences between this segmentation and theirs.

| This study | Heinrici | Betz |
| --- | --- | --- |
| 8.1-6(7) | 8.1-6 | 8.1-5 |
| | | 8.6 |
| 8.8-15 | 8.7-24 | 8.7-8 |
| | | 8.9-15 |
| 8.16-24 | | 8.16-22 |
| | | 8.23 |
| | | 8.24 |
| 9.1-5 | 9.1-5 | 9.1-2 |
| | | 9.3-5a |
| | | 9.5bc |
| 9.6-10 | 9.6-15 | 9.6-14 |
| 9.11-15 | | 9.15 |

There is no great disagreement with Heinrici, in so far as he is interested in presenting a structure, but Betz has a significantly different apportioning of units, making for a considerable disagreement in the rhetorical analysis. A detailed comparison with the work of Betz will be undertaken in Chapter 6, after the completion of the rhetorical analyses in Chapters 4 and 5, to which we now turn.

Chapter 4

RHETORICAL READING OF 2 CORINTHIANS 8–9

> The use of such clauses is full of risk. They do not suit the forceful
> speaker, since their studied artifice dissipates the force... For anger
> needs no artifice; in such invectives what is said should be, in a way,
> spontaneous and simple.
>
> Demetrius, De Elocutione 27

The purpose of this chapter is to undertake the next step in putting into
practice the methodology explained in Chapter 1. There we noticed that
the sequence in the rhetorical preparation of a speech was *Inventio*,
*Dispositio* and *Elocutio*, and in Chapter 1, it was proposed to take these
*constructive* moments in reverse order to lay bare the persuasive strategies of 2 Corinthians 8–9. This Chapter is divided, accordingly, into
four parts, under the headings *Elocutio*, *Dispositio* and *Inventio*[1] with a
brief discussion of *Genus* to conclude.

## 1. *Elocutio of 2 Corinthians 8–9*

*Elocutio* is divided, traditionally, into figures of speech and figures of
thought.[2] Figures of speech deal with the words 'materially', that is, as
regards the physical position and sound. Figures of thought deal with
techniques which affect the meaning. It is not always easy to keep
figures of thought and figures of speech theoretically distinct, as Quin-

---

1.    Quite a few technical terms have had to be introduced. On its first occurrence, each term is explained and further references may be found in the footnotes.

2.    'To confer distinction upon style is to render it ornate, embellishing it by
variety. The divisions under Distinction are Figures of Diction (*verborum exornatio*) and the Figures of Thought (*sententiarum exornatio*). It is a figure of diction
if the adornment is comprised in the fine polish of the language itself. A figure of
thought derives a certain distinction from the idea, not from the words' (*Herennium*
4.13.18).

tilian admits. Neither is the terminology stable, at least before Quintilian. In later rhetoric, as theory became more and more refined, the figures of speech and figures of thought were grouped according to similarities of technique and function. For example, figures of speech which achieved their effect by repetition (*geminatio, inclusio* and so forth) were theoretically associated and further distinguished. Figures of thought were likewise grouped and refined. For the sake of convenience, I have used two charts[3] of these later theoretical developments as a grid for the presentation of figures of speech and figures of thought. These charts are in the appendices and the number before each figure refers to the number on the appropriate chart. Not all the figures listed are present in 2 Corinthians 8–9 and so occasionally the numbering skips forward. For the sake of clarity, the algebraic illustrations of the figures employed by Lausberg and Mortara Garavelli are included where appropriate.

### 1.1. *Figures of Speech*
01 *Geminatio* (*epanalepsis*). *Geminatio* is a figure of repetition, which consists of the immediate repetition of a word or phrase (…xx…). The term is not found in our chosen authors, but Demetrius uses the broad term ἀναδίπλωσις for this phenomenon.[4] The phenomenon receives separate treatment in Quintilian.[5] The hearer or reader cannot avoid attending to the repetition, and so it is a figure of considerable force. There is just one example here.

9.6      Τοῦτο δέ, ὁ σπείρων **φειδομένως φειδομένως** καὶ θερίσει, καὶ ὁ σπείρων **ἐπ᾽ εὐλογίαις ἐπ᾽ εὐλογίαις** καὶ θερίσει.

---

3.    The charts are taken from Mortara Garavelli's *Manuale di Retorica*, but I have altered the technical terms to reflect the actual terms employed by the selected handbooks in use here.

4.    'Next figures of speech: these are themselves a form of composition, since it is practically a matter of rearrangement and redistribution when you say the same thing twice, through repetition or *anaphora* or *anthypallage*' (Demetrius, *Eloc.* 59). 'As for figures of speech, the more varied your choice, the more forceful their impact on what you say' (Demetrius, *Eloc.* 267). Demetrius does not distinguish *epanalepsis* from *anadiplosis*.

5.    'Words, for instance, may be doubled with a view to amplification, as in "I have slain, I have slain, not spurius Maelius" (where the first I have slain states what has been done, while the second emphasizes it), or to excite pity, as in "Ah! Corydon, Corydon" ' (Quintilian 3.9.29).

04 *Inclusio* (*redditio, epanadiplosis*).[6] *Inclusio* is a figure of repetition without contact (/x…x/). The term is not used in our handbooks, but is found in Quintilian. Heinrici notices the *effect* of *inclusio* between 8.1 and 9.15, but this effect seems too remote to be an example of *inclusio* in the technical rhetorical sense. There is, however, an *inclusio* in the first sentence of 2 Cor. 8.1-6, following on the initial address.

8.1     Γνωρίζομεν δὲ ὑμῖν, ἀδελφοί,

        **τὴν χάριν** τοῦ θεοῦ τὴν δεδομένην
        ἐν ταῖς ἐκκλησίαις τῆς Μακεδονίας,

8.6     εἰς τὸ παρακαλέσαι ἡμᾶς Τίτον,
        ἵνα καθὼς προενήρξατο οὕτως
        καὶ ἐπιτελέσῃ εἰς ὑμᾶς
        καὶ **τὴν χάριν** ταύτην.

05 *Repetitio* (*anaphora*).[7] *Repetitio* consists in the repetition of a word or phrase at the beginning of a series of sentences (x…/x…/). It has a certain natural climactic effect. There are three instances here.

8.18    **συνεπέμψαμεν δὲ** μετ᾽ αὐτοῦ **τὸν ἀδελφὸν**
        οὗ ὁ ἔπαινος ἐν τῷ εὐαγγελίῳ διὰ πασῶν τῶν ἐκκλησιῶν,…
8.22    **συνεπέμψαμεν δὲ** αὐτοῖς **τὸν ἀδελφὸν** ἡμῶν
        ὃν ἐδοκιμάσαμεν ἐν πολλοῖς πολλάκις σπουδαῖον ὄντα,
        νυνὶ δὲ πολὺ σπουδαιότερον πεποιθήσει πολλῇ τῇ εἰς ὑμᾶς.

8.23    **εἴτε** ὑπὲρ Τίτου, κοινωνὸς ἐμὸς καὶ εἰς ὑμᾶς συνεργός·
        **εἴτε** ἀδελφοὶ ἡμῶν, ἀπόστολοι ἐκκλησιῶν, δόξα Χριστοῦ.

9.6     Τοῦτο δέ,
        **ὁ σπείρων** φειδομένως φειδομένως καὶ θερίσει,
        καὶ **ὁ σπείρων** ἐπ᾽ εὐλογίαις ἐπ᾽ εὐλογίαις καὶ θερίσει.

---

6.    *Epanadiplosis, inclusio* and *redditio* all refer to the phenomenon of repeating a word or words at the beginning and at the end of a sentence. The terms are not found in the Hellenistic handbooks. The earliest explanation comes from Quintilian 9.3.34: 'Again the end may correspond with the beginning "Many grievous afflictions were devised for parents and for kinsfolk many".'

7.    'The verbal *anaphora* of the same word, Nireus, and the absence of connectives give an impression of a huge contingent, even though it is only two or three ships' (Demetrius, *Eloc.* 61). 'Epanaphora (*repetitio*) occurs when one and the same word forms successive beginnings for phrases and expressing like and different ideas, as follows' (*Herennium* 4.13.19).

06 *Conversio (epiphora).*[8] *Conversio* is a figure of repetition without contact. Its configuration is (/…x/…x). Its effect can be heavy insistence, as Heinrici has already observed using the term *conpar.*[9]

8.2    ὅτι ἐν πολλῇ δοκιμῇ θλίψεως ἡ περισσεία τῆς χαρᾶς **αὐτῶν**
        καὶ ἡ κατὰ βάθους πτωχεία **αὐτῶν**
        ἐπερίσσευσεν εἰς τὸ πλοῦτος τῆς ἁπλότητος **αὐτῶν·**

8.7    Ἀλλ᾽ ὥσπερ ἐν παντὶ **περισσεύετε,**
        πίστει καὶ λόγῳ καὶ γνώσει
        καὶ πάσῃ σπουδῇ καὶ τῇ ἐξ ἡμῶν ἐν ὑμῖν ἀγάπῃ,
        ἵνα καὶ ἐν ταύτῃ τῇ χάριτι **περισσεύητε.**

9.11   ἐν παντὶ πλουτιζόμενοι εἰς πᾶσαν ἁπλότητα,
        ἥτις κατεργάζεται δι᾽ ἡμῶν **εὐχαριστίαν τῷ θεῷ·**
9.12   ὅτι ἡ διακονία τῆς λειτουργίας ταύτης
        οὐ μόνον ἐστὶν προσαναπληροῦσα τὰ ὑστερήματα τῶν ἁγίων,
        ἀλλὰ καὶ περισσεύουσα διὰ πολλῶν **εὐχαριστιῶν τῷ θεῷ.**

8.11   νυνὶ δὲ καὶ τὸ ποιῆσαι <u>ἐπιτελέσατε</u>,
        ὅπως καθάπερ ἡ προθυμία **τοῦ θέλειν,**
        οὕτως καὶ τὸ <u>ἐπιτελέσαι</u> ἐκ **τοῦ ἔχειν.**

8.24   τὴν οὖν ἔνδειξιν τῆς ἀγάπης **ὑμῶν**
        καὶ ἡμῶν καυχήσεως ὑπὲρ **ὑμῶν**
        εἰς αὐτοὺς ἐνδεικνύμενοι εἰς πρόσωπον τῶν ἐκκλησι**ῶν.**

9.6    Τοῦτο δέ,
        ὁ σπείρων φειδομένως φειδομένως **καὶ θερίσει,**
        καὶ ὁ σπείρων ἐπ᾽ εὐλογίαις ἐπ᾽ εὐλογίαις **καὶ θερίσει.**

07 *Complexio (symploche).*[10] This combination of *anaphora* and *epiphora* is a figure of repetition without contact, with the configuration (/x…y/x…y). There is one example in 2 Corinthians 8–9.

9.6    Τοῦτο δέ,
        ὁ **σπείρων** φειδομένως φειδομένως **καὶ θερίσει,**
        καὶ ὁ **σπείρων** ἐπ᾽ εὐλογίαις ἐπ᾽ εὐλογίαις **καὶ θερίσει.**

The likely text being alluded to here is LXX Prov. 24.8, which reads:

    8.    'In Antistrophe (*scil. conversio*) we repeat not the first word in successive phrases, as in Epanaphora, but the last, as follows' (*Herennium* 4.13.19).
    9.    See Chapter 2.
    10.   'Interlacement (*scil. complexio*) is the union of both figures, the combined use of Antistrophe and Epanaphora, which are explained above. We repeat both the first word and the last in a succession of phrases, as follows' (*Herennium* 4.13.20).

*Prov. 22.8*   ὁ σπείρων φαῦλα θερίσει κακά
            πληγὴν δὲ ἔργων αὐτού συντελέσει
[8α]        ἄνδρα ἱλαρὸν καὶ δότην εὐλογεῖ ὁ θεός
            ματαιότητα δὲ ἔργων αὐτού συντελέσει

If this is the text and not Prov 11.24, then this is a case of Paul adjusting a text to construct a figure of speech (*symploche*) which he found neither in the LXX nor in the MT. The first line of the original is in the form (x…y/ x…y), this is the familiar parallelism of biblical poetry. The adjustment and expansion of the text constitute evidence of intentional awareness of the figures of speech.

08 *Adnominatio (paronomasis)*.[11] A figure of repetition by difference and change of form, a (pseudo-) etymological play on words with similar sounds. The author of *Ad Herennium* considers eight ways of achieving this—shortening and lengthening vowels, transposing letters and the like. Moderation is advised, especially if a speaker needs to project a certain solemnity because when technique becomes palpable credibility wanes.

8.2    ὅτι ἐν πολλῇ δοκιμῇ θλίψεως ἡ περισσεία τῆς χαρᾶς αὐτῶν
       καὶ ἡ κατὰ βάθους πτωχεία αὐτῶν
       ἐπερίσσευσεν εἰς τὸ **πλοῦτος** τῆς **ἁπλότητος** αὐτῶν·

It is not always easy to know how words were spoken in the past and so it is hard to judge if the similarity between θέλειν and ἐπιτελέσαι would have been noticed. The connection in content may support the identification of *adnominatio* here too.

8.10   τοῦτο γὰρ ὑμῖν συμφέρει,
       οἵτινες οὐ μόνον τὸ ποιῆσαι
       ἀλλὰ καὶ τὸ **θέλειν** προενήρξασθε ἀπὸ πέρυσι·
8.11   νυνὶ δὲ καὶ τὸ ποιῆσαι **ἐπιτελέσατε**,
       ὅπως καθάπερ ἡ προθυμία τοῦ **θέλειν**,
       οὕτως καὶ τὸ **ἐπιτελέσαι** ἐκ τοῦ ἔχειν.

09 *Commutatio (polyptoton)*.[12] This is a figure of repetition, which consists in using the *same words* in *different* forms e.g. an adjective in the

---

11. '*Paronomasia (scil. adnominatio)* is the figure in which, by means of a modification of sound, or change of letters, a close resemblance to a given verb or noun is produced, so that similar words express dissimilar things' (*Herennium* 4.21.29).
    12. 'There is a third form of *paronomasia*, depending on a change of case in one or more proper nouns' (*Herennium* 4.22.30-31).

simple and in *the* comparative *or* a noun in *a variety of cases. Ad Her. associates it with paronomasis, as does Heinrici.*

8.22     συνεπέμψαμεν δὲ αὐτοῖς τὸν ἀδελφὸν ἡμῶν
         ὃν ἐδοκιμάσαμεν ἐν **πολλοῖς** πολλάκις **σπουδαῖον** ὄντα,
         νυνὶ δὲ **πολὺ σπουδαιότερον** πεποιθήσει **πολλῇ** τῇ εἰς ὑμᾶς.

Another form of *commutatio*, distinguished only with difficulty from *commutatio* (polypton),[13] consists of using the *same roots* to construct not merely different forms of the same word but *different words*. For example, the same root can be used for a verb and for a noun. The later theorists distinguished this latter by the term 'etymological figure' or *derivatio* or παρηγμένον, but this distinction is not found in the authors being used here and hence the next heading is in parentheses. However, the phenomenon is present and occasionally significant.

10 *Etymological figure.*[14] Etymological figure (also *paregmenon* or *derivatio*) is a figure of repetition, using the same root to produce not merely different forms of the same word but different words as such. The writer uses the same root in different words, not simply different forms of the same word. It is a *later* theoretical refinement of *commutatio* and the difference is slight and is not found in the manuals used here. A few cases may be distinguished in 2 Corinthians 8–9; usually the play is between noun/adjectives and verbs. There should also be a a kind of 'coupling' between the realted words, which brings them syntactically together. The most obvious and sure example is 8.24 noted by both Heinrici[15] and Betz.[16] The Gorgian figure noticed by Heinrici in 9.8 resembles it.[17]

13. See Chapter 2.
13. Such scholastic distinctions made Quintilian impatient.
14. 'Cornificius calls this *traductio*, that is the transference of the meaning of one word to another Herennium It has, however, greater elegance when it is employed to distinguish the exact meanings of things, as in the following example: "This curse to the state could be repressed for a time, but not suppressed forever;" the same is true when the meaning of verbs is reversed by a change in the proposition with which they are compounded: for example, *Non emissus ex urbe, sed immissus in urbem esse videatur*. The effect is better still and more phatic when our pleasure is derived both from the figurative form and the excellence of the sense, as in the following instance: *emit morte immortalitatem*' (Quintilian 9.3.71).
15. See Chapter 2.
16. See Chapter 2.
17. See Chapter 2.

8.24    τὴν οὖν **ἔνδειξιν** τῆς ἀγάπης ὑμῶν
        καὶ ἡμῶν καυχήσεως ὑπὲρ ὑμῶν
        εἰς αὐτοὺς **ἐνδεικνύμενοι** εἰς πρόσωπον τῶν ἐκκλησιῶν.

8.2     ὅτι ἐν πολλῇ δοκιμῇ θλίψεως ἡ **περισσεία** τῆς χαρᾶς αὐτῶν
        καὶ ἡ κατὰ βάθους πτωχεία αὐτῶν
        **ἐπερίσσευσεν** εἰς τὸ πλοῦτος τῆς ἁπλότητος αὐτῶν·

This would be a clearer example of *figura etymologica* if ἡ περισσεία
were the subject of the verb ἐπερίσσευσεν. The linking of ἡ περισσεία
and ἡ κατὰ βάθους πτωχεία by καὶ means they are both in a way the
subject of the singular verb and this obscured the figure.

9.8     δυνατεῖ δὲ ὁ θεὸς **πᾶσαν** χάριν περισσεῦσαι εἰς ὑμᾶς,
        ἵνα ἐν **παντὶ πάντοτε πᾶσαν** αὐτάρκειαν ἔχοντες
        περισσεύητε εἰς **πᾶν** ἔργον ἀγαθόν,

11 *Interpretatio.*[18] *Interpretatio* or synonymy is a figure of repetition
which uses words of similar meaning to say the same thing. One goal is
variety in vocabulary, to lend colour to the expression. The second
example below, at 2 Cor. 9.10, resembles the use of parallelism in Hebrew poetry where the use of synonymy is especially striking.

8.19    οὐ μόνον δέ, ἀλλὰ καὶ χειροτονηθεὶς ὑπὸ τῶν ἐκκλησιῶν
        συνέκδημος ἡμῶν σὺν **τῇ χάριτι ταύτῃ**
        τῇ διακονουμένῃ ὑφ᾽ ἡμῶν
        πρὸς τὴν [αὐτοῦ] τοῦ κυρίου δόξαν καὶ προθυμίαν ἡμῶν,
8.20    στελλόμενοι τοῦτο, μή τις ἡμᾶς μωμήσηται
        ἐν **τῇ ἁδρότητι ταύτῃ** τῇ διακονουμένῃ ὑφ᾽ ἡμῶν·

9.10    ὁ δὲ ἐπιχορηγῶν σπόρον τῷ σπείροντι
        καὶ ἄρτον εἰς βρῶσιν χορηγήσει
        καὶ **πληθυνεῖ** τὸν **σπόρον** ὑμῶν
        καὶ **αὐξήσει** τὰ **γενήματα**[19] τῆς δικαιοσύνης ὑμῶν.

12 *Traductio. Traductio*[20] or *diaphora* is a figure of repetition without
contact. It refers to the use of the same word to mean different things.

18. 'Synonymy or Interpretation is the figure which does not duplicate the same
word by repeating it, but replaces the word that has been used by another of the
same meaning' (*Herennium* 4.28.38).
19. The two nouns are not quite synonyms, but belong together in terms of
cause and effect within the semantic field.
20. 'Transplacement (*scil. traductio*) makes it possible for the same word to be
frequently reintroduced, not only without offence to good taste, but even so as to

There is a certain cumulative effect as the various meanings are harvested. The classic example in 2 Corinthians 8–9 is the word χάρις, often noted by the exegetes without using the precise literary term *traductio*.[21]

Χάρις can mean gift (8.1, 4 and 9.14), generous undertaking (8.6, 7, 9, 19), thanks (8.16 and 9.15), blessing (9.8). This variety of meanings is fundamental to the persuasion in 2 Corinthians 8–9 because Paul wants to suggest that giving is itself a gift from God, which in turn resounds in greater thanksgiving to God.

| | |
|---|---|
| 9.5a | ἀναγκαινον οὖν ἡγησάμην παρακαλέσαι τοὺς ἀδελφούς, |
| 5b | ἵνα προέλθωσιν εἰς ὑμᾶς |
| 5c | καὶ προκαταρτίσωσιν τὴν προεπηγγελμένην **εὐλογίαν** ὑμῶν, |
| 5d | ταύτην ἑτοίμην εἶναι οὕτως ὡς **εὐλογίαν** καὶ μὴ ὡς πλεονεξίαν. |
| 6a | Τοῦτο δέ, ὁ σπείρων φειδομένως φειδομένως καὶ θερίσει, |
| 6b | καὶ ὁ σπείρων ἐπ᾽ **εὐλογίαις** ἐπ᾽ **εὐλογίαις** καὶ θερίσει.[22] |

By means of the word εὐλογία used in more than one sense, Paul effects a subtle shift in meaning here between the related concepts of freedom and bountifulness. In the first occurrence (2 Cor. 9.5c), it refers to the gift to come simply as a blessing. The second occurrence contrasts εὐλογία with πλεονεξία.[23] At this point a digression is necessary on the word πλεονιξία.

In standard modern versions of the Bible, this word is variously translated as extortion (NRSV, REB), as imposition (NJB) and as 'not as one grudgingly given' (NIV). The translators of the NRSV, REB and NJB have chosen a reading which supposes a feeling of being imposed upon. The NIV, on the other hand, tries to keep to the root meaning of πλεονεξία which is 'greed'. The problem is, howeaver, that it is not clear to whom πλεονεξία is being attributed—the Macedonians or the Achaians. (The KJV retains the ambiguity by settling for the word covetous-

render the style more elegant (*Herennium* 4.14.20). 'To the same type of figure belongs that which occurs when the same word is used first in one function and then in another Herennium' (*Herennium* 4.13.21). (The author does not use a separate term to distinguish repeated use and varied meaning.)

21. The various possible meanings of χάρις are noted by Allo 1937: 221, 212, 214 etc. Also by Danker—see Chapter 2.5—where he uses the term *paronomasia* for this effect.

22. Noted by Heinrici: see Chapter 2.2 above where he uses the term *antanaklasis*.

23. πλεονεξία has two meanings: 'greed' and 'exploitation'.

ness.) If it should be attributed to the Corinthians, then, the meaning is greed in the sense of meanness, holding on to what one has.

There is a problem of translation and interpretation here. In the dictionary attached to the Greek New Testament (*GNT*) two possible translations are offered (1) greed or covetousness, and (2) 'something one feels forced to do (2 Cor. 9.5)'. *The Exegetical Dictionary of the New Testament* (*EDNT*) notes:

> The context in 2 Cor. 9.5 suggests that πλεονεξία is there a 'gift wrested away [laboriously] from avarice'.[24]

According to *TDNT*, the classical range of meanings is (1) having more; (2) receiving more; and (3) wanting more.[25] In the LXX, the it comes to translate בצע, with the fundamental meaning of 'unlawful gain'. In *Testament of the Patriarchs* 12 the word denotes covetousness and taking advantage of. In the New Testament, it means striving for material possessions, and where 'this is the meaning, taking advantage of one's neighbour is obviously the main thought'.[26] This means that the 'desire for more' of 2 Cor. 9.5 is more reasonably attributed to the Macedonians (at least in the mind of the Corinthians) and inclines us towards the reading of 'taking advantage of' that is, giving freely and not as if you were forced. In this regard, it is interesting that Louw and Nida (*GELNTSD*) note two meanings of the word:

> **25.22 πλεονεξία**a, ας *f:* a strong desire to acquire more and more material possessions or to possess more things than other people have, all irrespective of need—'greed, avarice, covetousness.' καὶ τὴν πλεονεξίαν ἥτις ἐστὶν εἰδωλολατρία 'and greed, which is idolatry' Col. 3.5; καρδίαν γεγυμνασμένην πλεονεξίας ἔχοντες 'they are experts in greed' 2 Pet. 2.14.

> **88.144 πλεονεκτέω; πλεονεξία**b, ας *f:* to take advantage of someone, usually as the result of a motivation of greed—'to take advantage of, to exploit, exploitation'.[27]

This fundamental meaning of 'wanting more' *from others* is captured in Bauer's dictionary (*BAGD*: 667) when he reports Plummer's ICC trans-

24. *EDNT*, III: 103.
25. *TDNT*, VI: 266-74.
26. *TDNT*, VI: 271.
27. At the same time, their suggestion for 2 Cor. 9.5 is: 'then it will be ready as a gift, not as one grudgingly given'. Whatever πλεονεξία means, it does not mean 'a gift grudgingly given'.

lation of 'extortion'. This 'extortion' is surely an overtranslation,[28] but 'exploitation' might capture the sense of being imposed upon. In the Post-Apostolic Fathers, the root unambiguously means the coveting of the possessions of others.[29] The probability is, therefore, that the Corinthians may fear that the Macedonians have designs on Corinthian wealth; in that sense, a working translation would be 'exploitation' in the sense of taking advantage of. This sense of external compulsion is echoed two verses hence, where we read:

*2 Cor. 9.7* ἕκαστος καθὼς προῄρηται τῇ καρδίᾳ,
μὴ ἐκ λύπης ἢ ἐξ **ἀνάγκης**·
ἱλαρὸν γὰρ δότην ἀγαπᾷ ὁ θεός.

We now return to our discussion of the meanings of εὐλογία.

Finally, the generosity of the gift is underscored in the idiom ἐπ᾽ **εὐλογίαις**. The NRSV captures something of these shifts in meaning, by adding the adjective bountiful to the first occurrence and forcing a connection, thereby, with the third occurrence translated 'bountifully'.

9.5     So I thought it necessary to urge the brothers to go on ahead to you, and arrange in advance for this bountiful gift that you have promised, so that it may be ready as a voluntary gift and not as an extortion (*scil.* exploitation).

9.6     The point is this: the one who sows sparingly will also reap sparingly, and the one who sows bountifully will also reap bountifully.

The text also shows also the use of synecdoche (*abstractum pro concreto*) in 9.5 using εὐλογία and πλεονεξία. The synecdoche is part of his technique of avoiding all mention of money and specific amounts, thus avoiding as well any sense of an imperious demands, which, again, might make the Corinthians feel imposed upon. Given the subtle use of this (later) figure, the NRSV insertion of 'gift' is likewise misleading.

18 *Hendiadys*. Both as term and as idea, hendiadys does not occur in our authors. There is one case here in 8.4:

*2 Cor. 8.4* μετὰ πολλῆς παρακλήσεως δεόμενοι ἡμῶν
**τὴν χάριν καὶ τὴν κοινωνίαν**
τῆς διακονίας τῆς εἰς τοὺς ἁγίους.

28. It may be the cause of the use of the word in modern translations.
29. *TDNT*, VI: 273.

19 *Appositum*. *Appositum*[30] (*epitheton*) is a figure of addition by sub-ordinate accumulation, in the form of an adjective or an adjectival phrase. It is not distinguished in the writers we are using, but the use of adjectives and adjectival phrases is an important part of Paul's per-suasion. His mode of qualification, often oblique, reveals his interest.

God is mentioned ten times in these chapters. In three of those cases words to do with giving, giver and gift are used. Thus the initiative is consistently attributed to God.

*2 Cor. 8.1*     Γνωρίζομεν δὲ ὑμῖν, ἀδελφοί,
            τὴν χάριν τοῦ **θεοῦ** τὴν **δεδομένην**
            ἐν ταῖς ἐκκλησίαις τῆς Μακεδονίας,

*2 Cor. 8.16*   Χάρις δὲ τῷ **θεῷ** τῷ **δόντι**
            τὴν αὐτὴν σπουδὴν ὑπὲρ ὑμῶν
            ἐν τῇ καρδίᾳ Τίτου,

*2 Cor. 9.15*   Χάρις τῷ **θεῷ** ἐπὶ τῇ ἀνεκδιηγήτῳ αὐτοῦ **δωρεᾷ.**

The word διακονία is used of the collection, and twice Paul qualifies this collected as 'administered' by him.

*8.19*     οὐ μόνον δέ, ἀλλὰ καὶ χειροτονηθεὶς ὑπὸ τῶν ἐκκλησιῶν
        συνέκδημος ἡμῶν σὺν τῇ χάριτι ταύτῃ
        τῇ **διακονουμένῃ ὑφ' ἡμῶν**
        πρὸς τὴν [αὐτοῦ] τοῦ κυρίου δόξαν καὶ προθυμίαν ἡμῶν,
*8.20*     στελλόμενοι τοῦτο, μή τις ἡμᾶς μωμήσηται
        ἐν τῇ ἁδρότητι ταύτῃ
        τῇ **διακονουμένῃ ὑφ' ἡμῶν·**

Twice he qualifies the διακονία thus:

*8.4*     μετὰ πολλῆς παρακλήσεως δεόμενοι ἡμῶν
        τὴν χάριν καὶ τὴν κοινωνίαν
        τῆς **διακονίας τῆς εἰς τοὺς ἁγίους,**

---

30. 'Some also include under this head that form of propriety which is derived from characteristic epithets, such as in the Virgilian phrases, "sweet unfermented wine", or "with white teeth" ' (Quintilian 8.2.10). 'On the other hand, we admire Virgil when he says: "Oft hath the tiny mouse," etc. For here the epithet is appro-priate and prevents our expecting too much' (Quintilian 8.3.20). 'Wherefore, al-though these ornaments may seem to stand out with a certain glitter of their own, they are rather to be compared to sparks flashing through the smoke than to the actual brilliance of flame: they are, in fact, invisible when the language is of uni-form splendour, just as the starts are invisible in the light of day' (Quintilian 8.5.29). 'The epithetic as a rule, involves an element of antonomasis and conse-quently becomes a trope on account of this affinity' (Quintilian 9.1.6).

*9.1*            Περὶ μὲν γὰρ τῆς **διακονίας τῆς εἰς τοὺς ἁγίους**
                 περισσόν μοί ἐστιν τὸ γράφειν ὑμῖν·

For completeness' sake, the following remarks are made about the Christological titles used in 2 Corinthians 8–9. In 8.9, the full three part title is used for Jesus. This is frequent in Paul in general, but rare in 2 Cor. in being confined to four places: the greetings at the opening and close of the letter, 4.5 and 8.9. At 4.5 it functions emphatically to shift the emphasis from Paul the preacher to Christ the preached. Likewise in 8.9, it reminds the hearers of the basic preaching before going on to use the death and resurrection as a *exemplum*. And it further emphasized the status of Christ as rich (κύριος), so that his self-impoverishment is all the more remarkable.

23 *Dissolutio*. *Dissolutio* or asyndeton[31] is a figure of suppression in which conjunctions are omitted. Such economy of expression favours clarity, whereby it is impossible to miss the writer's meaning.

*8.13*           οὐ γὰρ ἵνα ἄλλοις ἄνεσις, ὑμῖν θλῖψις,
                 ἀλλ᾽ ἐξ ἰσότητος·[32]

28 *Conpar*. *Conpar*[33] (*isocolon*) is the figure in which the lines have virtually the same number of syllables. Appositely, *Ad Herennium* says that there is no need to count, because there is something trivial about precision in these matters. This feature of Hellenistic rhetoric is by no means limited to Greek and Latin as it is also found in Hebrew poetry, and there are several examples there. [34]

---

31. 'To show that asyndeton suits an actor's delivery, let this be an example: "I conceived, I gave birth, I nurse, my dear". In this disjointed form the words will, force anyone to be dramatic, however reluctantly—and the cause is the asyndeton' (Demetrius, *Eloc.* 194). 'Asyndeton (*scil. dissolutum*) is a presentation in separate parts, conjunctions being suppressed' (*Herennium* 4.30.41).

32. Noted by Heinrici.

33. 'We call *isocolon* (*scil. conpar*) the figure comprised of cola (discussed above) which consist of a virtually equal number of syllables. To effect the *isocolon* we shall not count the syllables—for that is surely childish—but experience and practice will bring such a facility that by a sort of instinct we can produce again a colon of equal length to the one before it, as follows' (*Herennium* 4.20.27).

34. *Isocolon* resembles the figure well known to biblical studies of the *parallelismus membrorum*. The example here is a *tricolon*.

8.2 ὅτι ἐν πολλῇ δοκιμῇ θλίψεως

|  |  |  |
|---|---|---|
| **ἡ περισσεία** | τῆς χαρᾶς | αὐτῶν |
| **καὶ ἡ κατὰ βάθους** | πτωχεία | αὐτῶν |
| ἐπερίσσευσεν |  |  |
| εἰς τὸ πλοῦτος | τῆς ἁπλότητος | αὐτῶν· |

8.7 Ἀλλ᾽ ὥσπερ  ἐν παντὶ    **περισσεύετε,**

πίστει καὶ λόγῳ καὶ γνώσει

καὶ πάσῃ σπουδῇ καὶ τῇ ἐξ ἡμῶν ἐν ὑμῖν ἀγάπῃ,

**ἵνα καὶ**   ἐν ταύτῃ τῇ χάριτι  **περισσεύητε.**

8.9 γινώσκετε γὰρ τὴν χάριν τοῦ κυρίου ἡμῶν Ἰησοῦ Χριστοῦ,

**ὅτι δι᾽ ὑμᾶς**  ἐπτώχευσεν  πλούσιος ὤν,

**ἵνα ὑμεῖς**   τῇ ἐκείνου πτωχείᾳ πλουτήσητε.

8.11 νυνὶ δὲ καὶ τὸ ποιῆσαι ἐπιτελέσατε,

**ὅπως καθάπερ** ἡ προθυμία   τοῦ θέλειν,

**οὕτως καὶ**   τὸ ἐπιτελέσαι   ἐκ τοῦ ἔχειν.

8.14 ἐν τῷ νῦν καιρῷ

       τὸ ὑμῶν περίσσευμα

              εἰς τὸ ἐκείνων ὑστέρημα,

ἵνα καὶ

       τὸ ἐκείνων περίσσευμα

γένηται

              εἰς τὸ ὑμῶν ὑστέρημα,

ὅπως γένηται ἰσότης,

8.15 καθὼς γέγραπται·

| ὁ | τὸ πολὺ | οὐκ ἐπλεόνασεν, |
|---|---|---|
| **καὶ ὁ** | τὸ ὀλίγον | οὐκ ἠλαττόνησεν. |

This last text is a reference to Exod. 16.18, which in the LXX reads:

καὶ μετρήσαντες τῷ γομορ
**οὐκ ἐπλεόνασεν ὁ τὸ πολύ**
**καὶ ὁ τὸ ἔλαττον οὐκ ἠλαττόνησεν**
ἕκαστος εἰς τοὺς καθήκοντας παρ᾽ ἑαυτῷ συνέλεξαν

At least in the LXX which is here an accurate rendition of the MT word order, this verse is not an example of *isocolon*, but of chiasm. It seems the translation has been adjusted here also to achieve an *isocolon*, which would be an argument for a conscious choice of literary figure. We shall see in the next chapter that the balanced phrases used here reflect the content which is 'balance' or 'equity'—almost an example of onomatopoeia!

8.21    προνοοῦμεν γὰρ καλὰ
      οὐ μόνον      ἐνώπιον      κυρίου
      ἀλλὰ καὶ      ἐνώπιον      ἀνθρώπων.[35]

9.5    ταύτην ἑτοίμην εἶναι
      οὕτως ὡς εὐλογίαν
      καὶ μὴ ὡς πλεονεξίαν.

9.6    Τοῦτο δέ,
      ὁ σπείρων      φειδομένως φειδομένως      καὶ θερίσει,
      καὶ ὁ σπείρων    ἐπ' εὐλογίαις ἐπ' εὐλογίαις      καὶ θερίσει.

30 *Homoeoptoton. Homoeoptoton*[36] is the ending of cola with like terminations, producing a rhyming effect.

8.14    ἐν τῷ νῦν καιρῷ τὸ ὑμῶν περίσσευ**μα** εἰς τὸ ἐκείνων ὑστέρη**μα**,
      ἵνα καὶ τὸ ἐκείνων περίσσευ**μα** γένηται εἰς τὸ ὑμῶν ὑστέρη**μα**, ὅπως
      γένηται ἰσότης,

8.15    καθὼς γέγραπται·
         ὁ τὸ πολὺ οὐκ ἐπλεόνα**σεν**,
      καὶ     ὁ τὸ ὀλίγον οὐκ ἠλαττόνη**σεν**.

Finally, in these chapters alliteration (the term is early modern) on π is frequent. This is not regarded as a figure of speech, but on the contrary as a fault of style. *Ad Herennium* uses no special term for it, but the best stylists avoid it.[37] It remains a (vulgar) figure of emphasis, common in Hellenistic writing, as the need to condemn it shows. In 2 Cor. the following verses show alliteration: on π the last phrase of 8.2; on π and ψ 8.22; on προ- 9.5; on π and πᾶς 9.8; on π 9.11a.[38]

<hr/>

35. Noted by Danker: see Chapter 2.5.

36. 'The figure called *homoeoptoton* when in the same period two or more words appear in the same case, and with like terminations, as follows' (*Herennium* 4.20.28).

37. 'We shall also avoid the excessive recurrence of the same letter, and this blemish the following verse will illustrate—for at this juncture, in considering faults, nothing forbids me to use examples from others: O Tite, tute, Tati, tibi tanta, tyranne, tulisti' (*Herennium* 4.12.18).

38. Allo 1937: 234 is not too happy with this. 'Remarquer les paronomases avec πᾶς (assez fréquentes), et toutes les allitérations en π, ce qui n'est pas très harmonieux, mais marque "insistance de l'affirmation".'

## 1.2. *Figures of Thought*

01 *Commoratio.* Commoratio[39] is a figure of amplification for the purposes of insistence. It is achieved by dwelling on a point and by returning to a point. Paul dwells on *giving* in a series of succinct arguments in 8.8-15 and on integrity in 8.16-24. He returns to the subject of giving in 9.6-10. These series of arguments in 8.8-15 would be an example. The repeated insistence on integrity in 8.16-24 is also an example. So also is the return to the theme of giving in 9.6-9. The topic of freedom is also insisted upon—8.8 and 12 and again in 9.5 (μὴ ὡς πλεονεξίαν, in the sense of exploitation)—is likewise *commoratio*.

02 *Descriptio.*[40] *Descriptio* or *hypotyposis* is vivid description of the consequences of an act so that it becomes engraved on the hearer's mind. There are three examples in 2 Corinthians 8–9. The dramatic poverty leads to the astonishing consequence of 8.3-5. Again, Paul sketches briefly what might happen if Macedonian envoys turned up and nothing had been done (9.4). Finally, the overflow into a great thanksgiving to God is vividly portrayed (9.12).

03 *Enthymeme.* Enthymeme[41] in our texts has a specific meaning. Traditionally the enthymeme is a rhetorical (incomplete) syllogism. Both *Ad Herennium* and the *De Elocutione* of Demetrius treat enthymeme as a proof by contraries, where statements are juxtaposed and the listener infers the connection. Demetrius, in particular, 'unpacks' an enthymeme to show that it consists in ideas, which are undisturbed when the verbal ornamentation is dropped. The *isocolon* in 8.14 is just such an example. Two things remain unspoken in this incomplete syllogism:

---

39. 'Dwelling on the point (*scil. commoratio*) occurs when one remains rather long upon and often returns to, the strongest topic on which the whole cause rests' (*Herennium* 4.45.58).

40. 'Vivid Description is the name for the figure which contains a clear, lucid, and impressive exposition of the consequences of an act' (*Herennium* 4.39.51).

41. 'The enthymeme differs from the period. The latter is a rounded structure (hence its name in fact), the former has its meaning and constitution in the thought. The period circumscribes the enthymeme in the same way as any other subject matter, the enthymeme is a thought, expressed whether controversially or in the form of a logical consequence' (Demetrius, *Eloc.* 30-33). 'Reasoning by Contraries is the figure which, of two opposite statements, uses one so as neatly and directly to prove the other' (*Herennium* 4.18.25).

firstly, the fact that prosperity is not guaranteed to last and, secondly, that a gift sets up a relationship of reciprocity, a guarantee against the future. Even if you removed the ornament of *isocolon*, the content would remain. The enthymeme is powerful because it triggers insight involuntarily and what arises within our own minds is more convincing than that which comes in from outside.

05 *Definitio. Definitio*[42] is a figure of semantic clarification, whereby a writer explains a concept more precisely. Paul reassures his hearers that ἐκ τοῦ ἔχειν in 8.11 does not mean they are expected to impoverish themselves—this was a possible inference from the example of Christ, who made himself poor. This is also the impression he gives in the Macedonian example in 8.3 where they went beyond their ability. This is not what Paul has in mind and he explains himself more fully in 8.12-13 and in 9.5c.

07 *Correctio. Correctio*[43] is a figure of semantic dilation by which a speaker seems to come up with a better way of saying something. It is a figure which lends apparent spontaneity and freshness while it protects from misunderstanding. There are several examples in 2 Corinthians 8–9: the first possible instance is in 8.3, in the change from κατὰ δύναμιν to παρὰ δύναμιν, where within the figure of *parenthesis* (see below), Paul corrects and improves what he wants to say. In. 8.8 Paul corrects the impression imperative imposition.[44] 2 Cor. 9.4 also exhibits this figure (ἵνα μὴ λέγω ὑμεῖς).

42. 'Definition in brief and clear-cut fashion grasps the characteristic qualities of a thing' (*Herennium* 4.25.35). 'The first topic in the prosecutor's argument is a brief, clear and conventional definition of the word whose meaning is sought...' (Cicero, *Inv.* 2.17.53). 'Definition is used in a case in which a document contains some word the meaning of which is questioned' (Cicero, *Inv.* 2.51.153). 'It is at all events clear that a definition is an explanation in the form of a statement of the class to which a thing belongs and of some special property that distinguishes it, or else a collection of common properties among which what its special property is comes into view' (Cicero, *Part. Or.* 12.41).
43. 'Correction retracts what has been said and replaces it with what seems more suitable' (*Herennium* 4.26.36).
44. Noted by Betz: see Chapter 2.3.

08 *Contentio. Contentio*[45] or antithesis is a figure of semantic dilation by means of opposing terms, usually within the same semantic field, such as suffering and joy, poverty and wealth.

This figure is found very powerfully in 8.2, where the juxtaposition of contraries forces the listener to think in other than material terms. The same figure is used in the *exemplum* of Christ in 8.9. It is likewise found in 8.14[46] and in 9.6.[47]

11 *Commutatio.* There are further figures under the heading of 'antithesis', such as oxymoron, *reversio* and *commutatio.*[48] *Commutatio* as a figure of thought is to be distinguished from *commutatio* as a figure of speech. It is a kind of refined antithesis, and in chiastic form, is known in the later literature as *antimetabole.* Antithesis, oxymoron, *reversio* and *commutatio* are all refinements of antithesis, but our authors do not anticipate the later precision. There are examples of chiastic juxtaposition in 2 Corinthians 8–9, where the chiastic arrangement of the pronoun and demonstrative adjective conveys the meaning.

8.7      Ἀλλ᾽ ὥσπερ ἐν παντὶ περισσεύετε,
         **πίστει** καὶ **λόγῳ**
         καὶ **γνώσει** καὶ πάσῃ **σπουδῇ**
         καὶ τῇ ἐξ ἡμῶν ἐν ὑμῖν ἀγάπῃ,
         ἵνα καὶ ἐν ταύτῃ τῇ χάριτι περισσεύητε.[49]

45. 'Through Antithesis contraries will meet. As I have explained above, it belongs either among the figures of diction, as in the following example: "You show yourself conciliatory to your enemies, inexorable to your friends"; or among the figures of thought, as in the following example: "While you deplore the troubles besetting him, this knave rejoices in the ruin of the state. While you despair of your fortunes, this knave alone grows all the more confident in his own". Between these two kinds of Antithesis there is this difference: the first consists in a rapid opposition of words; in the other opposing thoughts ought to meet in a comparison' (*Herennium* 4.45.58). 'Certes on peut y voir le poids des paradoxes et le choc des antithèses. Mais derrière ces mots chargés du contenu christologique le plus lourd, se profile dans cette société la figure de l'esclave. L'exhortation christologique de Paul vise à dire: ne vous installez pas dans les richesses même et surtout spirituelles! Regardez au Christ' (Carrez 1986: 183).
46. Noted by Heinrici.
47. Noted by Betz.
48. Quintilian 9.3.88 and 9.3.97; *Herennium* 4.28.39.
49. Noted by Danker.

8.9        γινώσκετε γὰρ τὴν χάριν τοῦ κυρίου ἡμῶν Ἰησοῦ Χριστοῦ,
           ὅτι δι' ὑμᾶς <u>ἐπτώχευσεν</u> **πλούσιος** ὤν,
           ἵνα ὑμεῖς τῇ ἐκείνου **πτωχείᾳ** <u>πλουτήσητε</u>.[50]

The action of becoming poor is in contrast with the action of becoming rich. The state of being rich is contrasted with poverty as a means of becoming rich.

8.14       ἐν τῷ νῦν καιρῷ τὸ **ὑμῶν** περίσσευμα εἰς τὸ <u>ἐκείνων</u> ὑστέρημα,
           ἵνα καὶ τὸ <u>ἐκείνων</u> περίσσευμα γένηται εἰς τὸ **ὑμῶν** ὑστέρημα, ὅπως
           γένηται ἰσότης,

12 *Sententia*. *Sententia*[51] or maxim is a commonplace, based on experience and considered universally, 'proverbially' valid. Verse 9.6[52] is just such a maxim. Although this particular *sententia* alludes to Scripture, and may derive some of its force from the allusion, the validity it carries is founded in the common experience. 9.7[53] also has a proverbial ring to it. Probably 2 Cor. 9.9, with it scriptural echo, functions in a similar way.

A further refinement of the *sententia* is the *epiphonemon*. The refinement is not found in our chosen authors, but Quintilian illustrates it from Cicero. The early practice means that it would have been 'available' in Hellenistic rhetoric in practice before the theorists came to account for it in theory. To indicate that it is not found as such in our authors, the heading is placed in parentheses.

13 *Epiphonemon*. *Epiphonemon*[54] is a *sententia* which is used to conclude a longer portion of argument, a concluding acclamation which functions like a *peroratio*, taking us back over the entire argument. Quintilian describes it as an acclamation. The very last verse of ch. 9 is such an acclamation, which has the appropriate aphoristic character and which takes us back over the preceding discussion very neatly. One

---

50. Noted by Betz: see Chapter 2.3. It does not fit the form ABB'A'.
51. 'A Maxim is a saying drawn from life, which shows concisely either what happens or ought to happen in life' (*Herennium* 4.17.24).
52. Noted by Betz.
53. Noted by Betz.
54. 'For an *epiphomena* is an exclamation attached to the close of a statement or a proof by way of climax. Here are two examples: "Such toil it was to found the Roman race!" and "The virtuous youth preferred to risk his life by slaying him to suffering such dishonour" ' (Quintilian 8.5.11).

consequence of identifying 9.15 as *sententia* with the special function of *epiphonemon* is that the ending is not necessarily epistolary (i.e. marking the end of a letter) but rather rhetorical (that is, marking the end of an argument). It is probable as well that 8.15 functions in the same manner—the other example of *epiphonemon* used by Quintilian is a citation from Virgil. Such an identification would confirm v. 15 as the end of a block of argument.

14 *Similitudo*. Similitude[55] is a figure of semantic dilation, which brings together things which do not belong together, in order to use some characteristics of one to illuminate the other. An image is established in 9.6, taken up again in 9.9, which is then developed in vv. 10-12.[56] The commonplace of agricultural phenomena, a cultural cliché convincing in itself, is used to remind the Corinthians that God who inspires generosity will not leave them without reward. The metaphor may have been familiar from the teaching of Jesus (cf. Mark 4) and would thus have enjoyed a particular resonance.

15 *Exemplum*. *Exemplum*[57] or παράδειγμα is a figure of similitude, effecting a comparison. An *exemplum* may appear at any point in an argument. The story of what God has achieved among the Macedonians is an *exemplum*[58], setting up an implied comparison, which is articulated at a safe remove in 9.1-5, where the question of shame and honour arises. It was recommended practice to plant seeds of proof (*semina confirmationum*) in the *exordium*. Here it has a subtle function: on their second appearance the Macedonians could have provoked rejection (who are they to spy on us?). But because they have already provoked envy, the seeds of comparison have already been sown. The other powerful *exemplum* is 8.9[59]. This is introduced as a reminder of their faith (γινώσκετε), i.e. what they are already persuaded of, in order to

---

55. 'Comparison (*scil. similitudo*) is a manner of speech that carries over an element of likeness from one thing to a different thing. This is used to embellish or prove or clarify or vivify' (*Herennium* 4.45.59).

56. Noted by Danker.

57. 'Exemplification (*scil. exemplum*) is the citing of something done or said in the past, along with the definite naming of the doer or author. It is used with the same motives as a comparison' (*Herennium* 4.49.62).

58. Noted by Betz: see Chapter 2.3.

59. Noted by Danker: see Chapter 2.5.

persuade them to further imitation. The preceding *appositum* (τοῦ κυριοῦ ἡμῶν Ἰησοῦ Χριστοῦ) underscores the force of the *exemplum*.

16 *Brevitas*. *Brevitas*,[60] or λακωνισμός is a figure of suppression: the language becomes spartan and only the minimum necessary comes to expression. It is the antithesis of *commoratio*, a figure of dilation. Paul's writing can be famously dense and concise; 8.13a is an example of his use of *brevitas* to let them know he anticipates their objection, but the expression is as concise as it could be to avoid the effect of *descriptio*. He does not want this possible negative reaction to seem any more real in their imaginations. The suppression of verbs in 8.23 creates a suspense which is resolved only by the exclamation δόξα Χριστοῦ (see below).

The later rhetorical theorists distinguished a further subdivision of *brevitas* entitled *percursio* (Quintilian) or *praecisio* (Cicero *De Or.* 3.52.202). It uses suggestion to cause more to be understood than was actually said.

17 *Percursio*.[61] *Percursio* is a particular instance of *brevitas* and so is again a figure of suppression. A thumbnail sketch of circumstances is given, leaving much to be understood. The suppression of names in 8.18 and 22 may well a figure of *percursio*, which, precisely by leaving much to be understood, persuades by evocation of the familiar. It thus contributes to the persuasiveness of presenting these individuals— assuming them to be already known to the community. The identification depends on the interpretation given.

18 *Occultati*. *Occultatio*[62] (*praeteritio*, παράλειψις) is a figure of suppression whereby one (merely) pretends to pass over something while in reality providing the essential features and giving considerable emphasis to it. There is a recognized example at 9.1:

---

60. 'Conciseness (*scil. brevitas*) is the expressing of an idea by the very minimum of essential words, as follows' (*Herennium* 4.54.68).

61. Cf. Quintilian 8.3.82.

62. 'Paralipsis (*scil. occultatio*) occurs when we say that we are passing by, or do not know, or refuse to say that which precisely now we are saying ... This figure is useful if employed in a matter which it is not pertinent to call specifically to the attention of others, because there is advantage in making only an indirect reference to it, or because the direct reference would be tedious or undignified, or cannot be made clear or can easily be refuted' (*Herennium* 4.27.37).

Περὶ μὲν γὰρ τῆς διακονίας τῆς εἰς τοὺς ἁγίους
περισσόν μοί ἐστιν τὸ γράφειν ὑμῖν·

The comment of Demetrius on this figure is interesting:

> 'I pass over Olynthus, Methone, Apollonia, and thirty-two cities in Thrace'. In these words, Demosthenes has actually stated everything he wanted, yet he claims to pass over them, to imply that he has other more forceful points to make (*Eloc.* 263).

It is precisely the case here that Paul has 'other more forceful points to make'. He does not use the word χάρις here because he is resuming one of the '*semina confirmationum*' from the *exordium* (τῆς διακονίας τῆς εἰς τοὺς ἁγίους).

21 *Interpositio. Interpositio*[63] (*interclusio*, παρένθεσις) is a figure of order which interrupts but does not stop the flow of thought. It is not found separately in our chosen authors, but Quintilian is able to give synonyms in Latin and Greek: in other words, the phenomenon is widely recognized.[64] The first example is in 8.3 (ὅτι κατὰ δύναμιν, **μαρτυρῶ**, καὶ παρὰ δύναμιν). Μαρτυρῶ emphasizes the *correctio* which follows. Heinrici regards οὐ καθὼς ἠλπίσαμεν as *interpositio* in 8.5. Rather more significantly, the entire verse 8 in ch. 8 is an *interpositio*. The *propositio* of the argument is v. 7 (see below) and the proof begins in v. 9 (see below). Most unusually between the *propositio* and the beginning of the proof, Paul inserts a denial, which combines *interpositio* with *correctio*. Finally, in 9.4 there is a fine example of *interpositio* which is not at all peripheral to his argument: ἵνα μὴ λέγω ὑμεῖς.[65] This apparently throwaway remark brings to delicate expression the purpose of the argument in 9.1-5. He has rendered this threat to their honour 'safe' by associating himself first with the shame which would follow any failure to match the efforts of the Macedonians.

23 *Significatio. Significatio*[56] (ὑπόνοια, συνέμφασις, *significatio*) is a figure of replacement, by which someone or something is named in a

---

63. 'The first is called interpositio or interclusio by us, and parenthesis or paremptosis by the Greeks, and consists in the interruption of the continuous flow of our language by the insertion of some remark' (Quintilian 9.3.23).

64. Noted by Heinrici.

65. Noted by Heinrici.

66. 'Emphasis (*scil. significatio*) is the figure which leaves more to be suspected

round about way, indirectly. It is a kind of *insinuation*, in which appeal is made to something familiar and is often an appeal to the hearer to share an experience with the speaker. The way the unnamed brothers are presented in 8.18 and 22 is just such an appeal to the familiar. As such, not naming them, apart from Titus, is covert persuasion because people are more likely to accept emissaries who are already familiar to them.

24 *Permutatio* (ἀλληγορία). *Permutatio*[67] or ἀλληγορία is a figure of replacement in the content. The relationship between metaphor and allegory is one of quantity, because an allegory is a sustained metaphor. The *similitudo* in 9.9-12[68] shows a tendency to allegory.

34 *Exclamatio.*[69] *Exclamatio* is a figure of replacement in the syntax, whereby one transforms one's argument into an exclamation. *Ad Herennium* confines *exclamatio* to apostrophe, but Quintilian is familiar with a wider usage. The hoped-for effect of *exclamatio* is to have the hearers share the emotion of the speaker. There is an example in 8.23, which may help unravel the sentence somewhat.

2 *Cor. 8.23*   εἴτε ὑπὲρ Τίτου, κοινωνὸς ἐμὸς καὶ εἰς ὑμᾶς συνεργός·
εἴτε ἀδελφοὶ ἡμῶν, ἀπόστολοι ἐκκλησιῶν,
δόξα Χριστοῦ.

Traditionally, εἴτε has been translated by 'as for' (see NRSV, NAB) and δόξα Χριστοῦ is usually taken to be somehow in apposition to ἀπόστολοι ἐκκλησιῶν. If, however, δόξα Χριστοῦ were to be taken as an exclamation, the verse could then be translated:

than has been actually asserted... This figure sometimes possesses liveliness and distinction in the highest degree; indeed it permits the hearer himself to guess what the speaker has not mentioned' (*Herennium* 4.53.67).

67. 'Allegory (*scil. permutatio*) is a manner of speech denoting one thing by the letter of the words, but another by their meaning' (*Herennium* 4.34.46).

68. Noted by Betz: see Chapter 2, section (3).

69. 'Apostrophe (*scil. exclamatio*) is the figure which expresses grief or indignation by means of an address to some man or city or place or object' (*Herennium* 4.15.22). 'The figures best adapted for intensifying emotion consist chiefly in simulation. For we may feign that we are angry, glad, afraid, filled with wonder, grief or indignation, or that we wish something, and so on... To this some give the name of *exclamatio*, and include it among the figures of speech' (Quintilian 9.2.26).

whether [we are dealing with] Titus...
or with...
[what matters is] Christ's [be] glory!

This reading may be confirmed by two considerations. In the first place, Paul is expressing a certain impatience with these administrative details. He anticipates the resistance such an imposition could cause and tries to minimize this by showing that he shares their impatience. In this case δόξα Χριστοῦ is not a further description of the emissaries, a kind of apposition, but on the contrary, places Christ's glory as the object of all this planning.

Second, he goes on in v. 24 to invite proof of their love and his boasting, by which he means generous participation in the collection. This service, the collection, is supposed to bring glory to Christ (2 Cor. 8.19: 'we are administering this generous undertaking for the glory of the Lord'). This means the issue at stake is not so much the emissaries, but rather Christ's glory, that is, something distinct from, and above the status of, the emissaries.

There are two other examples of *exclamatio* which resemble each other. The opening of 8.16 and the closing of 9.13. Both are possibly familiar from the liturgical usage, although this is, of course, a conjecture.

8.16    Χάρις δὲ τῷ θεῷ τῷ δόντι τὴν αὐτὴν σπουδὴν
        ὑπὲρ ὑμῶν ἐν τῇ καρδίᾳ Τίτου,

9.15    Χάρις τῷ θεῷ ἐπὶ τῇ ἀνεκδιηγήτῳ αὐτοῦ δωρεᾷ.

## 2. *Dispositio of 2 Corinthians 8–9*

As explained in Chapter 2, the uncovering of the *dispositio* depends on the convergence of indicators. Is there an *exordium*? Is there a *propositio*? How much of the argument does the *propositio* account for? Where does Paul start 'proving'? The following analysis of the *dispositio* of 2 Corinthians 8–9 depends on a convergence of these indicators. It is really only at the end, when all text units have been named, that one can say that the rhetorical *dispositio* is coherent. My proposal here is that we begin by asking 'where does Paul start proving.' (This is not the same as asking where Paul starts persuading, because every element of the speech has a function within the persuasion.) This proposal upsets the 'natural' order of the *dispositio* for the sake of analysis, and it takes the risk of looking at the *propositio* after the proof. The hope is

that functions of the *exordium, propositio* and *peroratio* will be clari-
fied by looking first at the *probatio*. It seems to me that Paul does not
begin to prove anything until he comes to ch. 8, v. 9.[70] In our authors,
the terms for the stages of the *dispositio* are these:[71]

| Cic. *Part. Or.* | Cic. *Inv.* | *Her.* | *Rhet. ad Alex.* |
|---|---|---|---|
| *initium* | *exordium* | *exordium* | προοίμιον |
| *narratio* | *narratio* | *narratio* | διήγησις |
| | *partitio* | *divisio* | |
| *confirmatio* | *confirmatio* | *confirmatio* | βεβαίωσις |
| *reprehensio* | *refutatio* | *confutatio* | προκατάληψις |
| *peroratio* | *peroratio* | *conclusio* | παλιλλογία |

In chs. 8–9, Paul begins to argue his case in v. 9, by introducing the
*exemplum* of our Lord Jesus Christ. An *exemplum* in itself does not
prove that what follows is part of the *confirmatio*, because an *exemplum*
may be found also in the *exordium*. However, not only is this *exemplum*
introduced with the first explanatory γὰρ,[72] but is itself exploited in the
subsequent verses.

8.9    γινώσκετε **γὰρ** τὴν χάριν τοῦ κυρίου ἡμῶν Ἰησοῦ Χριστοῦ,
       ὅτι δι' ὑμᾶς ἐπτώχευσεν πλούσιος ὤν,
       ἵνα ὑμεινς τῇ ἐκείνου πτωχείᾳ πλουτήσητε.

### 2.1. *Confirmatio 1: 8.8-15*

We saw in Chapter 2 that on the evidence of the vocabulary, it is possible to think of 8.8-15 as a unit of text. It may likewise be seen as a
unit of argument, involving several steps and closing with a Scripture
citation (a favourite Pauline technique). Citation of authoritative religious texts is regarded as conclusive and concluding evidence.

The unit 2 Cor. 8.8-15 forms a threefold argument, which begins and
ends with strong arguments—faith in Christ and God's word in Scripture, which are 'clinching' arguments. Paul follows sound rhetorical
advice which recommends putting your best arguments at the beginning

---

70. As observed by John Chrysostom and by H.D. Betz.
71. Compare with the terms used at the close of Chapter 1 in this volume.
72. There are eight occurrences of γὰρ in 2 Cor. 8–9. 2 Cor. 8.9, 10, 12, 13, 21
and 9.1, 2, 7. I hope to show below that the *exordium* takes up 8.1-6 and the *peroratio* 9.11-15. If this turns out to be persuasive, then γὰρ is used only in the *confirmatio* of 2 Cor. 8–9. This indicates 'proving' in these verses.

and end, but because these arguments are of themselves persuasive, there is no need to develop them. On the other hand, there is a need to develop the central argument touching on the awkward question of how much is expected. Christ made himself poor and the Corinthians no doubt wonder if they are expected literally to impoverish themselves.

Earlier, Betz's opinion on the proofs here was reported. According to Betz, Paul has three points, following closely on rhetorical theory: the honourable (8.9), the expedient (10-12) and the fair (13-15). There are indeed three *probationes* here and the text does deal with the expedient and the fair, but it is difficult to see how the honourable plays a role in the *exemplum* of Jesus. Rather than relying on impressions it is methodologically more correct to examine the figures of speech already uncovered in the paragraph. The *exemplum* in verse 9 is matched by the *sententia* in v. 15. The 'expedient' in vv. 11 and 12 is in vv. 13-14, where Paul explains they are not to impoverish themselves. The *sententia* confirms the appeal to ἰσότης.

On the level of style, vv. 9-15 show an high concentration of balanced phrases (*isocola*), the form of which neatly reflect the content of the argument, which is all about ἰσότης.

## 2.2. *Confirmatio 2: 8.16-24*

*Confirmatio 2* begins by making explicit mention of God (in the exclamation, Χάρις δὲ τῷ θεῷ), whose authority was implicit in the immediately preceding *sententia*, and ends with an exclamation (δόξα Χριστοῦ), before a final challenge to prove 'your love before all the churches'.

Official representatives are to be sent to look after the collection. One can ask at this point why Paul did not come himself, when the project is so dear to him? There are two possibilities: (1) He wants to come, but cannot, and as a result he resorts to emissaries; (2) He can come, but does not want to, and in this case we must ask why? For what reason would Paul distance himself so signally from the practical achievement of the collection and involve himself in complex arrangements so that effectively three sets of emissaries finally are sent? As we want the progress of the next two *confirmationes* this is something to bear in mind.

The argument in between is about ethos or good character, an essential concern of all rhetoric, forensic, deliberative or celebratory. By sending emissaries, Paul has added to the problem of his absence:

already it is not certain that the Corinthians are going to contribute and a plausible excuse would be that one cannot be sure of those collecting the actual money. The good character of these people, therefore, has to be vouched for as above reproach. The possible feeling of being imposed upon is anticipated in Paul's own ethos where he claims that the emissaries are to protect *his* good name, before God and man. He portrays himself as being under examination, thus mollifying any negative feeling the Corinthians might have about him. After all, they themselves have already felt free to question his reliability.

The role played by *epitheton* here (16b, 18b, 19 and 22b), combined with *ethopoeia* (these are brief character sketches: Titus in 17, the brother in 18-19, our brother in 22) and the concern for the ethos of Paul in v. 21 tell us that what is at stake is the virtue of those who will actually handle the money. But the ethos is at the service of the collection: the integrity of the envoys is meant to anticipate one kind of practical objection to taking part.[73]

Verse 23 presents the two 'teams' being sent, but the exclamation relativizes their importance in relation to the glory which is due to Christ. Thus Paul effects a reminder of the Christ, who was rich and made himself poor. The concluding v. 24 resumes the theme of the collection, but anticipates the question of the honour of the Corinthian community, a theme to be undertaken in the next *confirmatio*.

## 2.3. *Confirmatio 3: 9.1-5*

In the text unit 9.1-5, the proof undertaken is complex. Shame and honour are the themes. In effect, the Corinthians are threatened—an approach which risks losing the *benevolentia* of the audience. It begins with a *praeteritio* in 9.1, which is amplified by the flattery in 9.2. The emissaries of 8.16-24, whose apparent function there was to keep a check on the probity of Paul, now become in 9.3-5 observers of the generosity (or lack thereof) of the Corinthians. Worse still, they are being sent ahead, which separates them from Paul. The risk of alienation in this argument is great, as no one likes to be under scrutiny. Between the Scylla of flattery and the Charybdis of threat, Paul sails a

---

73. 'Anticipation is the device by which we shall remove ill-feeling that we encounter by anticipating the criticisms of our audience and the arguments of those who are going to speak on the other side...anticipation is the method by which you anticipate the objections that can be advanced against your arguments and sweep them aside' (*Rhet. ad Alex.* 33.1439b.3).

craft which could founder, if overblown on either side. Paul offsets this risk by affecting to be still under scrutiny himself while leaving the Corinthians in no doubt in the parenthesis of v. 4, that they too are being tested. But anger against Paul is defused because he himself, *even before them*, is under scrutiny. Any possible feeling of alienation towards these arrivals is anticipated by dropping all names and referring to them at the beginning and end of vv. 3-5 as 'brothers'. Finally, the possible offence given by the absence of Paul is avoided by turning the absence into an opportunity for freedom—he won't be there to see who gives what. His absence is a problem, which is met in two steps. Firstly, in 2 Cor. 8.16-24, he is represented by the emissaries. Secondly, in 9.1-5 it was necessary to send them ahead. The particle οὖν in v. 5 seems to indicate that he is concluding his series of arguments about his absence.

Although Paul makes a virtue of this necessity, by claiming his absence is an opportunity for greater freedom, the reason to the absence remains unclear. It could be that he himself was not free on account of other demands or simply judged it unwise. Forced change of cherished plans is already familiar in the Corinthian correspondence. A speculation may be permitted. If it were the case that Paul simply *chose* to absent himself, why would he so choose? It may be that he wishes, even in this case, not to approach even the appearance of being the recipient of funds. It could be, as Murphy-O'Connor suggests (1995: 316), that things are so delicate between Paul and the Corinthians at this stage that he finds it better to let his message be aired and discussed, and if need be, defended by Titus, before he himself arrives on the scene. It is this absence which creates the need to send emissaries, and which threatens to heighten the feeling of imposition. The subtlety of Paul's strategy is clear. He turns this *chosen* necessity into a positive virtue. In *confirmatio 2*, the representatives are truly representative in that a broad coalition is activated, thus enhancing the sense that the collection is to be a means of increased communion between the church.[74] Finally, his absence is construed to mean that their freedom to give is enhanced by his not being there. It is ironic that at the very moment he is putting greatest pressure on them, he asserts that their freedom is what is at

---

74. The broad coalition is made up of the 'saints' in Jerusalem, the 'churches' in Greece and Paul's 'apostles and fellow-workers'. Cf. 1 Cor. 10.32: 'Give no offence to Jews or to Greeks or to the church of God.'

stake. In the light of 2 Cor. 2.1, it is clear that Paul is well capable of choosing to change his mind.[75]

It is illuminating to read, in this context, an earlier text of 2 Cor. 1.15-17:

> 15 Since I was sure of this, I wanted to come to you first, so that you might have a double favour; 16 I wanted to visit you on my way to Macedonia, and to come back to you from Macedonia and have you send me on to Judea. 17 Was I vacillating when I wanted to do this? Do I make my plans according to ordinary human standards, ready to say 'Yes, yes' and 'No, no' at the same time?

## 2.4. *Confirmatio 4: 9.6-10*

Paul often closes arguments with citations from Scripture. 2 Corinthians 9.6-10 is the last portion of the *confirmatio* and, appropriately, it is full of citations and allusions. It also enjoys a single semantic field (sowing, producing and harvesting), and it is likewise framed by the only verbs in the future-tense in 2 Corinthians 8–9: twice in v. 6 and three times in v. 10.

The 'proof' here still has to do with the collection, but this time from the point of view of God's reward in the future. It depends for its credibility on the faith of the Corinthians and their acceptance of the authority of the proof texts.

Having looked first at the four *probationes* which make up the argument of 2 Corinthians 8–9 we now return to look at the *propositio*, followed by the *exordium* and *peroratio*.

## 2.5. *Propositio: 8.7-8*

Even though Aristotle said that a speech requires only two moments—the *propositio* and the proof—the subsequent tradition up to Quintilian did not develop any extensive theories about the *propositio*. Furthermore, the terminology fluctuates somewhat. In *Ad Herennium* 2.18.28 it is called the *propositio*, and there it is described most plainly: 'through the proposition we set forth summarily what we intend to prove'. Later in the same text (2.20.32) the *propositio* is entitled the *expositio* and earlier on in the same work (1.3.4) the term *divisio* was used. The

---

75. Compare: 2 Cor. 2.1: 'So *I made up my mind* not to make you another painful visit' with 2 Cor. 9.5: 'So *I thought it necessary* to urge the brothers to go on ahead to you, and arrange in advance for this bountiful gift that you have promised, so that it may be ready as a voluntary gift and not as an extortion.'

*divisio* is properly a particular kind of *propositio*, in which several points to be taken up are announced.

How can a *propositio* be identified? It can be recognized by position, coming just before the proof and immediately after the *narratio* (if there is one) or the *exordium* (if there is no *narratio*). It can be identified if the subsequent arguments, in their variety, may be derived from it or seem to substantiate it. It can be identified by style: the *propositio* should be succinct and clear. Let us take each one of these.

If proving proper begins in 2 Cor. 8.9, then we should look for the *propositio* in the verses preceding. The immediately preceding verse 8 has been analysed as *interpositio* containing a *correctio*. It therefore briefly interrupts the flow and clarifies v. 7. The opening word Ἀλλ᾽ creates a break with the preceding. Furthermore, the ἵνα clause expresses a direct wish of the writer. It is the equivalent of an imperative, an excellent way to proclaim a proposal.

As noted above, a *propositio* ought to be succinct and clear. 2 Cor. 8.7 is one of the most carefully constructed sentences in 2 Corinthians 8–9, exhibiting *conversio, isocolon* and possibly *commutatio*.

| | | |
|---|---|---|
| *2 Cor. 8.7* | Ἀλλ᾽ **ὥσπερ ἐν παντὶ περισσεύετε,** | a |
| | πίστει καὶ λόγῳ καὶ γνώσει | b |
| | καὶ πάσῃ σπουδῇ | c |
| | καὶ τῇ ἐξ ἡμῶν ἐν ὑμῖν ἀγάπῃ, | d |
| | **ἵνα καὶ ἐν ταύτῃ τῇ χάριτι περισσεύητε.** | e |

The flattery of 7b is amplified in c and d.[76] Furthermore, it is somewhat unexpected if the critical reading is to be accepted. Indebtedness takes the place of flattery. But there is no risk of losing the thread, because the writer has carefully balanced the opening Ἀλλ᾽ ὥσπερ ἐν with the concluding ἵνα καὶ ἐν.

Again, a *propositio* ought to sustain and, in another sense, be sustained by the subsequent *probationes*. We have to look at each part of the argument. The first *confirmatio* argues by example, by proportionality and by scriptural authority that they should take part in the collection. In particular, the περισσεύητε of 8.7 is echoed in 8.14 by the word περίσσευμα. Even if one were to agree with *confirmatio 1* in theory, there are questions of probity and practicality. *Confirmatio 2*

---

76. The unkind comment of Demetrius in *Eloc.* 295 is relevant: 'Everyone likes to be his own example and is eager to add praise to praise, or rather to win one uniform record of praise.'

and *confirmatio 3* belong together and deal with a specific question not so easily derived from the *propositio*.

*2 Cor. 8.7* Ἀλλ᾽ ὥσπερ ἐν παντὶ περισσεύετε, πίστει καὶ λόγῳ καὶ γνώσει καὶ πάσῃ **σπουδῇ** καὶ τῇ ἐξ ἡμῶν ἐν ὑμῖν **ἀγάπῃ**, ἵνα καὶ ἐν ταύτῃ τῇ χάριτι περισσεύητε. 8 Οὐ κατ᾽ ἐπιταγὴν λέγω ἀλλὰ διὰ τῆς ἑτέρων **σπουδῆς** καὶ τὸ τῆς ὑμετέρας **ἀγάπης** γνήσιον δοκιμάζων·

*2 Cor. 8.16* Χάρις δὲ τῷ θεῷ τῷ δόντι τὴν αὐτὴν **σπουδὴν** ὑπὲρ ὑμῶν ἐν τῇ καρδίᾳ Τίτου,

*2 Cor. 8.24* τὴν οὖν ἔνδειξιν τῆς **ἀγάπης** ὑμῶν καὶ ἡμῶν καυχήσεως ὑπὲρ ὑμῶν εἰς αὐτοὺς ἐνδεικνύμενοι εἰς πρόσωπον τῶν ἐκκλησιῶν.

The important words of the *propositio* and its *correctio*, σπουδή and ἀγάπη, recur only in *confirmatio 2*, at the beginning and the end. Thus the second proof takes up from 8.8 the topic of the zeal of others (Titus) and ends with the notion of love being tested, a mutual love, as we seen in 8.7 and 8.24. This second proof then deals with the practical business of sending envoys.

The highly public nature of the collection is used to offset any potential suspicion of possible misdemeanour, while the ethos of those sent becomes an element in the ethos of Paul himself. In terms of the ethos of Paul, 2 Cor. 8.21-22 could not be plainer. But again, these very public arrangements are there also so that their love and his boasting might be seen before all the churches. This takes us back to the thesis 8.7b-c, where Paul has spoken of the Corinthians in flattering terms. In 8.24 we find the third of only three uses of the word ἀγάπη in 2 Corinthians 8–9. The other uses are in 8.7 and in the amplification of that verse in 8.8.

*Confirmatio 3* continues the difficult task of making the possibly offensive imposition of envoys and their early arrival palatable to the Corinthians. The verbal connections here are looser. Thus the σπουδή of the *propositio* is echoed in the semantically similar word ζῆλος, found only 9.2. Paul challenges them to let their zeal be seen, and not only their zeal, but their freedom as well (9.1-2 and 9.5). It is a complicated rhetorical achievement, the purpose of which is, again, to ensure that they do give to the project. The boasting of 9.1-2 (προθυμία, ζῆλος) echoes the boasting in 8.7b-c (σπουδή)[77] The insistence on

77. 'After re-establishing his own credentials, Paul celebrates the Corinthians in a veritable explosion of accolades at 7.11 "What concern (σπουδή), what support you gave me (ἀπολογία), what indignation (ἀγανάκτησις), what fear (φόβος), what

generosity (which implies freedom) in 9.5 is a echo of the *correctio* of 8.7 in 8.8, where Paul insists he is not commanding them.

Finally, in the last *confirmatio* (9.6-10), the issue of abundance is taken up again, also using the vocabulary of περισσεύω. Thus, under different guises, Paul has been continually pressing his case: the example of Christ, their honour before the church, their freedom because only the free gift is truly a gift, God's blessing on such generosity. I conclude that the *propositio* in 8.7[78] does in fact account for the four subsequent *probationes*, both governing them and sustained by them.

This overarching function of the *propositio* is confirmed by the careful verbal continuities as we move from *confirmatio* to *confirmatio*. *Confirmatio 4* begins with the theme of εὐλογία, which forms the ending of *confirmatio 3*. *Confirmatio 3* takes up the topic of honour/ shame before the eyes of the churches—the very subject which closes *confirmatio 2* in 8.24. *Confirmatio 2* begins with a thanksgiving to God, thus making explicit the authority behind the citation which closes *confirmatio 1* at 8.15. The careful sequence of the proofs is a question which will be taken up again, under the auspices of the *quaestio infinita* and the *quaestio finita*.

---

longing (ἐπιπόθησις), what zeal (ζῆλος), what vindication (ἐκδίκησις)! In everything you prove yourselves above reproach in the way you handled the matter at hand". Then he adds, "I bragged about you to Titus" (7.13-14), and in 9.2 states that he notified the Macedonians of Corinthians' enthusiasm. In effect, Paul gives the Corinthians an opportunity to view themselves within the Hellenistic reciprocity structure. They, too, are people of excellence, and the stage is set for the discussion of a delicate matter: the collection for God's people in Jerusalem (Chs. 8–9)' (Danker 1991: 274-75).

78. The importance of the verse is recognized by Carrez 1986: 182: 'Ce verset intervient comme un verset-crochet dans le raisonnement. Il sert de petite conclusion à la description du comportement généreux des Macédoniens (1–5) et en même temps permet à Paul de commencer une exhortation adressée aux Corinthiens (8–12).' At the same time the difficulty of this verse is recognized by Danker 1989: 123: 'Paul's use of the theme of escalated beneficence in v. 7 helps explain what the RSV evidently considers a rough patch of syntax. The Greek text concludes this verse with a clause introduced by the conjunction *hina*. This clause parallels the *hina* clause of v. 6. Between these two clauses Paul inserts in colloquia fashion the accolade that serves as the basis for the conclusion expressed in the second purpose clause. Thus v. 7 is in effect an amplification of the *hina* ("that") clause of v. 6 and completes the thought initiated by the verb *parakaleó* ("urged") in v. 6.'

2.6. *Exordium and Peroratio 8.1-6 and 9.11-15*
As already seen in the delimitation, 2 Cor. 8.1-6 and 9.11-15 are joined
by shared vocabulary and *inclusio*. It remains to be asked if these
'blocks' exhibit the characteristics of the classical *exordium* and
*peroratio*.

Because 8.1-6 begins by recounting the history of the Macedonians,
it is tempting to think it constitutes a *narratio*. However, it is not a classical *narratio* which was supposed to recount the agreed facts, as a
foundation for the *forthcoming* interpretation and argument. But the
past actions of the Macedonians do not constitute the substance of the
*confirmationes 1–4*. So why is the whole first sentence (as in Nestlé-
Aland[27]) devoted to them?

In general, the *exordium*[79] could be in two styles, the *principium*
which was direct or *insinuatio* which was oblique.[80] *Insinuatio* was to
be used when the speaker is not sure of the goodwill of the audience,
for whatever reason. Here, Paul is asking them for money—the Corinthians are not sure they should give money at all, not to mention to
Paul. Thus he starts by recounting what God has achieved among the
Macedonians and how it was their example which led Paul to encourage
Titus to come to Corinth. Thus Paul as agent is concealed. The independence of the Macedonians is expressed in two short phrases, the
*correctio* (καὶ παρὰ δύναμιν) in v. 3 and the *parenthesis* (καὶ οὐ
καθὼς ἠλπίσαμεν) in v. 5. This wonderful story of the Macedonians
serves to excite pathos in the Corinthians—admiration (for their
achievement) and envy (of Paul's unqualified praise).

An *exordium* was also supposed to plant the seeds of the future proof
(*semina probationum*; Quintilian 4.2.54). Wealth and poverty are taken
up in *confirmatio 1*, as does the inspiration of the example of Christ
(ἔδωκαν πρῶτον τῷ κυρίῳ); the role of Titus (and others) in *confirmatio 2*; the implied comparison between Macedonia and Corinth is
made more explicit in *confirmatio 3*; the agency of God, present from

---

79. 'There are two kinds of Introduction: the Direct Opening, in Greek called
the *prooimion*, and the Subtle Approach, called the *ephodos*' (*Herennium* 1.4.6).

80. 'Now I must explain the Subtle Approach. There are three occasions on
which we cannot use the Direct Opening, and these we must consider carefully: (1)
when our cause is discreditable, that is, when the subject itself alienates the hearer
from us; (2) when the hearer has apparently been won over by the previous speakers
of the opposition; (3) or when the hearer has become wearied by listening to
speakers' (*Herennium* 1.6.9).

8.1 and throughout, receives especial emphasis in *confirmatio 4*.

The *peroratio*[81] had two purposes: recapitulation and emotional appeal. The recapitulation takes the form of an assertion (2 Cor. 9.11) followed by two explanatory sentences, which 'cover' the various aspects of the argument. Thus, Paul starts in v. 11 with a conviction that all will be well—thus he begins the final part with a link to the immediately preceding section (2 Cor. 9.6-10). The first explanation in v. 12 is as follows:

> ὅτι ἡ διακονία τῆς λειτουργίας ταύτης
> οὐ μόνον ἐστὶν προσαναπληροῦσα τὰ ὑστερήματα τῶν ἁγίων,
> ἀλλὰ καὶ περισσεύουσα διὰ πολλῶν εὐχαριστιῶν τῷ θεῷ.

Verse 12a captures what Paul sees to be the dignity of the collection—the administration of a public service.[82] 12b takes us back to *confirmatio 1*, the supplying of the needs of the saints and 12c takes us to *confirmatio 4*, where God acts in such a way as to provoke thanksgiving.

Verse 13 takes up reference to other parts of the proof:

> διὰ τῆς δοκιμῆς τῆς διακονίας ταύτης
> δοξάζοντες τὸν θεὸν ἐπὶ τῇ ὑποταγῇ τῆς ὁμολογίας ὑμῶν
>     εἰς τὸ εὐαγγέλιον τοῦ Χριστοῦ
> καὶ ἁπλότητι τῆς κοινωνίας
>     εἰς αὐτοὺς καὶ εἰς πάντας,

---

81. 'The peroration is an easier matter to explain. It falls into two divisions, amplification and recapitulation' (Cicero *Part. Or.* 15.52). 'Amplification therefore is a sort of weightier affirmation, designed to win credence in the course of speaking by arousing emotion' (Cicero *Part. Or.* 15.53). 'By these means in our perorations we shall make the audience well-disposed towards ourselves and ill-disposed towards our opponents; and by all the methods already stated we shall construct both speeches in accusation and speeches in defence scientifically' (*Rhet. ad Alex.* 36.1445a.27). One of functions of the peroration was summing up, as we read in Cicero: 'The summing-up is a passage in which matters that have been discussed in different places here and there throughout the speech are brought together in one place and arranged so as to be seen at a glance in order to refresh the memory of the audience' (Cicero, *Inv.* 1.52.98).

82. Allo 1937: 236 defends the religious sense of this word: 'Le substantif λειτουργία signifiait "service public" dans les cités grecques; d'abord profane, il a pris occasionnellement, chez les Juifs...et dans l'hellénisme, le sens religieux de "service sacré". Le verbe λειτουργῆσαι est dit de notre collecte (peut-être au sens neutre?) *Rom.* 15, 27; mais le sens religieux de λειτουργία est hors de doute.'

This time Paul takes up the secondary argument—that this is a testing of their sincerity. In 2 Cor. 9.12, he calls the whole διακονία a testing—the word itself mentioned in the *correctio* of 8.8. But the real place where this testing occurs is in the arguments is in 8.16-24 and 9.1-5.

A general argument for connecting elements of 2 Cor. 9.13 with the central *confirmationes* could be made as follows. (1) That some the practical testing of the Corinthians is to be found in 2 Cor. 16-9.10, is indicated by the end of the argument of *confirmatio* 2, τὴν οὖν **ἔνδει-ξιν** τῆς ἀγάπης ὑμῶν καὶ ἡμῶν καυχήσεως ὑπὲρ ὑμῶν εἰς αὐτοὺς **ἐνδεικνύμενοι** εἰς πρόσωπον τῶν ἐκκλησιῶν. Similarly, *confirmatio 3* ends with the words: ἵνα προέλθωσιν εἰς ὑμᾶς καὶ προκατα-ρτίσωσιν τὴν προεπηγγελμένην εὐλογίαν ὑμῶν, ταύτην ἑτοίμην εἶναι οὕτως ὡς εὐλογίαν καὶ μὴ ὡς πλεονεξίαν. Furthermore, the vocabulary of shame and honour in these two chapters is found mostly in the two central proofs.[83] Thus the idea of testing first before Titus and the brothers and finally before the other Macedonians is a subsidiary persuasion in the *peroratio*. (2) There is a direct verbal link with 2 Cor. 8.16-24 in the word εὐαγγέλιον which occurs only in 9.13 and 8.18. (3) There is a direct link between 2 Cor. 9.1-5 in the word δια-κονία, which begins the third proof.

The main arguments, *confirmationes 1* and *4*, are echoed in v. 12, the minor, perhaps less creditable, arguments, *confirmationes 2* and *3*, in v. 13. Paul is here following the advice of Nestor that one should place the weaker troops in the middle.

The *peroratio* was intended to end the discussion on the high note of appeal and emotion. The language of 'liturgy' attempts to insert this final appeal in a semantic field of special resonance. It ends appro-

---

83. δοκιμάζω: **8.8, 22**; 13.5.
   δοκιμή: 2.9; **8.2; 9.13**; 13.3.
   ἐνδείκνυμι: **8.24**.
   ἔνδειξις: **8.24**.
   ἔπαινος: **8.18**.
   καταισχύνω: 7.14; **9.4**
   καυχάομαι: 5.12; 7.14; **9.2**; 10.8, 13, 15, 16, 17 (×2); 11.12, 16, 18 (×2), 30 (×2); 12.1, 5 (×2), 6, 9.
   καύχημα: 1.14; 5.12; **9.3**.
   καύχησις: 1.12; 7.4, 14; **8.24**; 11.10, 17.
   κενόω: **9.3**.
   μωμάομαι: 6.3; **8.20**.

priately on an up-beat note of praise and thanksgiving.[84] It is also significant that the grace of God, so effective among Macedonians, according to the *exordium*, comes in the *peroratio* to refer to the Corinthians.

What of the emotional appeal? An inventory of the emotional language may help:

| | |
|---|---|
| 9.11 | εὐχαριστίαν τῷ θεῷ· |
| 9.12 | εὐχαριστιῶν τῷ θεῷ. |
| 9.13 | δοξάζοντες τὸν θεὸν |
| 9.14 | αὐτῶν δεήσει...διὰ τὴν ὑπερβάλλουσαν χάριν τοῦ θεοῦ |
| 9.15 | Χάρις τῷ θεῷ |

The emotional appeal is first of all in the style: the alliteration in v. 11 (π) and the repetition of πᾶς. In 9.12 he reminds them that this action is not only horizontal but also has a vertical dimension. The use of the intensive form προσαναπληροῦσα instead of the simple πληρόω. The vocabulary of 'liturgy' is present throughout. The creation of κοινωνία leads to an overtly emotional instance: καὶ αὐτῶν δεήσει ὑπὲρ ὑμῶν ἐπιποθούντων ὑμᾶς. There is a climax in the repetition of εὐχαριστίαν τῷ θεῷ in 9.11 and εὐχαριστιῶν τῷ θεω in 9.12, and in the substitution of that expression by the longer δοξάζοντες τὸν θεὸν ἐπὶ τῇ ὑποταγῇ τῆς ὁμολογίας ὑμῶν εἰς τὸ εὐαγγέλιον τοῦ Χριστοῦ in 9.13. Finally, Paul risks an echo of 8.8 in 9.13. In v. 8 he denied he was commanding them, rather testing them (οὐ κατ᾽ ἐπιταγὴν and δοκιμάζων). Here he still speaks of testing (διὰ τῆς δοκιμῆς), but goes on to speak of obedience (ἐπὶ τῇ ὑποταγῇ), thus reminding them that their obedience in any case is not to him, but to Christ. Finally, this description of the gift of God as indescribable (ἐπὶ τῇ ἀνεκδιηγήτῳ αὐτοῦ δωρεᾷ) is emotional—words fail him! Yet he manages to end with the word which synthesises exactly what he has been saying: χάρις. It was God's χάρις which achieved such wonderful effects among the Macedonians; it is the χάρις of Christ which is the fundamental example to follow; it is χάρις which moved the heart of Titus; it will be by God's χάρις that

---

84. In a sentence (v. 14) noted for the pile-up of prepositions. See Percy 1946: 211-14: 'In stilistischer Hinsicht ist zuerst der eben erwähnte grosse Reichtum an Präpositionsausdrücken sowie an anderen Nebenbestimmungen zu erwähnen, besonders Eph 1,3... Zwar kommnt es mitunter auch bei anderen Schriftstellern vor, dass sie an einer einzelnen Stelle drei oder mehr Präpostitionsausdrücke aneinanderreihn—so z.B. Apg 12,5...2Kor 1,11..., 7,12...9,14.'

their generosity will be rewarded. This is the ὑπερβάλλουσαν χάριν which is to stir them to great deeds.

Cicero recommends keeping one's outstanding appeal until the end. Paul's strongest appeal here is the creation of a wider communion—hence the repetition of the word κοινωνία from the *exordium*. It is only in this wider communion that *his* claim to authority makes any sense. It is here we have the emotional appeal inherent in the special vocabulary of 8.1-5 and 9.11-13: κοινωνία (8.4 and 9.13), ἁπλοτῆς (8.2 and 9.11,13) and δοκιμή (8.2 and 9.13). Finally, there are two expressions which, as we saw above, function as an inclusion:

τὴν χάριν τοῦ θεοῦ (8.1) and
τὴν ὑπερβάλλουσαν χάριν τοῦ θεοῦ (9.14);

εἰς τὸ πλοῦτος τῆς ἁπλότητος αὐτῶν (8.2)
ἐν παντὶ πλουτιζόμενοι εἰς πᾶσαν ἁπλότητα (9.11)

*Rhetorical Structure.* If the considerations thus far are accurate, then, the *dispositio* of 2 Corinthians 8–9 would be as follows:

| | | |
|---|---|---|
| **Exordium** | 8.1-6 | History, people, issue |
| **Propositio** | 8.7 (8) | Donate! |
| **Confirmationes** | | |
| *Confirmatio 1* | 8.9-15 | Why give? |
| *Confirmatio 2* | 8.16-24 | Emissaries appointed |
| *Confirmatio 3* | 9.1-5 | Emissaries sent ahead |
| *Confirmatio 4* | 9.6-10 | God's reward |
| **Peroratio** | 9.11-15 | Thanksgiving to God |

According to this structure, there is no *narratio* here. In deliberative oratory, the statement of facts was not considered necessary.[85] If we may, for a moment, anticipate *in nuce* the fuller discussion in Chapter 6[86] of Betz's theories, the *narrationes* proposed by him (8.6 and 9.3-5a) are, of course, part of the overall persuasion, but do not constitute the statement of facts of the matter under dispute. If 8.6 were the statement of facts, then the *propositio* (8.7-8, for ch. 8 according to Betz) should

85.  'Opening passages either brief or often absent altogether—for members of a deliberative body are prepared to listen for their own sake. Nor indeed in many cases is much narration needed; for narrative deals with matters past or present, but persuasion deals with the future' (Cicero, *Part. Or.* 4.13).

86.  Chapter 6 below contains a full discussion of Betz.

take issue with some aspect of the statement of facts. But Titus' role in the collection is not under dispute—it is first of all the collection itself and then Paul's ethos. Titus has only a minor role in the *confirmatio* of 8.15-24. Again, if 9.3-5a were the statements of facts, then the *propositio* (9.5bc) should take issue with some aspect of the statement of facts, but this is not the case. In any case, the statement of facts belongs to a discussion of the past—what are the agreed events before we dispute the interpretation. But in 9.3-5 we are dealing with an event in the future and possible outcomes. A discussion of Betz's important alternative *dispositiones* (for there are two) is postponed until Chapter 6 of this study.

### 3. *Inventio*[87]

*Inventio* is the task of finding arguments which will convince. To come up with arguments which are appropriate to both the topic and the hearers, it was necessary to be clear, first of all, on what the problem was.[88]

It may be helpful to distinguish two levels of discourse here. First of all there is the surface question of the collection—which is indeed dealt with in theological and practical terms as we have seen. In these cases, the things which Paul thinks will be convincing are examples, faith, reputation and probity. At the same time, there are two deeper questions: Paul's authority and the union of the Corinthian church with the wider church. These merit separate treatment.

Paul's authority is presented in a carefully oblique way in these verses. The good example of the Macedonians shows the proper theo-

---

87. 'In as much then as the first of the speaker's functions is to invent, what will be his aim? ... To discover how to convince the persons whom he wishes to persuade and how to arouse their emotions' (Cicero *Part. Or.* 2.5). 'Invention is used for the six parts of a discourse: for Introduction, Statement of Facts, Division, Proof, Refutation and Conclusion' (*Herennium* 1.3.4). 'The parts of it, as most authorities have stated, are Invention, Arrangement, Expression, Memory, Delivery. Invention is the discovery of valid or seemingly valid arguments to render one's cause plausible' (Cicero, *Inv.* 1.7.9).

88. 'It is not that every speech does not always turn on some *constitutio* (or issue), but there are certain topics that are peculiar to these speeches; they are not distinct from the "issues", but are particularly appropriate to the ends proposed for these types of speeches. For example, it is generally agreed that the end in the forensic type is equity, i.e. a subdivision of the larger topic of "honour". In the deliberative type, however, Aristotle accepts advantage as the end, but I prefer both honour and advantage' (Cicero, *Inv.* 2.51.155-56).

logical order—they gave themselves first to God and then to Paul, which can be differently 'weighted' thus—to God first and only then to Paul, or, to God, yes, but then also to Paul (8.5). The exercise of the authority is very gentle; it is not a command but a test (8.8)—in fact it is offered as advice (8.10). At the same time Paul fears the Corinthians will suspect him of seeking his own advantage (8.20); an alienating admission, which could make him 'lose' his audience, which is balanced by the confession of their shared reputation (9.4). Paul is also the agent through which thanksgiving will go to God, i.e. he represents an opportunity for a deepening relationship with God (9.11, matching 8.5). Thus while there is a very negative moment—they suspect him—this is buried in the midst of practical arrangements to obviate any such suspicion and in any case not at all dwelt upon.

The question of communion with other churches is vital for the Corinthian church, given its tendency to sectarianism. The good example of Macedonian churches and the responsibility towards the Jerusalem church are intended to reweave the threads binding Corinth to the church catholic. This is again very delicately handled: Paul starts by talking of God's grace operative elsewhere (2 Cor. 8.1), which expresses itself in a desire for κοινωνία—a pregnant word, the meaning of which is expanded later. The delicate question of self-interest is treated in 2 Cor. 8.14—you too may one day be in need, but the minatory tone is mollified by the citation from Scripture. In the second *probatio* dealing with Paul's probity, the mistrust of the Corinthians is set aside by the use of representatives *of the other churches*. Thus, their presence is to the advantage of the Corinthians. Paul is so sure of this that he can make the appeal in 2 Cor. 8.24, which in a positive vein anticipates the rather self-centred motive of 9.4. Finally, participation in this service is seen as part of belonging to Christ—which is meant to provoke generosity and sharing on a grand scale. Thus the relationship with the other churches is a concrete step to living the gospel more deeply.

All this is done with consummate rhetorical skill, so that the arguments constitute a careful balance of flattery, threat and opportunity. None is allowed to dominate.

It was customary to distinguish two types of argument: the *quaestio finita* and the *quaestio infinita*.[89] The *quaestio finita* is a practical dis-

---

89. Cicero, *Inv.* 1.6.8, distinguishes special cases (*causa*) and general questions (*quaestio*): 'Next, what exactly are the divisions of the question? One unlimited,

cussion about some particular project or happening or crime; it is the more difficult, because the *quaestio infinita* is a discussion of something in principle or in theory. Because it is relatively easy to establish something in principle, Cicero[90] points out that the *quaestio infinita* is usually a means of amplification. But that is not what is happening here. Paul starts with the *quaestio infinita* because it is easier to begin with general principles about Christian giving before descending into the detail of how this is to take place. It is more difficult to begin with the how rather than the why: to start with the why already disposes the hearer to listen favourably. In any case, some discussion of 'why' most logically precedes the discussion of 'how'.

In 2 Corinthians 8–9, the first *confirmatio* deals with the principle of giving—the example of Christ, the value of equality, the authority of Scripture. The fourth *confirmatio* resembles it: scriptural allusion and citation return as persuasive techniques. The inspiration of Christ and the future reward by God are generalized arguments in favour of charity. In a sense, they would fit any situation and there is no real denying what is being said if you are a believer in the first place. The challenge is to persuade people to charity in a concrete instance. The second *confirmatio* sets up an administrative procedure designed to facilitate the collection and obviate any reluctance to trust Paul. The administration of the funds will be very public indeed—entrusted to no less than three people with various recommendations. Not only that, but Paul himself will be absent when the collection is being made. And finally, the question of their own good name, the question of shame and honour arises

which I call a discussion, and the other limited, to which I give the name of a cause' (Cicero, *Part. Or.* 1.4). 'Having found your arguments, to put them together; and in an unlimited inquiry the order of arrangement is almost the same as that in the arrangement of topics which I have explained; but in a limited inquiry we must also employ the means designed to excite the emotions' (Cicero, *Part. Or.* 3.9). 'Questions, as I said at the beginning, are of two kinds; one kind is limited by its referring to particular occasions and persons, and this I call a cause; and the other is unlimited, that is, marked by no persons or occasions, and this I designate a thesis' (Cicero, *Part. Or.* 18.61).

90. 'Well then, the most ornate speeches are those which take the widest range and which turn aside from the particular matter in dispute to engage in an explanation of the meaning of the general issue, so as to enable the audience to base their verdict in regard to the particular parties and charges and actions in question on a knowledge of the nature and character of the matter as a whole' (Cicero, *De Or.* 3.30.120).

in the third *confirmatio*. These various considerations would suggest the following overall structure of the argument:

**A.** *Quaestio infinita*
8.8-15:   Give generously; example of Christ; principle of equality; in time of
          need your want will be supplied; citation from Scripture to conclude.

>   **B.** *Quaestio finita*
>   8.16-24 Paul's integrity is at stake: he sends others; uses the
>           churches as witnesses.
>   **B′** *Quaestio finita*
>   9.1-5     Paul's integrity is at stake: he distances himself from the
>             administration by time and space; the witnesses may be-
>             come witnesses to the shame of the Corinthians.

**A′** *Quaestio infinita*
9.6-10:   Give generously; it is part of your relationship with God; citations from
          Scripture form the basis of the whole argument.

A and A′ belong together—Paul starts with the example of Christ and ends with the gift of God. Likewise both conclude with the Scripture citations. Both show balanced figures of speech, both are on the level of the *quaestio infinita*. B and B′ deal with the consequences of Paul's absence. The two sections are concerned, apparently, with practical arrangements, that is, *quaestio finita*—but again it is wise not to place the emphasis only on the integrity of Paul, but their shared honour/shame. Paul stresses, in this regard, that they truly represent him with the same zeal he himself would have shown (2 Cor. 8.16: τὴν αὐτὴν σπουδὴν). The emotional argument is found at the centre of each unit— 8.20 and 9.4, while a resumption of the *propositio* concludes each of these units—8.24 and 9.5. This organization of the arguments follows the regular advice of the rhetoricians that weaker arguments should be placed in the middle, while strong arguments should be placed at the beginning and end. This opinion is classically expressed in the text:

> In the Proof and Refutation of arguments it is appropriate to adopt an Arrangement of the following sort: (1) the strongest arguments should be placed at the beginning and at the end of the pleading; (2) those of medium force, and also those that are neither useless to the discourse nor essential to the proof, which are weak if presented separately and individually, but become strong and plausible when conjoined with the others, should be placed in the middle. For immediately after the facts have been stated the hearer waits to see whether the cause can by some means be proved, and that is why we ought straightaway to present some strong argument. (3) And as for the rest, since what has been said last is easily

committed to memory, it is useful, when ceasing to speak, to leave some very strong argument fresh in the hearer's mind. This arrangement of topics in speaking, like the arraying of soldiers in battle, can readily bring victory (*Herennium* 3.10.18).

Paul follows these instructions carefully here. A refinement can be noticed too, in that there is a temporal development in the argument as well. We start with the past (Christ's example) and end with the future (God's reward). In between, practical arrangements are made about the present (Paul's representatives). This chronological analysis supports the unity of 8-9.[91]

The collection, in one sense, is merely a vehicle for other concerns of Paul. These are his own authority (exercised in the matter of the collection) and the Corinthian church's experience of wider communion. It is this latter issue which arises as a 'desideratum' in the *exordium* and the *peroratio*. In both parts we hear the word κοινωνία.

### 4. *Genus of 2 Corinthians 8–9*

It seems clear that the genre of the rhetoric here is deliberative, rather than forensic or epideictic. There are several indicators: the different rhetorical genera are divided into three, and distinguished according to the time-frame encompassed: forensic (past), epideictic (present) and deliberative (future). Clearly this is not epideictic: nobody is being praised in the main burden of the discourse, nor is the past being judged. Instead, the Corinthians are being urged about the future. In general, deliberative rhetoric makes use of the *quaestio infinita*, the indefinite and general question, without reference to facts, persons, time and the like. Here the main issue under discussion is not *how much* the Corinthians should donate, but whether they should; in other words, it

91. Among others on the unity of the chapters see Allo 1937: 222: 'La fin du ch. V2I et les cinq premiers versets du ch. IX forment véritablement un tout (id. Hofmann, al.); dans la première péricope (V2I, 16-24), Paul recommande ses envoyés et décrit leur mission générale; dans la seconde (IX, 1-5), il explique pourqoui il a fait entrer Corinthe dans le champ de leur action quoique la collect y eût déjà mise ein train par l'église elle-même. Ainsi le chapitre IX ne se présente pas du tout, à qui sait bien le lire, comme un doublet du précédent, et nous rejetterons très délibérément les opinions de Semler ou de Halmel, et autres, d'après qui IX supposerait une autre situation que V2I, ou aurait une destination plus générale (l'Achaïe entière), et ferait donc partie d'une autre lettre; ou bien celle de Neander, Reuss, qui suppose que Paul aurait fait une absence entre V2I et 9.'

is a general theoretical question, as we saw in *confirmationes 1* and *4*. The mentions of individuals are not part of a proof, but rather subsidiary consideration affecting the ethos of the rhetor and the ethos of the auditors, thus supporting the question of whether rather than simply how. *Confirmatio 2*, dealing with the good names of Titus, the brothers and Paul, has something epideictic in it, but, I think, always at the service of the overall persuasion, which is deliberative. It is worth mentioning that deliberative rhetoric uses most conveniently examples and comparisons, and implied comparisons of examples as we have here. Deliberative rhetoric involves giving advice, persuasion and dissuasion, and one of its goals is the advantageous or the harmful. Paul here certainly gives advice (2 Cor. 8.10 : καὶ γνώμην ἐν τούτῳ δίδωμι· τοῦτο γὰρ ὑμῖν συμφέρει[92]) regarding the advantageous (8.14; 9.10), touching on the good name, ethos of the Corinthians (8.8, 24), while leaving them absolutely free (8.8; 9.5). All of this matches the suggestions made regarding deliberative rhetoric by the theorists.[93]

92. Allo 1937: 217 writes: 'συμφέρει: le sens n'est pas ici "aider" ou "être avantageux", mais "s'accomoder [à leurs dispositions]".'

93. 'Well, the purpose in deliberating is to obtain some advantage, to which the whole procedure in giving advice and pronouncing an opinion is directed in such a manner, that the primary considerations to be kept in view by the giver of advice for or against a certain course are what action is or is not possible and what course is necessary or not necessary' (Cicero, *Part. Or.* 24.83). 'There is, furthermore, something which unites qualities from both these classes; by its own merit and worth it entices us and leads us on, and also holds out to us a prospect of some advantage to induce us to seek it more eagerly. Examples are friendship and a good reputation' (Cicero, *Inv.* 2.52.157). 'Now I think I should speak of that which is also coupled with advantage; which, nevertheless, we call honourable. There are then many things that attract us not only by their intrinsic worth but also by the advantage to be derived from them; this class includes glory, rank, influence, and friendship' (Cicero, *Inv.* 2.55.166). 'Now that we have discussed honour and advantage, there remain to be described the qualities that go with these, namely, necessity and affection' (Cicero, *Inv.* 2.56.170). 'The greatest necessity is that of doing what is honourable; next to that is the necessity of security and third and last the necessity of convenience; this can never stand comparison with the other two' (Cicero, *Inv.* 2.58.173-74). 'The orator who gives counsel will throughout his speech properly set up Advantage [τὸ συμφέρον] as his aim, so that the complete economy of his entire speech may be directed to it. Advantage in political deliberation has two aspects: Security and Honour' (*Herennium* 3.2.3). 'Since in causes of this kind the end is Advantage, and Advantage is divided into the consideration of Security and the consideration of Honour, if we can prove that both ends will be

## 5. *Conclusion*

Part of the project of this study has been completed. A method was proposed in the first Chapter, which involved careful delimitation of text on the basis of verbal and narrative indicators before undertaking research into the rhetoric of 2 Corinthians 8–9. It was further proposed that the least arbitrary methodology would be to use the steps for the construction of a speech, but in reverse order. The purpose of such caution was to avoid the arbitrary imposition of a *dispositio* on the text itself. In any case, there is more to the persuasion than the *dispositio*, as we have seen. Thus far, the tentative delimitation of text units made in Chapter 2 has been confirmed by the identification of a coherent *dispositio* in Chapter 3. As always, a convergence of indicators is required and this is what we have here. The identification of figures of thought and speech has been completed, as has the work of exposing the *inventio*. However, the mere identification of figures, arrangement and invention is not yet interpretation. The next chapter consists of an exposition of 2 Corinthians 8–9 in the light of these observations.

served, we shall promise to make this twofold proof in our discourse; if we are going to prove that one of the two will be served, we shall indicate simply the one thing we intend to affirm' (*Herennium* 3.4.8). 'Deliberative speeches are either of the kind in which the question concerns a choice between two courses of action, or of the kind in which a choice among several is considered' (*Herennium* 3.2.2). 'We shall be using the topics of Justice if we say that we ought to pity innocent persons and suppliants; if we show that it is proper to repay the well-deserving with gratitude; if we explain that we ought to punish the guilty' (*Herennium* 3.3.4).

Chapter 5

SYNTHESIS

> The summing-up is a passage in which matters that have been discussed
> in different places here and there throughout the speech are brought
> together in one place and arranged so as to be seen at a glance in order to
> refresh the memory of the audience.
>
> Cicero, *Inv.* 1.52.98.

The *peroratio* of an argument ought, according to the rhetorical manuals, to amplify, to recapitulate the arguments and to increase credence
by arousing emotion. Leaving that aside, the purpose of this fifth Chapter is twofold: to synthesize the argument so far and to offer an exposition of 2 Corinthians 8–9 in the light of the rhetorical observations.
The wider consequences are reserved for the final Chapter.

### 1. *The Persuasion in 2 Corinthians 8–9*

The language chosen for 2 Corinthians 8–9 generally enhances the persuasion of the chapters. In a society where benefaction was a powerful,
all-pervasive cultural assumption, the vocabulary of benefaction would,
of itself, have inclined the hearer to attend favourably to the argument.[1]
As Danker points out (1982: 317) the vocabulary of benefaction identified those praised as people of uncommon excellence and virtue. Part
of the function is to bring this excellence to the attention of others.

---

1. The force of *assumed* arguments is well captured in Perelman 1971: 8. 'Our
treatise will consider only the discursive means of obtaining the adherence of
minds: in the sequel, only the technique which uses language to persuade and convince will be examined. This limitation, in our opinion, by no means implies that
the technique in question is the most efficacious way of affecting minds. The contrary is the case—we are firmly convinced that the most solid beliefs are those
which are not only admitted without proof, but very often not even made explicit.
And, when it is a matter of securing adherence, nothing is more reliable than external or internal experience and calculation conforming to previously admitted rules.'

Using language like this means that Paul is offering the Corinthians an opportunity to attain prestige, for their contributions to the welfare of the saints in Jerusalem. One can image the appeal especially to people who were not necessarily extraordinarily rich, who might otherwise never be able to dream of such a good reputation. The 'pull', therefore, of this language is quite powerful.

The generic description of the benefits bestowed by benefactors are (1) relief from guilt and oppression; (2) stability and common welfare; (3) healing; (4) familial relations; (5) monetary donations; and (6) relief from suffering (Danker 1982: 393-409). By means of a monetary donation, Paul's hopes to relieve the suffering of the saints in Jerusalem. The instability they experience (not uncommon in the Mediterranean at the time) will be met by a commitment from the Corinthians to their common welfare (*probatio 1*) which at the same time is an assertion of familial nature of the Christian church (cf. use of brothers, other officials and the *peroratio*). By offering the Corinthians this concrete occasion to be part of an esteemed cultural given, Paul in turn becomes a kind of benefactor of the Corinthians. One of advantages for Paul in using this kind of language is that he is able to appeal for money without ever having to use the term. It may be part of the reason why he himself will not be there, namely, to allow them the full prestige of what is achieved.

The same is true of the metaphor of economy (emphasized by Young and Ford 1987) and of *amicitia* (underlined by Witherington 1995). These various semantic fields are not in fundamental contradiction with each other or with a rhetorical reading, and, indeed, help deepen our appreciation of the resonance of the vocabulary of chs. 8 and 9. (Semantic fields which are specific to textual units will be treated under those units.) The resonance of these broad linguistic phenomena, recoverable today by painstaking observation and comparison, would originally have been instinctive, immediate and persuasive. To them we must add what is specific: the shared Christian faith in God and in Christ.

The markedly distinctive theological outlook of these chapters is both christological and theological. Christ is present chiefly in the *exemplum* of *confirmatio 1* where the theme of self-emptying occurs, echoing a theme found more fully in Philippians 2. God, however, is altogether more richly described. We noted earlier the semantic field of giving, which includes the notion of χάρις; in these chapters there is a theology of grace. It is not a theology which is in reaction to (later) controversies between grace and good works (both expressions are used). It is rather a theology which reflects a more primordial experience in which God's action and human response are not distinguished in terms of initiative and merit. Neither is it a theology which speculates on grace. Rather, the metaphor of favour or *amicitia* is used to portray God as one who 'favours'[2] us and whose 'favour' 'favours' a like response in us. We give thanks for the good works achieved by his grace, as Augustine succinctly puts it. By using language drawn from the cultural codes of social relations in the Mediterranean world generally to express the divine goodness, his own and the church's role and the expected response of the Corinthians, Paul shows just how evocative and persuasive his writing could be. Finally, he speaks directly to his Corinthians in using the language of χάρις to a community where the χαρίσματα were so highly esteemed and played so much a part in the community's identity.

Thus, by using language of profound cultural and religious resonance, that essential prerequisite for all argumentation, an 'effective community of minds', is realized.[3] We now move our consideration from the background of the persuasion to the foreground.

### 1.1. *Exordium: 2 Cor. 8.1-6*

All beginnings are difficult *and decisive*. The first portion of argument, the *exordium*, reveals a great deal, not only about what Paul wanted to say, but also about what he felt the Corinthians might feel about him. The *exordium* is an example of *insinuatio*, the indirect opening. It is indirect because Paul does not begin by saying openly and in a straightforward way, 'I want you to do this'. This would be possible in a setting in which the speaker is sure of his audience. Paul was not sure how the Corinthians would take his appeal. If the setting of chs. 8 and 9 is indeed to be found within 1–9, as many authors today hold, then as he writes he is not sure whether the *potential* reconciliation of 2 Corinthians 7 actually had been effective. On the contrary, it could be

---

2. The awkward language is an attempt to capture the force of 'grace' in these chapters.

3. 'For argumentation to exist, an effective community of minds must be realized at a given moment. There must first of all be agreement, in principle, on the formation of this intellectual community, and, after that, on the fact of debating a specific question together: now this does not come about automatically' (Perelman 1971: 14).

undermined by any perceived high-handedness. The indirect approach is achieved concretely by focusing the attention of the hearer/reader on God, on the Macedonians and on Titus.

*2 Cor. 8.1-6* 1 Γνωρίζομεν δὲ ὑμῖν, ἀδελφοί, τὴν χάριν τοῦ θεοῦ τὴν δεδομένην ἐν ταῖς ἐκκλησίαις τῆς Μακεδονίας, 2 ὅτι ἐν πολλῇ δοκιμῇ θλίψεως ἡ περισσεία τῆς χαρᾶς αὐτῶν καὶ ἡ κατὰ βάθους πτωχεία αὐτῶν ἐπερίσσευσεν εἰς τὸ πλοῦτος τῆς ἁπλότητος αὐτῶν· 3 ὅτι κατὰ δύναμιν, μαρτυρῶ, καὶ παρὰ δύναμιν, αὐθαίρετοι 4 μετὰ πολλῆς παρακλήσεως δεόμενοι ἡμῶν τὴν χάριν καὶ τὴν κοινωνίαν τῆς διακονίας τῆς εἰς τοὺς ἁγίους, 5 καὶ οὐ καθὼς ἠλπίσαμεν ἀλλὰ ἑαυτοὺς ἔδωκαν πρῶτον τῷ κυρίῳ καὶ ἡμῖν διὰ θελήματος θεοῦ 6 εἰς τὸ παρα-καλέσαι ἡμᾶς Τίτον, ἵνα καθὼς προενήρξατο οὕτως καὶ ἐπιτε-λέσῃ εἰς ὑμᾶς καὶ τὴν χάριν ταύτην.

| v. | Figures of speech | Figures of thought |
|---|---|---|
| 1 | inclusio, traductio (passim), appositum | exemplum |
| 2 | conversio, adnominatio, figura etymo-logica, conpar | contentio |
| 3 | isocolon, epitheton | descriptio, correctio, interpositio |
| 4 | appositum, hendiadys | |
| 5 | | |
| 6 | inclusio | |

Paul's ploy is to report first of all on the success of the collection in Macedonia. Lest this seem to be a purely Macedonian affair, the agent of this success is God. It is the χάρις *of God* which has brought this about—as we see from the adjectival phrase τὴν δεδομένην. Both this adjectival phrase and the genitive emphatically portray God as the agent in what has taken place. The next appearance of this 'agent' is, there-fore, significant.

> 5 and this, not merely as we expected; they gave themselves first to the Lord and, by the will of God, to us, 6 so that we might urge Titus that...

Deliberative oratory is to do with influencing people and causing them to (choose to) act in accordance with the will of the speaker. But the first 'willing' in this persuasion is God's will. It is by the will of God that the Macedonians gave themselves to Paul in order that he might urge Titus. There is no denying that giving yourself first to the Lord is a good thing. Following that by 'and...to us' is in effect associating Paul with God and constitutes a high claim in itself which risks rejection. However, the initiative does not lie with Paul, but belongs to God and to the Macedonians. And that initiative is specifically that Titus should be persuaded to go to Corinth. Finally, God is associated throughout with χάρις (*inclusio* of 8.1 and 8.5-6) and with the semantic field of gift, as we saw in Chapter 3.

The benefit of beginning with God is immediately apparent: the *exemplum* of the Macedonians is given the highest authority. The account of their response to the collection is given added force by a concentration of figures: *conversio, adnominatio, figura etymologica, conpar, descriptio* and *contentio*. Their extreme poverty overflowed, paradoxically, into a generosity beyond their means. This graphic account is affirmed by an oath[4] in parenthesis ('I swear'), making God a witness to this. Finally, the use of *conversio* (the threefold αὐτῶν) serves to bring forward *their* joy, *their* poverty, *their* sincerity. This is very high praise, but, because God is the chief protagonist, the impression of human boasting is avoided. Thus the figures employed serve the purpose of the *insinuatio*, that is, the understatement of Paul's own role.

Titus, who will be the leader in the delegation, is without apparent initiative. A possible negative reaction to him is side-stepped by making the 'election' of Titus a matter of divine grace. Nevertheless, lest his authority seem less, he is mandated thrice—by God, by the Macedonians and by Paul.

By relocating the focus of attention, the author has captured the attention of the Corinthians. Yet, Paul himself, who is after all making the request, sending a delegation and placing the Corinthians under the observation of foreigners, is hardly present in the *exordium*. He is represented only by an unfocused plural, not as an individual.

A task of the *exordium* was to lay the ground for the forthcoming discussion. How is this achieved? The agency of God is taken up in *confirmatio 4*, where God is portrayed as the origin of prosperity, both material and spiritual. The implied comparison with the Macedonians is taken up in *confirmatio 3*, at which point the reputation of the Corinthians is at stake. The role and commissioning of Titus as representative forms the content of *confirmatio 2*, at which point the delegation is also expanded to include the other representatives. Finally, the completion (ἐπιτελέσῃ) of the χάρις is explicitly undertaken in *confirmatio 1* (ἐπιτελέσατε and ἐπιτελέσαι). These topics are then taken up in reverse order and so the *exordium/insinuatio* fulfils its function.

---

4.   An oath is an unproved statement supported by an appeal to the gods (*Rhet. ad Alex.* 17.1432a).

This anticipation of items in the argument from 2 Cor. 8.9–9.10 shows two things. First, the *exordium* sows the *semina probationum* for the whole argument, not only in terms of content and vocabulary, but also in terms of sequence. Second, it means that the identification of the mention of Titus as *narratio* is mistaken, *pace* Betz. It does not function as a *narratio*—the statement of facts to be disputed—it functions as a *semen probationis*.[5]

### 1.2. *Propositio: 8.7 (8)*

*2 Cor. 8.7-8*  7 Ἀλλ᾿ ὥσπερ ἐν παντὶ περισσεύετε, πίστει καὶ λόγῳ καὶ γνώσει καὶ πάσῃ σπουδῇ καὶ τῇ ἐξ ἡμῶν ἐν ὑμῖν ἀγάπῃ, ἵνα καὶ ἐν ταύτῃ τῇ χάριτι περισσεύητε. 8 Οὐ κατ᾿ ἐπιταγὴν λέγω ἀλλὰ διὰ τῆς ἑτέρων σπουδῆς καὶ τὸ τῆς ὑμετέρας ἀγάπης γνήσιον δοκιμάζων·

The *propositio* employs two main figures: *conversio* (περισσεύέτε and περισσευήτε) and *conpar* or *isocolon* between 7a and 7e. The intervening 7b-d is in part flattery and in part recall of indebtedness. Danker thinks it shows a certain effect of climax—and it might, in the manner that all lists do, but it is not a climax in the technical sense used by the Hellenistic rhetoricians whose work we have used. Nevertheless, the care in construction is clear. In Chapter 4, the manner in which the *propositio* governs the subsequent argument was laid out and need not be repeated in detail.

It is unexpected to find a *correctio* immediately after the *propositio* and this might count against the reconstruction of the argument proposed in this study. Properly speaking, for the sake of clarity and to satisfy the hearer's curiosity at that point, the *probatio* should follow immediately, as Aristotle says. The *correctio* (a figure of emphasis and improved expression) serves two purposes. When someone goes to the trouble of saying something in a better way, or even some part of it in a better way, then not only is the expression improved but added emphasis made. The presence of *correctio* in this unusual position reveals as well the nervousness of Paul in proposing the collection to the Corinthians. This anxiety is apparent in the way he subordinates himself to other agents in the *exordium*. It is apparent too in the significant but slight references to himself in 8.20 and 9.4. If the *propositio* proper is v. 7 and v. 8 constitutes an emphasizing correction, then, while Betz is

5.    This will be taken up fully in the next Chapter.

right to see a *propositio* here, he is mistaken (1) in including the *correctio* and (2) in limiting the proposition to ch. 8, as we shall see. Verse 8, however, sets a tone for the proofs.

### 1.3. *Confirmatio 1: 2 Cor. 8.9-15*

*2 Cor. 8.9-15*   9 γινώσκετε γὰρ τὴν χάριν τοῦ κυρίου ἡμῶν Ἰησοῦ Χριστοῦ, ὅτι δι᾽ ὑμᾶς ἐπτώχευσεν πλούσιος ὤν, ἵνα ὑμεῖς τῇ ἐκείνου πτωχείᾳ πλουτήσητε. 10 καὶ γνώμην ἐν τούτῳ δίδωμι· τοῦτο γὰρ ὑμῖν συμφέρει, οἵτινες οὐ μόνον τὸ ποιῆσαι ἀλλὰ καὶ τὸ θέλειν προενήρξασθε ἀπὸ πέρυσι· 11 νυνὶ δὲ καὶ τὸ ποιῆσαι ἐπιτελέσατε, ὅπως καθάπερ ἡ προθυμία τοῦ θέλειν, οὕτως καὶ τὸ ἐπιτελέσαι ἐκ τοῦ ἔχειν. 12 εἰ γὰρ ἡ προθυμία πρόκειται, καθὸ ἐὰν ἔχῃ εὐπρόσδεκτος, οὐ καθὸ οὐκ ἔχει. 13 οὐ γὰρ ἵνα ἄλλοις ἄνεσις, ὑμῖν θλῖψις, ἀλλ᾽ ἐξ ἰσότητος· 14 ἐν τῷ νῦν καιρῷ τὸ ὑμῶν περίσσευμα εἰς τὸ ἐκείνων ὑστέρημα, ἵνα καὶ τὸ ἐκείνων περίσσευμα γένηται εἰς τὸ ὑμῶν ὑστέρημα, ὅπως γένηται ἰσότης, 15 καθὼς γέγραπται· ὁ τὸ πολὺ οὐκ ἐπλεόνασεν, καὶ ὁ τὸ ὀλίγον οὐκ ἠλαττόνησεν.

This passage is especially rich in figures and it may help to lay them out clearly:

| v. | Figures of speech | Figures of thought |
|----|-------------------|---------------------|
| 9  | *conpar*          | *contentio, commutatio, exemplum* |
| 10 | *paranomasia*     |                     |
| 11 | *conversio, conpar* | *definitio*       |
| 12 |                   | *definitio, sententia* |
| 13 | *dissolutio*      | *definitio, brevitas* |
| 14 | *conpar*          | enthymeme, *commutatio* |
| 15 | *conpar*          | *sententia*        |

As noted in Chapter 4, there are basically three arguments presented, which are the example of Christ (v. 9), the advice given (vv. 10-14) and the support of Scripture (v. 15). The counsel given in v. 10 is amplified by the rich combination of figures in vv. 11-13. It is noticeable that in comparison to other passages there is a high proportion of *isocola*, balanced phrases by which Paul mirrors the content (ἰσότης) in the rhythm of speech. The verses where this balance is absent are explanatory verses marked by *definitio* and *sententia*, because there the mirroring of content and form is not required. The rough change to *dissolutio* in v. 13 is a figure of emphasis designed to acknowledge and give due weight to their fears that he means them to impoverish themselves, according to the example of both the Macedonians (who gave beyond their ability) and of Christ (who made himself poor).

Beyond the level of the figures of thought, it is clear that the example of Christ and the citation from Scripture are both concluding and conclusive arguments. These are things which are always true. The very apparent effort in vv. 10-14 to allay fears takes up the attractive argument of creating *amicitia*, a relationship of mutual favour. This is culturally a very strong argument (see Witherington 1995: 414-19), as well as prudent practice.

### 1.4. *Confirmatio 2: 2 Cor. 8.16-24*

*2 Cor. 8.16-24*  16 Χάρις δὲ τῷ θεῷ τῷ δόντι τὴν αὐτὴν σπουδὴν ὑπὲρ ὑμῶν ἐν τῇ καρδίᾳ Τίτου, 17 ὅτι τὴν μὲν παράκλησιν ἐδέξατο, σπουδαιότερος δὲ ὑπάρχων αὐθαίρετος ἐξῆλθεν πρὸς ὑμᾶς. 18 συνεπέμψαμεν δὲ μετ᾿ αὐτοῦ τὸν ἀδελφὸν οὗ ὁ ἔπαινος ἐν τῷ εὐαγγελίῳ διὰ πασῶν τῶν ἐκκλησιῶν, 19 οὐ μόνον δέ, ἀλλὰ καὶ χειροτονηθεὶς ὑπὸ τῶν ἐκκλησιῶν συνέκδημος ἡμῶν σὺν τῇ χάριτι ταύτῃ τῇ διακονουμένῃ ὑφ᾿ ἡμῶν πρὸς τὴν [αὐτοῦ] τοῦ κυρίου δόξαν καὶ προθυμίαν ἡμῶν, 20 στελλόμενοι τοῦτο, μή τις ἡμᾶς μωμήσηται ἐν τῇ ἁδρότητι ταύτῃ τῇ διακονουμένῃ ὑφ᾿ ἡμῶν· 21 προνοοῦμεν γὰρ καλὰ οὐ μόνον ἐνώπιον κυρίου ἀλλὰ καὶ ἐνώπιον ἀνθρώπων. 22 συνεπέμψαμεν δὲ αὐτοῖς τὸν ἀδελφὸν ἡμῶν ὃν ἐδοκιμάσαμεν ἐν πολλοῖς πολλάκις σπουδαινον ὄντα, νυνὶ δὲ πολὺ σπουδαιότερον πεποιθήσει πολλῇ τῇ εἰς ὑμᾶς. 23 εἴτε ὑπὲρ Τίτου, κοινωνὸς ἐμὸς καὶ εἰς ὑμᾶς συνεργός· εἴτε ἀδελφοὶ ἡμῶν, ἀπόστολοι ἐκκλησιῶν, δόξα Χριστοῦ. 24 τὴν οὖν ἔνδειξιν τῆς ἀγάπης ὑμῶν καὶ ἡμῶν καυχήσεως ὑπὲρ ὑμῶν εἰς αὐτοὺς ἐνδεικνύμενοι εἰς πρόσωπον τῶν ἐκκλησιῶν.

In this argument we move from the *quaestio infinita* of *confirmatio 1*, to the *quaestio finita* of the practical administration in *confirmatio 2*. The figures are as follows:

| v. | Figures of speech | Figures of thought |
| --- | --- | --- |
| 16 | *appositum* | *commoratio* (on ethos) *passim; exclamatio* |
| 17 | | |
| 18 | *repetitio* | *percursio, significatio* |
| 19 | *interpretatio, appositum* | |
| 20 | *appositum* | |
| 21 | *conpar* | |
| 22 | *commutatio* | *percursio, significatio* |
| 23 | *repetitio,* | *brevitas, exclamatio* |
| 24 | *conversio, figura etymologica* | |

This is an administrative argument and deals with the practical arrangements regarding the collection. However, the argument begins, not with human plans but with divine χάρις, that is, with a resumption of the starting point in the *exordium*. This is not without its importance, if the envoys are to enjoy authority. In fact, the practical arrangements are minimal, giving way to the more important question of the ethos or good character of those being sent. Ethos and *ethopoiia* are commonplaces of rhetoric. The envoys here enjoy great authority: from God, from the churches and from Paul himself. This emphasis on authority could be counter-productive and provoke a negative reaction among the Corinthians who might feel imposed upon. Paul offsets any negative reaction by claiming that it is he himself who is being protected by such elaborate arrangements. This claim in v. 21 functions as a *captatio benevolentiae*, which, while especially suitable in the *exordium*, is appropriate at any point in a speech. It is an important moment because these envoys are soon to be transformed into 'observers' of the Corinthians, sent in effect to spy on them. The position of this *captatio* is also important: it comes after the representatives of the church and before the representative of Paul himself, that is, he does not exercise his authority (in sending a representative) until he has placed himself in a weaker position. His own probity is not best proclaimed by a representative of his own choosing. Verses 21-22 will also remind the Corinthians of that striking feature of Paul's ministry, the fact that he is self-supporting and takes no money for himself. This option to be self-supporting probably created more problems than it solved and the risk taken by underlining it here serves to show how keen Paul is to proclaim his probity. The *exclamatio* which concludes v. 23, is likewise a kind of *captatio*, in that it serves to relativise these envoys: the glory belongs to Christ. Verse 24 concludes with an anticipation of the honour challenge to be taken up in 9.1-5.

The lack of names for the brothers being sent (other than Titus) has occasioned a good deal of study and speculation. There may be a rhetorical explanation. It is an example of *significatio*—an insinuation which obliges the audience to recall *within their own minds* who it is that is meant. Such a technique triggers a recollection of the familiar. The familiarity of the envoys should then contribute to their acceptability.

## 1.5. *Confirmatio 3: 2 Cor. 9.1-5*

*2 Cor. 9.1-5* 1 Περὶ μὲν γὰρ τῆς διακονίας τῆς εἰς τοὺς ἁγίους περισσόν μοί
ἐστιν τὸ γράφειν ὑμῖν· 2 οἶδα γὰρ τὴν προθυμίαν ὑμῶν ἣν ὑπὲρ
ὑμῶν καυχῶμαι Μακεδόσιν, ὅτι Ἀχαΐα παρεσκεύασται ἀπὸ
πέρυσι, καὶ τὸ ὑμῶν ζῆλος ἠρέθισεν τοὺς πλείονας. 3 ἔπεμψα
δὲ τοὺς ἀδελφούς, ἵνα μὴ τὸ καύχημα ἡμῶν τὸ ὑπὲρ ὑμῶν
κενωθῇ ἐν τῷ μέρει τούτῳ, ἵνα καθὼς ἔλεγον παρεσκευασμένοι
ἦτε, 4 μή πως ἐὰν ἔλθωσιν σὺν ἐμοὶ Μακεδόνες καὶ εὕρωσιν
ὑμᾶς ἀπαρασκευάστους καταισχυνθῶμεν ἡμεῖς, ἵνα μὴ λέγω
ὑμεῖς, ἐν τῇ ὑποστάσει ταύτῃ. 5 ἀναγκαῖον οὖν ἡγησάμην
παρακαλέσαι τοὺς ἀδελφούς, ἵνα προέλθωσιν εἰς ὑμᾶς καὶ
προκαταρτίσωσιν τὴν προεπηγγελμένην εὐλογίαν ὑμῶν, ταύτην
ἑτοίμην εἶναι οὕτως ὡς εὐλογίαν καὶ μὴ ὡς πλεονεξίαν.

| v. | Figures of speech | Figures of thought |
|---|---|---|
| 1 | *appositum* | *occultatio* |
| 2 | *figura etymologica* (2-4) | |
| 3 | | |
| 4 | *correctio* | *descriptio, interpositio* |
| 5 | *traductio, homoeoptoton, isocolon* | *definitio, synecdoche* |

The sequence of ideas here is carefully constructed to echo preceding
argument thus seeming to say the same thing, but with a different object
in mind. The emphatic figure of *occultatio* uses the expression already
familiar and repeated from the *exordium* (8.4): τῆς διακονίας τῆς εἰς
τοὺς ἁγίους. The flattery found in the *propositio* (7b) is taken up again,
but it is the implied comparison between the Macedonians and the
Achaians (regional toponyms used to encourage comparison) which
comes to fullest expression. The words chosen show that Paul has
boasted to the Macedonians about them and as a result the brothers of
the preceding argument become 'observers' of the goodwill of the
Corinthians.

The awkward business of placing the community under the observation of outsiders is made palatable by two techniques. Just as Paul
has felt the need to protect his integrity in *confirmatio 2*, so also here,
he speaks as if his honour were at stake. The honour of the Corinthians
is what is really at stake, but feelings of unwarranted imposition are
excluded by the fact that both the Corinthians and Paul are in the same
position. This emerges in a potent aside, using the figure of *interpositio*.
The final claim that he sends the envoys *ahead*, which was also a risk,
is covered by a declaration that it is Corinthians' freedom he is

concerned with, expressed by means of *traductio*, because εὐλογία has
two meanings here: the deed of benefaction and the attitude of blessing.
The theme of freedom is resumption of the *correctio* in 8.8—another
indication that these chapters do belong together.

### 1.6. *Confirmatio 4: 2 Cor. 9.6-10*

*2 Cor. 9.6-10*  6 Τοῦτο δέ, ὁ σπείρων φειδομένως φειδομένως καὶ θερίσει,
καὶ ὁ σπείρων ἐπ᾽ εὐλογίαις ἐπ᾽ εὐλογίαις καὶ θερίσει. 7
ἕκαστος καθὼς προῄρηται τῇ καρδίᾳ, μὴ ἐκ λύπης ἢ ἐξ
ἀνάγκης· ἱλαρὸν γὰρ δότην ἀγαπᾷ ὁ θεός. 8 δυνατεῖ δὲ ὁ θεὸς
πᾶσαν χάριν περισσεῦσαι εἰς ὑμᾶς, ἵνα ἐν παντὶ πάντοτε
πᾶσαν αὐτάρκειαν ἔχοντες περισσεύητε εἰς πᾶν ἔργον ἀγα-
θόν, 9 καθὼς γέγραπται· ἐσκόρπισεν, ἔδωκεν τοῖς πένησιν, ἡ
δικαιοσύνη αὐτοῦ μένει εἰς τὸν αἰῶνα. 10 ὁ δὲ ἐπιχορηγῶν
σπόρον τῷ σπείροντι καὶ ἄρτον εἰς βρῶσιν χορηγήσει καὶ
πληθυνεῖ τὸν σπόρον ὑμῶν καὶ αὐξήσει τὰ γενήματα τῆς
δικαιοσύνης ὑμῶν.

| v. | *Figures of speech* | *Figures of thought* |
|---|---|---|
| 6 | *complexio, traductio, conpar* | *similitudo, sententia* |
| 7 | *interpretatio* (possibly) | *sententia* |
| 8 | [alliteration] | |
| 9 | *correctio* | *sententia* |
| 10 | *interpretatio, epitheton* | |

Five verbs in the future tense frame this section and make it clear that
both the future and attitudes towards the future constitute the substance
of the section framed by vv. 6 and 10. Now, the future is portrayed in
two ways: by means of sententia and in a similitudo. The sententia
describes whatever everyone accepts—here a proverb in v. 6 and Scripture citation in vv. 7 and 9. Verse 8, in the centre, is decorated speech,
the fault of alliteration on πᾶς notwithstanding. The motivation here is
that everything is possible with God—generous giving in the present,
confident hope in the future. The similitudo of seeds (probably familiar
from Jesus' teaching) remains marvellously polyvalent: it could mean
assurance of material prosperity and it certainly means 'spiritual' prosperity. Thus, the Corinthians are encouraged, again, to take part in this
enterprise, even for their own advantage.

The fourth *confirmatio* relates well to what goes before. The second
appearance of the aorist subjunctive of περισσεύω takes us directly
back to the *propositio* while the emphasis on freedom recalls the

*correctio* which followed the *propositio*. Furthermore, the *complexio* in 9.6 recalls the balanced phraseology of *confirmatio 1*, as does the explicit citation of Scripture.[6] Again, the vocabulary of 2 Cor. 9.5 is resumed in 9.6, while 2 Cor. 9.10 leads naturally to 9.11. In argumentative terms, the central verse is at the centre: v. 8. But we know already from the *exemplum* of the Macedonians that God can achieve great things. In 2 Corinthians 8–9, God is giver, and the giving God loves the giver, who thus comes to be like God.

All deliberation is oriented to the future, as regards the action to be undertaken. The arguments themselves may be from a variety of sources and of various kinds, such as is the case here: the arguments in the first *confirmatio/quaestio infinita* are taken from the past—mainly the *exemplum* of Jesus. The arguments in the fourth *confirmatio*, also a *quaestio infinita*, are taken from the future, based on the providence of God and the implicit faith of the Corinthians in such a 'God'.

*1.7. Peroratio: 2 Cor. 9.11-15*

2 Cor. 9.11-15   11 ἐν παντὶ πλουτιζόμενοι εἰς πᾶσαν ἁπλότητα, ἥτις κατεργάζεται δι᾽ ἡμῶν εὐχαριστίαν τῷ θεῷ· 12 ὅτι ἡ διακονία τῆς λειτουργίας ταύτης οὐ μόνον ἐστὶν προσαναπληροῦσα τὰ ὑστερήματα τῶν ἁγίων, ἀλλὰ καὶ περισσεύουσα διὰ πολλῶν εὐχαριστιῶν τῷ θεῷ. 13 διὰ τῆς δοκιμῆς τῆς διακονίας ταύτης δοξάζοντες τὸν θεὸν ἐπὶ τῇ ὑποταγῇ τῆς ὁμολογίας ὑμῶν εἰς τὸ εὐαγγέλιον τοῦ Χριστοῦ καὶ ἁπλότητι τῆς κοινωνίας εἰς αὐτοὺς καὶ εἰς πάντας, 14 καὶ αὐτῶν δεήσει ὑπὲρ ὑμῶν ἐπιποθούντων ὑμᾶς διὰ τὴν ὑπερβάλλουσαν χάριν τοῦ θεοῦ ἐφ᾽ ὑμῖν. 15 Χάρις τῷ θεῷ ἐπὶ τῇ ἀνεκδιηγήτῳ αὐτοῦ δωρεᾷ.

| v. | Figures of speech | Figures of thought |
|----|----|----|
| 11 | [alliteration] | *commoratio* |
| 12 | *isocolon* | *descriptio* |
| 13 | *isocolon* | |
| 14 | | |
| 15 | *appositum* | *epiphonemon, exclamatio* |

The closing part of the speech was meant to recapitulate, to amplify and to increase credence by kindling emotion. Emotion *is* aroused: (1) by the vocabulary of 'excess' (πλουτιζόμενοι, προσαναπληροῦσα, περισσεύουσα and ὑπερβάλλουσαν); (2) by the repeated insistence on

---

6. A similarity between the two *quaestiones infinitae* is not surprising.

thanksgiving and prayer, which creates communion; (3) by mentioning the longing of the Macedonians for the Corinthians and finally (4) by means of the *exclamatio* at the end, closing the *peroratio* confidently and joyfully. The text amplifies in an astute manner: the vocabulary of catechesis appears (εὐχαριστία, ὁμολογία, εὐαγγέλιον, κοινωνία, possibly λειτουργία and διακονία), a vocabulary which is new to these two chapters (apart from κοινωνία). The effect is to remind the hearers not only of the basics of the faith, but of the beginnings of the faith—that first ardour. It may well serve as an oblique reminder of their indebtedness to Paul: the one father they have.

The *peroratio* recapitulates the argument in a very complete way. The similarities with the *exordium* have already been noted and need not be repeated, except to recall that it includes the vocabulary of riches, sincerity, communion, abundance and grace. The language of 'excess' takes us back to the *propositio*. The mention of Christ takes us back to *confirmatio 1*, as does the recall of mutuality (v. 14). A delicate hint at the testing proposed in *confirmationes 2* and *3* may be found in the small word δοκιμή, although the word itself is not found in the *quaestiones finitae*. And God's action in bringing about this good work (διὰ τὴν ὑπερβάλλουσαν χάριν τοῦ θεοῦ ἐφ᾽ ὑμῖν) reflects back to the centre of *confirmatio 4* which was v. 8. Thus a rather exhaustive, yet discrete, recapitulation is achieved, while mere repetition is avoided. This shows that the *peroratio* does indeed consist of 9.11-15 and that the recapitulation takes us back over both chs. 8 and 9, *pace* Betz.

This may be the point to observe that while the links connecting the *quaestiones infinitae* with both the *propositio* and the *peroratio* are strong, the connections between the latter two and the *quaestiones finitae* are less marked. This possible problem is best understood in the light of the following considerations. First, it seems clear that some foreshadowing of the four proofs may be found in the *semina probationum*, with the result that when the issues appear they are not entirely without preparation. Second, Paul may have wished to postpone *fleshing out* these administrative proposals until after the first proof (the *quaestio infinita* of 8.9-15), in order that their enthusiasm might be kindled before broaching anything negative which might quench the flame of their commitment. Something similar may be said of the light way Paul echoes the practical issues in the *peroratio*. It is the time to drum up enthusiasm, and while not losing sight of the forthcoming test, he returns to the theme of kindling enthusiasm.

A comment by Cicero elucidates the mixture of gratitude and communion evinced in the *peroratio*: 'Gratitude embraces the memory of friendships and of services rendered by another, and the desire to requite these benefits' (Cicero, *Inv.* 2.53.161). A related comment from *Rhet. ad Alex.* is likewise apposite:

> If we are urging our audience to render assistance to certain parties, whether individuals or states, it will also be suitable briefly to mention any friendly feeling or cause for gratitude or compassion that already exists between them and the members of the assembly (*Rhet. ad Alex.* 34.1439b.15).

## 2. *The Portrayal of Paul and the Corinthians*

In these two chapters, Paul, the man trumpeting his authority in 2 Corinthians 1–7 seems unaccountably to have disappeared. A sentence from Demetrius struck me forcibly in relation to 2 Corinthians 8–9.

> The use of such clauses is full of risk. They do not suit the forceful speaker, since their studied artifice dissipates the force... For anger needs no artifice; in such invectives what is said should be, in a way, spontaneous and simple (Demetrius, *Eloc.* 27).

If *anger* needs no artifice, *anxiety* does. The hard-won yet only recently reconciled authority of 2 Corinthians 1–7 is deliberately suppressed in chs. 8 and 9. From the beginning, Paul hides behind the plural and a higher authority. God is the one who initiates the collection and promotes generosity—even the administrative details are under divine grace. The occasional appearance of Paul is carefully calibrated: in *confirmatio 2*, he portrays himself as the one being tested. In *confirmatio 3*, this continues, although the *interpositio* of 9.4 conveys the underlying intention. All of which constitutes a conscious use of *captatio benevolentiae*. The significance of this undertaking for Paul can hardly be overestimated and to undermine it by an overbearing (cf. βαρεῖαι καὶ ἰσχυραί) epistolary παρουσία would be foolish. Hence the anxious style, full of artifice and concealed persuasion.

All we have, of course, is Paul's interpretation of who his hearers/readers are but that, in itself, although not necessarily objective, is a valuable insight into what he thinks the Corinthians need. The persuasion in 2 Corinthians 8–9 serves three purposes: to test how genuine their commitment is; to re-establish the authority of Paul; and to bring this fractious, sectarian community back into the wider κοινωνία of the gospel. All three purposes are to be achieved by means of the practical step of the collection.

The rhetorical tradition recognized as appropriate to deliberation the themes of advantage, security, honour and virtue.[7] But the choice of exactly what to say to which audience depended on the particular circumstances.

> Consequently, in exhorting and advising, although our aim will be to teach by what method it is possible for us to attain the good and avoid the evil, nevertheless in addressing well educated people we shall speak most of glory and honour, and shall give our chief attention to the kinds of virtue that are exercised in protecting and increasing the common advantage of mankind. Whereas if we are speaking in the presence of the unlearned and ignorant, it is profits and rewards, pleasures and modes of avoiding pain that must be put forward...[8]

Paul appeals to honour, glory and virtue, showing thereby that he is dealing with well educated people and not the unlearned and the ignorant.

### 3. *Is the Text Rhetorical in Intention?*

The careful employment of figures and the clear sequence of the *dispositio* lead to the claim that the rhetoric here is consciously applied. The *exordium* and the *peroratio* closely match the theory in the handbooks. In the *dispositio*, the *confirmationes* are ordered not only according to the *quaestiones finitae* and *infinitae*, but also chronologically (past–present–future). We saw too the adaptation of LXX citations to make them into *isocola*, an effort which discloses mindfulness of the techniques. Taken together, all the indicators favour a very experienced, almost certainly trained user of rhetoric.

It is surely the case that more than once Paul spoke to communities in various places about the collection, his great project: such speaking experience would account for the condensed, structured style, a fruit of practice and experience. It could well be that he had used elsewhere the *quaestiones infinitae* in *confirmationes 1* and *4*, while adapting to the particular occasion here the weaker *quaestiones finitae*, found here in *confirmationes 2* and *3*. Such a speculation takes us back to the question

7.   Cicero, *Part. Or.* 24.83; *Inv.* 2.51.155-56; 2.55.166; 2.56.170; 2.58.173-74; *Herennium* 2.2.3.
8.   Cicero, *Part. Or.* 26.91-92.

of whether we are dealing with a letter or a speech. Here, it could well be a speech already very familiar to Paul which he has made use of and adapted in letter form to the Corinthians. It has also been recognized that much of the rhetoric in the New Testament has an oral background and this is especially significant in texts which, in any case, were meant to be read aloud.[9]

## 4. *Conclusion*

Having uncovered and commented on the persuasive structures and techniques in 2 Corinthians 8–9, we now turn to a comparison with Betz, and finally, a discussion of Paul's place in the Hellenistic culture of his times in the light of the implications of this study. These matters constitute the substance of the final Chapter.

9.  See Achtemeier 1990. Hester 1996: 253-54 writes: 'Paul's letters acted as a substitute for the writer's presence and were oral (or, perhaps, "aural") in their immediate context. His letters were a way of bringing the speech, instead of the speaker, to the audience. They were read out loud to the audience by the letter carriers—those mentioned in the opening greeting—who acted also as interpreters of his thought and messengers to the audience when they didn't understand something or didn't react to the effect Paul tried to create.'

Chapter 6

CONCLUSION

> To think of Paul as either Jewish or Greek is not only superficial but
> wrong.
>
> Malherbe 1994: 243

This Chapter has as its goal a discussion of some of the consequences
which follow from the preceding analysis. The dialogue with the broader issues which scholarship raises in relation to 2 Corinthians 8–9 and
to Paul in general should serve not only to investigate the wider reper-
cussions of this study but also to probe further its validity and utility.

## 1. *Rhetorical Structures Compared*

Following the brief outline of Betz's rhetorical *dispositio* of 2 Corinthians 8 and 9 in Chapter 2, and having delayed until now a detailed
account of his rhetorical structure, the time has come to compare and
contrast his rhetorical *dispositio* with the one arrived at in this study. A
certain awkwardness attends this procedure because Betz sees two letters with two rhetorical *dispositiones*, whereas this study holds that
there is only one letter and, therefore, only one rhetorical *dispositio* in
these verses. This means that some of the details of comparison really
make sense only now, after the full presentation of our rhetorical reading and it is for this reason that the comparison has been delayed until
now.

H.D. Betz begins his analysis by identifying the *exordium* (2 Cor.
8.1-5) and a *narratio* (8.6). In this study we arrived at only an *exordium*, without the embellishment of a *narratio*. Betz is correct in identifying in these opening verses the 'virtues' of the *exordium*. The only
difference between this study and Betz's outline is the extent of the
*exordium* and the presence of a *narratio* in v. 6. Betz's grounds for
claiming that here we have a distinct unit are (1) this is a different form
of narrative and (2) it explains the occasion of the first letter (8.1-24).

| Betz | | This study | | |
|---|---|---|---|---|
| **The Letter to the Corinthians** | | | | |
| omitted | [I. Epistolary prescript] | | | |
| 1-24 | II. Body of the letter | | | |
| 1-5 | *Exordium* | *Exordium* | 8.1-6 | History, |
| 6 | *Narratio* | | | people, issue |
| 7-8 | *Propositio* | *Propositio* | 8.7(8) | Donate! |
| 9-15 | *Probatio* | *Confirmationes* | | |
| | 9. *First proof* | *Confirmatio 1* | 8.9-15 | Why give? |
| | 10-12 *Second proof* | | | |
| | 13-15 *Third proof* | *Confirmatio 2* | 8.16-24 | Emissaries |
| 16-22 | Commendation | | | appointed |
| 23 | Authorization | | | |
| 24 | *Peroratio* | | | |
| omitted | [Epistolary postcript] | | | |
| **The Letter to the Achaians** | | | | |
| omitted | [I. Epistolary prescript] | | | |
| | | *Confirmatio 3* | 9.1-5 | Emissaries |
| 1-15 | II. Body of the letter | | | sent ahead |
| 1-2 | *Exordium* | | | |
| 3-5a | *Narratio* | | | |
| 5bc | *Propositio* | *Confirmatio 4* | 9.6-10 | God's reward |
| 6-14 | *Probatio* | | | |
| | 6 *Thesis* | | | |
| | 7 *First proof* | | | |
| | 8 *Second proof* | | | |
| | 9-11 *Third proof* | | | |
| | 12 *Fourth proof* | | | |
| | 13-14 *Fifth proof* | *Peroratio* | 9.11-15 | Thanksgiving |
| 15 | *Peroratio* | | | to God |
| omitted | [Epistolary postcript] | | | |

Against the presence of a *narratio* at this point is the *general principle*[1] (which need not be slavishly followed in all cases) that deliberative oratory does not require a *narratio*. The function of a *narratio* is best seen in forensic rhetoric, where the *narratio* is an account of the *agreed facts* before one goes on to dispute the interpretation, either

1. Cicero, *Part. Or.* 4.13.

because of other evidence or because of questions of law. The *narratio* points to the focal point of the discussion, the very issue of dispute requiring interpretation, in the light of laws or universal human experience. The subsequent argument should then go on to promote the speaker's interpretation of the *narratio*, proposed in the *propositio*.

It seems obvious that while the appointment of Titus does indeed have a role in the following discussion, nevertheless, it does not form the *substance* of the subsequent arguments, nor indeed does it lie at the core of the *propositio* (vv. 7-8). Of course, it is true that the emissaries are taken up in ch. 8, but, even if one were to take 8.1-24 as a single rhetorical unit, *pace* Betz, the interpretation of v. 6 is not the issue which governs the *entire* argument which follows. Hence, properly speaking, there is no *narratio* here.

Betz thinks of v. 6 as distinct because it recounts the most recent fact which led to the writing of the letter which lies behind 2 Cor. 8.1-24. It is true that the decision to appoint Titus functions as a consequence of the enthusiasm in Macedonia, as Paul says, and in that sense, v. 6 is to a degree chronologically distinct from the preceding report. But there is continuity as well: it is the great magnanimity of the Macedonians which urges Paul to appoint Titus, so that the splendid Macedonian example might provoke comparable generosity among the Corinthians. (In fact, it is this implied comparison which makes us think the *exordium* prepares the reader for 2 Corinthians 9, as in ch. 9 the comparison is made explicit.) When we bear in mind that the issue in the *propositio* is whether or not the Corinthians should take part in the collection and to what extent, then it is clear that the agency of Titus is significant enough to be part of the argument, but nevertheless, secondary to the larger question of participation in the collection. In fact, in the subsequent argument in 2 Cor. 8.16-24, it is not so much the agency of Titus which is at stake, but rather the reputation of Paul, as we saw above.

Furthermore, as we saw, the *exordium* makes use of the '*semina probationum*', that is, the laying out of the seeds of the argument. Briefly, this points to and anticipates the presence of four arguments, hinted at in 8.1-6 and taken up in *reverse order* in 8.9-9.10, as follows:

| ↓ 8.1 | God's agency | 9.6-10 | God's agency |
|---|---|---|---|
| 8.2 | Macedonian *exemplum* | 9.1-5 | Competition with Macedonians |
| 8.6 | Titus's role | 8.16-24 | The representatives |
| 8.6 | Completion | ↑ 8.9-15 | Completion |

The pattern of reverse order is hardly fortuitous. As a result, 2 Cor. 8.6 cannot be singled out as a *narratio* which informs the argument from 2 Cor. 8.9-24.

Betz has identified the *propositio* as contained in 8.7-8, and here we agree with him. The only point of disagreement touches on the quantity of text 'governed' by the *propositio*. As the *propositio* itself is somewhat general, and contains no *partitio*, it could be said to cover at least the remainder of ch. 8. Because it is somewhat general, there is no reason to think it could not cover the arguments we have discovered in 9.1-10, which continue to deal with the question of motivation under different aspects. Of course, the argument from the generality of the *propositio* could prove counter-productive, were we not to bear in mind that the *probationes* deal concretely with motivations for taking part— the example of Christ, Paul's probity, the reputation of the Corinthians and the agency of God. Positively, the extent of the subsequent argument depends on the *semina probationum* in the *exordium*, i.e. the anticipation of four distinct areas of argument to be touched upon. Traces of a *partitio*, or a least an ordered anticipation of the subsequent proofs, are to be found not in the *propositio*, but in the *exordium*. While this resembles the *semina probationum*, it is, nevertheless, not found in classical rhetoric.

As regards the proofs in 2 Cor. 8.9-15 and 16–23 there is no substantial disagreement with Betz. Verse 24 is identified as the *peroratio* to the preceding argument on the basis of a Semitic reading of the participle ἐνδεικνύμενοι, which Betz reads as an appeal. A *peroratio* should also look back over the preceding argument. Betz has some right on his side here. For instance the important word ἀγάπη takes us back to the *propositio*. Likewise, the key word ἐκκλησία occurs only in 8.16-24. At the same time, however, the root καυχ- *otherwise absent* in ch. 8, propels us forward to its highly significant presence in 9.1-5. In its occurrence in v. 24 it is accompanied by the expression ὑπὲρ ὑμῶν, the very expressions which recur with the same root in 9.2-3.

2 *Cor.* 9.2 2 οἶδα γὰρ τὴν προθυμίαν ὑμῶν ἣν **ὑπὲρ ὑμῶν καυχῶμαι** Μακεδόσιν, ὅτι Ἀχαΐα παρεσκεύασται ἀπὸ πέρυσι, καὶ τὸ ὑμῶν ζῆλος ἠρέθισεν τοὺς πλείονας. 3 ἔπεμψα δὲ τοὺς ἀδελφούς, ἵνα μὴ τὸ **καύχημα** ἡμῶν τὸ **ὑπὲρ ὑμῶν** κενωθῇ ἐν τῷ μέρει τούτῳ, ἵνα καθὼς ἔλεγον παρεσκευασμένοι ἦτε,

The verbal connections, therefore, look both backwards and forwards, which is exactly the Janus function of a transitional phrase. It would be more adequate to the data to think of the looking forward as not simply a general orientation towards the future, but as a particular and immediate looking forward to the next unit of argument, which follows immediately in 9.1-5, in which the reputations of the Corinthians and of Paul are united in risk.

Betz is quite brief is his reasons for thinking that 9.1-2 forms an *exordium*. He relies on a reference to the literature on rhetoric and on the support of Windisch, who thinks vv. 1-2 have the character of an 'Einleitung'. However, he adds an extended note on the character of the *exordium*, which he sees as a response to the boredom (*taedium*) of the Corinthians. This is really his explanation of the unusual beginning to chapter 9. He notes as well that the *exordium* includes a *captatio benevolentiae* in the form of his praise for them before the Corinthians.

Of course, Betz is right about the *captatio benevolentiae* and about the figure of *occultatio* at 9.1. However, just because the text has an 'introductory' feel does not mean it is an *exordium*. Paul may simply be bringing us into a new argumentative unit—in this case to do with boasting, shame and honour. This is a delicate subject calling for an appropriately oblique preparation. As we saw in Chapter 5, the opening vv. 1-2 do prepare the reader/listener for the risky notion that the emissaries are to become observers of the Corinthians. On the other hand, the verses do *not* prepare us for the remainder of the argument—God rewarding the good and the general blessings at the end of the chapter. Betz's *exordium*, if correct, would be a rather weak one, which would take us only to v. 6. It is, therefore, more adequate to think of vv. 1-2 as introducing only this unit of argument with which it is so intimately bound.

Betz then goes on to think of 9.3-5b as fulfilling the role of the *narratio*. Paul, apparently, feels obliged to explain why other brothers are being sent, and he hopes that anticipated negative reception, perhaps precipitated by the first letter (8.1-24) may be evaded. Again, Betz thinks of two different addressees—in the first letter the Corinthians, in the second letter the Achaians.

If this truly were a statement of facts, that is, a state of affairs in need of interpretation, then we would anticipate that the role of the emissaries would be the substance of the following argument. But this is not the case in the rest of ch. 9, because 9.6-10 does not deal with the emissaries, who are effectively forgotten from v. 6 onwards. The role of *narratio* is not fulfilled here either.

On the other hand, the claim to take all of 9.1-5 as a single unit of *argument* is sustained by our analysis of the vocabulary in Chapter 3 above. Betz seems to have missed the point that Paul is taking up in 9.1-5 and now making explicit in the implied comparison from the real *exordium* of these two chapters in 8.1-6. This implicit comparison is made explicit by the change of nomenclature from Corinthians in 2 Cor. 6.11 to Achaians in 2 Cor. 9.2. Macedonia is a region, so the use of Achaia is perhaps more appropriate. This is a simpler explanation, rhetorically comprehensible, calling for fewer hypotheses and no redactional reconstructions.

Continuing the application of his rhetorical *dispositio*, Betz finds in 9.5b-c the *propositio* of the remaining argument. This is identified on three grounds. Firstly, Paul passes from past decisions to future requirements. Secondly, the *propositio* is where one would expect to find it, after the *narratio*. Thirdly, it fulfils the functions of a *propositio*, 'to set forth both the points of agreement and those which continue to be regarded as tasks or challenges'. We take each comment in turn.

The move from past to future, which Betz uses to distinguish 5b-c from the preceding material, is not so clear. The future is not absent in the preceding verses, as we see from the fear that embarrassment may result. The second argument falls if there is no *narratio*, although there could still be a *propositio* between the *exordium* and the *probatio* (as we have found in 2 Corinthians 8–9).

The third argument needs clarification. Certainly 5b-c resembles a *propositio*, in that it proposes something, as do many sentences and phrases in Paul. Furthermore some of the language in 5b-c is taken up immediately in the following verses (εὐλογία and the language of the cheerful giver). However, it was not the purpose of the *propositio* to set forth points of agreement—that was the function of the *narratio*. Rather the *propositio* had to state succinctly and unmistakably the case to be made. The question to be asked is whether the contents of 5b-c form the nucleus of the argument in the following verses. It might seem that it does, in that the notion of freely/generously giving is indeed a theme from v. 6 onwards. It depends on how you divide up the verse. Betz is somewhat ambivalent—the *narratio* is 3-5b and the *propositio* is 5b-c—so that the text shades over from the *narratio* into the *propositio*. This would mean that the *propositio* is found in a result clause, depending on the main thought at the start of the sentence, ἀναγκαῖον οὖν ἡγησάμην. If we are following the indications given by Betz, then

v. 5b-c can be read as looking back over 9.1-5. This is indicated first of all by the continued reference to the emissaries (προέλθωσιν, προκα-ταρτίσωσιν) and to his boasting about the Corinthians (προεπηγγελ-μένην). This means that if we include 5b in the *propositio* then it looks chiefly *backwards* over the preceding text unit. If we go on to think of 5c alone as the *propositio*, then even there the notion of preparedness, so much a function of the arrival of the Macedonians, is still present and in fact it brings us back into the semantic field of preparedness which we found in 9.1-5. As a result, the only phrase of the purported *propositio* which looks forward is the last phrase, οὕτως ὡς εὐλογίαν καὶ μὴ ὡς πλεονεξίαν. This phrase functions two ways. First of all it is an attempt to deal with any possible feeling of threat or pressure in 9.1-5. Already Paul has tried to obviate that by two means: (1) the portrayal of himself as under examination in 8.16-24, and (2) by the association of himself with the potential shame incurred should the Corinthians not live up to their reputation (9.4). Any residual resentment is faced by his claim that he wants them to be free in their giving. In v. 5 εὐλογία primarily means 'gift'. Giving as a gift, freely and generously, is developed in 9.6-7. But the main subject of 9.6-10 is that God is present in the giving and will reward the generous giver—a slight shift in nuance between εὐλογία which points to freedom and εhπ᾽ εὐλογίαις which points to the related attitude of generosity. It is this generosity, inspired and rewarded by God, which is the real topic of 9.6-10. In that sense, if the last phrase of v. 5 is meant to be the *propositio*, it fails to govern fully the subsequent argument. Given these various considerations and bearing in mind the slightness of the phrase, it would seem to be more cautious and more adequate to think of v. 5c as a transition between two blocks of argument, underlining freedom and generosity (9.5-7) in the light of a possible feeling of pressure caused by the *preceding* argument (9.1-4). I am in agreement with Betz in seeing a block of argument beginning in 9.6. However, he confuses the issue somewhat when he states (1985: 102, 111) that the *probatio* 'begins... with that statement of the thesis in v. 6'. This is not a 'thesis' in the rhetorical sense, but a *sententia*, that is, proverbial wisdom of some kind *which does not need to be proved* but rather functions itself as part of a proof.

Anticipating the order a little, in the last verse of ch. 9, there is a sharp difference between Betz and the model proposed here. Betz holds that the proofs continue through 9.9-11 and on to 9.14, with 9.15 as the *peroratio*. Taking 9.9-11, Betz says that here we have a three step development (1) a proof from Scripture; (2) an allegorical interpretation; and (3) ethical conclusions. We may agree with Betz v. 9 and v. 10 constitute a proof from Scripture followed by an allegorical interpretation. However, as we saw above, the language of v. 11 is entirely different to the language of vv. 9-10. In this study, the *peroratio* begins with v. 11 and continues to the end, whereas for Betz, the *peroratio* consists only of the last exclamation in v. 15. Apart from its brevity, there are problems with v. 15 as a *peroratio*. The offices of the *peroratio* are well known: it is meant to recapitulate and to affect the emotions. It is true, of course, that an exclamation is an emotional form of expression. But as recapitulation, 9.15 is laconic to a fault. It does not take us back to Betz's *exordium* in 9.1-2, which is not about God's agency, but rather begins to make explicit the comparison between the Macedonians and the Achaians. Neither does it reflect the *propositio* in Betz's structure which is to be found in 9.5b-c or perhaps just 5c. There the emphasis is on the freedom of the Corinthians rather than the agency of God. For these reasons, while 9.15 does indeed end the entire argument and thus may be *part* of the *peroratio*, on its own it is simply too concise to be securely identified. It was considerations such as these which made us look to a more extensive text as the *peroratio* of 2 Corinthians 8–9.

As regards the presence of 'proofs' in 2 Cor. 9.11-14, it should be recalled that all moments in a rhetorical text are persuasive in intention, but this does not necessarily mean they are all *probationes* in the technical sense. It is clear that vv. 10-14 are indeed meant to persuade, but this time by looking beyond the simple issue of giving as such (to which four *probationes* have been dedicated, according to our *dispositio*), which is the topic of the *propositio* in 2 Cor. 8.6-7, to the wider benefits accruing thereto. Rather than dealing with a proof as such, which would touch on the causes for giving, 2 Cor. 9.11-14 deal with the wider question of a broad thanksgiving to God from whom all blessings flow, that is, the consequences of giving. This wider, future-oriented, hortatory section fits better with the offices of the peroration while bearing in mind that all moments in rhetoric are meant to be persuasive. Finally, not only is the expected correspondence between the *exordium* (2 Cor. 9.1-2) and the *peroratio* (9.15) absent, but neither does the *propositio* (2 Cor. 9.5b-c), touching on freedom in giving, govern that section named *probatio* in 2 Cor. 9.11-14. This is because that last section broaches, however delicately, the issue of self-interest, which is surely not quite consistent with ὡς εὐλογίαν, which here means 'freely, as a blessing' and, as such, would seem to preclude not only extortion but also self-interest.

Bearing in mind these various considerations and keeping in view the rhetorical structure proposed in this study, supported by its own internal logic and by the delimitation of Chapter 3, the rhetorical structures of the two letters proposed by Betz are found to be unconvincing. In general, simpler hypotheses which nevertheless adequately account for the data are to be preferred to complex hypotheses. The rhetorical structure uncovered in Chapter 4 and commented on in Chapter 5, is a simpler hypothesis, making fewer presuppositions about editorial exclusion of epistolary conventions and dependent on no reconstruction of events between the two supposed letters. Occam's razor is not without its uses.

Finally, in this his analysis of the *language* of 2 Corinthians 8–9, Betz (1985) sees the vocabulary of administration. The vocabulary he selects to represent this reading of 2 Corinthians 8–9 is as follows (page numbers in parentheses refer to Betz 1985). The order is the sequence of occurrence.

| | | |
|---|---|---|
| παράκλησις | = | 'official request' or *mandatum* (71) |
| παρακαλέω | = | 'appoint' (71) |
| σπουδή | = | 'characteristics of the ideal administrator' (70) |
| συμπέμπω | = | 'to send someone with someone' (72) |
| ὑπέρ | = | 'authorization' (79) |
| ὑποταγή | = | 'submission' (122-23) |
| ὁμολογία | = | 'contractual agreement' (123) |

We need to look at the interpretation of each term and ask whether the reading proposed here supports or undermines Betz's use of these terms.

### 1.1. Παρακαλέω / παρακλήσις

The common Greek usage of παρακαλέω reflects the root meaning of 'to call'. Even in its legal usage it means 'to summon' (*TNDT*, V: 775). Commonly, it also means 'to beseech', 'to exhort' and 'to comfort'. In the LXX, the dominant meaning is 'to comfort'. The New Testament range of meanings is different from classical use and focuses firmly on the events of salvation: asking for help, exhortation, consoling help and comfort. The sense of 'summons', according to *TDNT*, is retained in 2 Corinthians 8–9 (*TDNT*, V: 793). There seems to be, therefore, no verbal connection between the *mandatum* and this Greek verb. In the

*EDNT* (III: 26-27), a special section is devoted to the use of the verb and the noun in 2 Corinthians, without noting any special 'administrative' sense. Neither is there any suggestion of this meaning in BAGD (617).

### 1.2. Σπουδή / σπουδαῖος

The root meaning is 'haste' or 'zeal'. Both the verb and the noun show a similar shift in meaning from 'haste' to 'exertion' and 'seriousness'. In stoic circles it comes to mean morally 'good'. *TDNT* (VIII: 566) offers zealous concern as a translation of σπουδή in 2 Cor. 7.11. In particular, the σπουδή of 2 Cor. 8.16 is perceived to be a gift from God. The *EDNT* and BAGD are both rather concise on the verbs and nouns deriving form this root and offer no hint of this special meaning detected by Betz.

### 1.3. Συμπέμπω

This form is found only twice in the New Testament, in both in 2 Corinthians 8. The compound form receives no treatment in *TDNT* and only a slight notice in *EDNT*. The simple form (*EDNT*, III: 68) does convey the idea of a mandate, but not particularly connected with an official mandate in Graeco-Roman administration.

### 1.4. Ὑπέρ

This preposition has a wide band of meanings in the New Testament. BAGD (838-39) lists the following:

1.   (a) on behalf of; (b) with the genitive of the thing (variously); (c) in place of; (d) because of; (e) above and beyond; (f) about, concerning.
2.   over and above, beyond
3.   adverbial use (cf. 2 Cor. 11.23).

No special 'administrative' use is found. BAGD interprets the use in 2 Cor. 8.23 in terms of 1.(f) i.e. where it is taken to be the equivalent of περί which seems a natural meaning in the context. *EDNT* does not deal with our text. Neither, apparently, does *TDNT* (III: 514) although I wonder if the reference to 2 Cor. 8.24 under meaning 4 (c) in *TDNT* (VIII: 514) 'with reference to' should not read 8.23. The meaning of 'regarding' is supported by Blass *et al.* §§231.1 where the substitution of περί by ὑπέρ is discussed. Again, there is no hint of a special technical sense and in any case gives too great a weight to a preposition.

## 1.5. Ὑποταγή and ὁμολογία

I treat these terms together because Betz does. Ὑποταγή does mean submission and acquiescence (*TDNT*, VIII: 46). It can also mean simply obedience (BAGD: 847; *EDNT*, II: 407). The *EDNT* suggests that the obedience required here is religious obedience to the proclamation made by the apostles. Such a reading coheres with the normal meaning of ὁμολογία. There are two basic sense to ὁμολογία, confession and acknowledgment (BAGD: 568-69). *TDNT* says the term is used very broadly here (2 Cor. 9.13) and 'has no precise sense' (V: 215). *EDNT* contains a special note saying that it could be just the general meaning here, in the sense that the Corinthians obedience would testify to their acknowledgment of the gospel (II: 514). It is interesting that Betz has to appeal to Erasmus for support for his interpretation of this word to mean 'contract'.

It would seem that the special interpretation of Betz of these terms is a function of his overall interpretation of 2 Corinthians 8 as an administrative letter. If, however, we do not need to think in those terms and if the study presented here is accurate in seeing 2 Corinthians 8–9 as a rhetorical unit, then it should be possible to read all these terms in the more or less usual sense.

Paul is issuing no commands in these chapters, as he himself says. It is possible to take παράκλησις and παρακαλέω in their second ordinary sense of to exhort, to encourage. The σπουδή of Titus is not an administrative virtue: it is a gift and a gift by which he imitates the σπουδή of Paul. Titus will represent Paul, not as a bureaucrat, but rather as someone who has in his heart the same enthusiasm and keenness which Paul himself has. My interpretation of 2 Cor. 8.23 as an exclamation seems already an adequate basis for taking ὑπὲρ in the sense of περί. Finally, the terms ὑποταγή and ὁμολογία are more easily taken in Christian sense given the presence in the *peroratio* of so many terms which belong to the kerygmatic vocabulary of emergent Christianity. In a word, the administrative vocabulary discovered by Betz seems not to have a solid foundation, either linguistically or rhetorically.

## 2. *The Wider Question of Paul's Education*

This study began with the question of the possibility and utility of a rhetorical reading of Paul's letters. At this point, it would seem safe to maintain that a rhetorical reading is both possible and useful. A remaining issue is whether a conservative Jew like Paul would have been likely to have received the necessary education which the skilled use of rhetoric implies.

In the sciences, it is possible to reconstruct theoretically a picture of an entire body, even a life, from a single bone. An identikit picture of the person can be approximated in terms of size, age, sex, nutrition, medical history and so forth. While so complete a reconstruction of Paul's life on the basis of two chapters from one of his letters would be over-ambitious, nevertheless such a restricted text can be a window, an aperture, a lens which permits its own perspective on a larger panorama. That larger panorama is the complex domain of Hellenism and Hellenistic Judaism, and their influences on him. In this concluding chapter, our purpose is to see what light our interpretation of 2 Corinthians 8–9 may shed on the cultural heritage and education of Paul, in a word, on his particular position in the broad landscape which constitutes Hellenistic Judaism.

Although that analysis takes only one text, 2 Corinthians 8–9, it affords an insight, however limited, on the world which Paul inhabited, because it combines his dual interests of Gentile and Jew—if not 'Athens and Jerusalem', then Jerusalem and Corinth. Paul must be understood in terms of this hybrid cultural background. In turn, his particular achievement can serve to extend our understanding of what was possible within that cultural framework. All the terms of the discussion are disputed: 'Judaism', 'Hellenism' and 'universalism' do not yield univocal, simple meanings, but represent instead a broad band of possibilities, differently realized by different people in different circumstances.

According to an older type of scholarship, it was common to contrast the typical mindsets of the Jew and the Greek; sometimes Greek culture was regarded as superior and Semitic culture as inferior. At oher times, the Semitic, regarded—perhaps romantically—as better able to deal with human nature as an integrated whole, was held to be superior to the 'intellectualism' and 'rationalism' of the classical tradition. Neither position is free from its own *Tendenz* (sometimes very unacceptable when made explicit) and neither is adequate to the complex and variable reality which made up society in the first century of the Common Era, whether in general or more specifically in the Diaspora and in Palestine (Engberg-Pedersen 1994a: xix). A consensus regarding both Hellenism and Judaism in the Hellenistic period is emerging which means that the previous understanding will no longer serve as a map for touring these first-century societies. The emerging common opinion on Judaism and Hellenism and their interpenetration could be outlined as follows.

Even before Hengel, Tcherikover had dismissed the conventional distinction between Judaism in Palestine and in the Diaspora, noting that expectations are often overturned. Diaspora Judaism could be very traditionalist and Jerusalem could be highly Hellenized.[2] It was, nevertheless, Hengel's great work, *Judaism and Hellenism*, however much criticized later, which had the strongest influence in spreading the opinion that this facile distinction could not be sensibly maintained (Hengel 1974: 2). More recent writers such as Borgen (1987: 7; 1994: 30), Grabbe (1992: 151), Overman (1992: 65), Engberg-Pedersen 1994b: 256), Segal (1994: 23 n. 23) and Barclay (1996: 84) have trenchantly refuted the validity of the distinction. Accordingly, the cry of 'no opposition' has since been extended to other, related, areas of research. Thus, for example, any attempt to distinguish a Hellenistic, philosophical Philo and a later, Jewish, exegetical Philo is dismissed by Borgen (Borgen 1987: 44). Jewish writings of the time do not provide a sound basis for a distinction based on geographical location (Collins 1983: 10), neither does a distinction on the basis of the type of debate held support the separation, as we see from the discussion about circumcision—as much a question in Palestine as in the Diaspora (Borgen 1987: 249). The abandonment of the distinction has found its way into the history of Christian origins, where any schematic distinction into a Jewish and Hellenistic period in early Christianity is questioned, using the evidence of the Fourth Gospel.[3] In particular, in the case of Paul, a Hellenistic Paul cannot be played against a Jewish Saul.[4]

---

2.  Tcherikover 1979: 344-45. Koester had already voiced this in 1966. See Koester 1966: 194. Likewise Davies 1965: 179.

3.  Munck 1966: 169; Borgen 1987: 207. Borgen 1987: 169 writes: 'Thus the ideas of the heavenly figure who sees God (Israel) and ascent/descent are found in both Philo and John. Similarities have also been found between John and the rabbinic halakah about agency. The fourth Gospel, therefore, shows that no sharp distinction can be drawn between rabbinic and Hellenistic Judaism.'

4.  Munck 1966: 174; more recently Engberg-Pedersen 1994a: xvi. Malherbe 1994: 243 writes: 'To think of Paul as either Jewish or Greek is not only superficial but wrong.' The influence of exegetes' own theological positions always has a highly significant influence on their reconstructions of the past. The work of E.P. Sanders (1977) and J. Christiaan Beker (1980) should also be noted here.

If one asks why has such a consensus been reached and why has its effect been increasingly felt in different areas of study, then the answer has to be that our understanding of what both the terms Judaism and Hellenism mean has changed considerably.

Writers, especially perhaps theologians, have found it convenient to express themselves in broad-brush strokes when speaking of Judaism, as if it were a fairly monochrome, homogeneous reality. This is certainly not true of Judaism today. It becomes increasingly apparent that neither is it true of Judaism in the past. Judaism is and was a polychrome, varied and complex reality,[5] with a rich range of possible ways of being Jewish.[6] This is true not only of Diaspora Judaism, but also of Judaism within Palestine, where even the Samaritans had four different sects (Overman 1992: 70). A consequence of this is that there was no so-called normative Judaism, a monolithic, identifiable structure in terms of doctrine and praxis against which other varieties—so-called 'deviations'—may be measured.[7] Barclay recommends thinking of Judaism as a social and not just as an intellectual phenomenon[8] and such an observation receives support from Segal when he claims that the words '*Ioudaios*', '*Iudaeus*' and '*Yehudi*', meant originally someone from Judaea and probably had, in antiquity, a greater national connotation than the predominantly religious connotation of today (Segal 1990: 88) However, even within this variety of expression, a common thread of Hellenism has been recognized. Hengel wrote in 1974:

> From about the middle of the third century BC *all Judaism* must really be designated 'Hellenistic Judaism' in the strict sense, and a better differentiation could be made between the Greek-speaking Judaism of the Western Diaspora and the Aramaic/Hebrew-speaking Judaism of Palestine and Babylonia. But even this distinction is one-sided. From the time of the Ptolemies, Jerusalem was a city in which Greek was spoken to an increasing degree (Hengel 1974: 104).

And even though Hengel has been criticized for seeing too much Greek influence in Palestine, Segal could write in 1990:

---

5.    Kraabel 1992: 13 writes: 'The most striking impression from these new data is of the great diversity of Diaspora Judaism.'

6.    Barclay 1996: 4; Segal 1990: 32-33.

7.    Kraabel 1992: 9; Overman 1992: 63; Collins 1983: 244.

8.    Barclay 1996: 410 writes: 'If Judaism is defined—as it should be—as a social and not just an intellectual phenomenon, it is hard to see how the plural "Judaisms" could apply to the Diaspora.'

Hellenistic Judaism, deeply influenced by classical thought, was the maj-
ority Jewish culture of the day. Even within the small area of Judea and
the slightly larger area of the land of Israel, which included Samaria and
the Galilee, we have evidence of a large number of Hellenized Jews (84).

Writing in 1994, Engberg-Pedersen uses the word 'interpenetration'
to describe the relation between, or better the new reality born of, Hellenism and Judaism (Engberg-Pedersen 1994a: xix). Speaking perhaps
too strongly, he writes:

As an important corollary of this, the term 'Hellenistic' itself should not
be understood as signifying those elements in the Hellenistic cultural
melting-pot that were specifically and originally Greek. Rather, it is a
substantively empty term designating the mixture of cultural elements
that one is likely to find when one considers a certain phenomenon in the
Hellenistic period proper (as defined above in political terms)—and in
the Roman period too as long as one is talking about the eastern
Mediterranean area. Judaism (Engberg-Pedersen 1994a: xx).

The point is well taken, even if provocatively expressed. 'Hellenistic'
points to that dynamic process (Grabbe 1992: 153) and to those cultural
phenomena characteristic of the 'Hellenistic' period. Hellenistic Judaism is one such phenomenon, which can only with difficulty and by
abstraction be distinguished into its 'originally' Greek and Semitic
components. In any case, it is good for scholars of a literary bent to be
reminded that Hellenism was not just a matter of, or even primarily a
matter of, 'high' culture—it had also to do with land holdings, govern-
ment, the function of law, the perception of the individual and a certain
tendency to systematization in education, among other areas (Grabbe
1992: 155). Such a broad sense of Hellenism does not exclude assessing
its variable presence according to place and time.

As noted above within this Hellenistic period, Judaism is itself a Hellenistic phenomenon. Naturally, Judaism has roots in 'pre-Hellenistic'
Palestine. But the Judaism of the Second Temple Period was thoroughly influenced by Hellenism,[9] that 'cultural perspective which has its
roots in Greece and is manifest in historical texts and phenomena' (Betz
1994: 84). The dominant cultural influence in the Diaspora was Greek
(Tcherikover 1979: 348) and the extent to which accommodation could
go may be seen in Philo's claim that Plato's ideas came originally from
Moses (Borgen 1987: 21). Two areas may be used to assess the degree

---

9.   Davies 1966: 189; Segal 1994: 22-23; Grabbe 1992: 152; and many others.

of 'interpenetration': participation in education and attitudes to the Gentiles. They are not unrelated.

The Hellenistic period was marked specifically by παιδεία ('instruction')[10] and a renewed interest in systematization, of which the rhetorical manuals are examples. Jews resident not only in the Diaspora but also in Palestine were not impervious to the benefits of this cultural richness and social opportunity. The attraction of the Jews to Greek education was already noted by Tcherikover, when he wrote,

> Greek education also cast its spell upon the Jews. We have already seen…that, at the beginning of the Roman period, the Jews made various efforts to penetrate the citizen-class, and one of their ways of doing this was to obtain an education in the gymnasium… All these examples indicate the keen ambition of the Diaspora Jews to emulate the Greeks in the most important branches of original Greek cultural life, and there is no doubt that the education of young Jews in the gymnasia opened to them the way to a deeper understanding of Greek culture as a whole (Tcherikover 1979: 350).

The same attraction is noted by Collins in his much later work:

> It is evident from the literature of the diaspora that Jews were educated, by whatever means, in Greek literature and philosophy. The open attitude of the Diaspora Jews to their Hellenistic environment is amply shown in their use of Greek names and their recourse of Hellenistic law. The struggle of the Jews in Alexandria for parity with the Greek citizens typifies the aspirations of the Hellenistic Diaspora. The Hellenistic Jews were not reluctant exiles. They were attracted by Hellenistic culture, eager to win the respect of the Greeks and adapt to their ways (Collins 1983: 4).

The extent to which Jews were drawn to the educational opportunities afforded by Hellenistic society is confirmed by the attempt of the Emperor Claudius to ban Jews from future gymnasium education (Barclay 1996: 58). Egyptian Judaism was enthusiastic as a whole towards the dominant culture.[11] At the same time, for our period, the freedom to enjoy a wide education was most likely confined to the well-off—and there is evidence that the Jews in Asia Minor, for instance, were in a position to educate their sons (Barclay 1996: 266). Participation in

10. Hengel 1974: 65; the *Letter of Aristeias* praises specifically the virtues of παιδεία. See Roetzel 1992: 171.

11. Hengel 1974: 39; Borgen 1987: 19. The example of Philo is outstanding (Barclay 1996: 172-73) but not unique.

pagan society could occur at different levels of intensity[12] and we might expect that in Palestine the cultural exchange would be least marked. However, two observations may raise a question about that. First of all, Hengel thinks the influence of Hellenism on later Rabbinic tradition is extensive, both in regard to teaching functions and exegetical methods:

> Even the master–pupil relationship in the Rabbinate, bound up with the principle of tradition, has its model less in the Old Testament, where it was not known in this strict form, than in Greece. The διδάσκαλος corresponded to the *rab* and the *talmid* to the μαθητής. The dialectical form of instruction which could almost be termed 'Socratic', with its sequence of question and answer, and *solutiones*, may have been influenced by the model of the Greek rhetorical schools. The same is true of the exegetical methods developed by the rabbis after Shemaiah and Abtalion and their pupil Hillel; this applies both to halachic exegesis which, on the basis of the seven *middot* of Hillel in the controversy with the Sadducees, anchored the prescriptive right of the oral Torah in the Torah, and to haggadic exegesis, which, like the Homer exegesis of the Alexandrian grammatists, was meant to abolish and explain contradictions and stumbling blocks in the texts (Hengel 1974: 81).

He notes that the anti-Hellenistic scribal movement, which culminated in the development of the Rabbinate, made use of the methods and forms of Greek educational theory (Hengel 1974: 103). Thus, even in opposing Hellenism, the dominant culture prevailed in some sense. Although, as noted above, Hengel has been criticized for over-estimating the extent of Hellenistic penetration into Palestine, the evidence of the literature is still telling and conceded by Hengel's more recent critics:

> [T]he major strength of Hengel's work is that it sets out a context in which the Jews were bound to be influenced by a Greek culture and in which Hellenization was inevitable, barring a strong, conscious effort to reject all Greek influences (Grabbe 1992: 152).

This is the world of Paul of Tarsus, into which he fits as a Greek-speaking Asian Jew, widely travelled and familiar with the cultural codes and praxis of the Graeco-Roman world.

---

12. Borgen 1987: 228 writes: 'As for the problem area of participation in pagan society, there existed corresponding spectrums of thought and practices within both the synagogue and the church.'

## 3. *Conclusion*

This study began in Chapter 1 with a double purpose: to test a proposed method on the sample text of Paul, 2 Corinthians 8–9. The method itself was designed to reply to and overcome some of the criticisms levelled at rhetorical criticism. In particular, it was hoped that a combination of techniques (delimitation and rhetoric) would help meet the charge of arbitrariness, something very apparent in critics who begin their rhetorical analyses with the identification of the *dispositio*. The method uses the stages of rhetorical composition in reverse order, starting with the surface phenomena, and then to go deeper to the *dispositio* and the issue(s) at stake. It is my hope that the sample text has shown that such a method can work and helps to give a firmer footing to the rhetorical analysis of these two chapters.

After the introductory discussion in Chapter 1 and the historical survey in Chapter 2, Chapter 3 began the application of the proposed methodology with a detailed delimitation of the text of 2 Corinthians 8–9 and of the units within those two chapters. Passing reference was made to Paul's familiarity with the cultural codes of benefaction and of honour and shame. Chapter 4 presented a rhetorical analysis proper, starting with the *elocutio*, and working backwards through the *dispositio* to the *inventio*. The results of the delimitation in Chapter 3 were confirmed by the rhetorical *dispositio* in Chapter 4. The following Chapter 5 then went on to present a reading of 2 Corinthians 8–9 on the basis of the rhetoric employed. It is not without significance that a controverted issue such as the integrity of 2 Corinthians 8–9 can be illuminated by a rhetorical reading.

Finally, in this chapter we have tried to show (1) that Betz's rhetorical reading, although rich in detail and background, fails to deal adequately with the data; and (2) that the evidence from Hellenistic Judaism shows that Paul could very well have received an extensive education and challenges the assumption that it was limited, in rhetoric, to the progymnasmata. The reading made here stands in favour on an extensive Hellenistic education, if not quite to the ultimate level of Philo and his like.

Understanding ancients ruins is greatly assisted by the surviving theories of Vetruvius. We hope we have shown here that understanding the extant remains of the correspondence of Paul of Tarsus is enabled and enlightened by Hellenistic rhetorical theory and practice.

APPENDIX: FIGURES

*(Adapted from Mortara Garavelli)*

The figures in **bold** are to be found in 2 Corinthians 8–9.

*Figures of Speech*

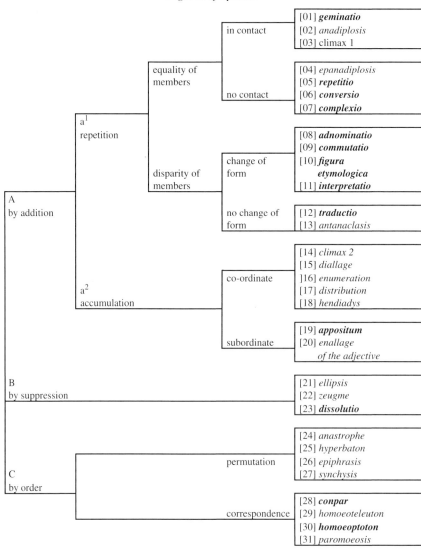

*Figures of Speech*

| | | | | |
|---|---|---|---|---|
| | | | [01] **commoratio** | *interpretatio* |
| | a¹ amplification | | [02] **descriptio** | *expolitio* |
| | | | [03] **enthymeme** | |
| | | | [04] *epiphrasis* | |
| | | | [05] **definitio** | |
| | a² semantic clarification | | [06] *dubitatio* | |
| | | | [07] **correctio** | |
| A Addition | | | [08] **contentio** | |
| | | antithesis | [09] *oxymoron* | |
| | | | [10] *reversio* | |
| | | | [11] **commutatio** | *chiasm* |
| | a³ semantic dilation | common-places | [12] **sententia** | |
| | | | [13] **epiphonemon** | |
| | | similitude | [14] **similitudo** | *comparison* |
| | | | [15] *exemplum* | |
| B Suppression | | | [16] **brevitas** | |
| | | | [17] **percursio** | |
| | | | [18] **occultatio** | |
| | | | [19] *aposiopesis* | |
| C Order | | | [20] *hysteron-proteron* | *hysterologia* |
| | | | [21] **interpositio** | |
| | | | [22] *subnexio* | |
| | in the content | | [23] **significatio** | |
| | | | [24] **permutatio** | |
| | | | [25] *prosopopeon* | |
| | | | [26] *dissimulation* | |
| | | speaker | [27] *sermocinatio* | *ethopesis* *diagolism* *percontatio* *subjectio* |
| D Replacement | in situation of | subject | [28] *digression* | |
| | | | [29] *licence* | |
| | | | [30] *concessio* | |
| | | | [31] *dubitatio et communicatio* | |
| | | listener | [32] *apostrophe* | |
| | in the syntax | | [33] *rhetorical question* | |
| | | | [34] **exclamatio** | |

# BIBLIOGRAPHY

Achtemeier, P.
    1990      '*Omne verbum sonat*: The New Testament and the Oral Environment',
              *JBL* 109: 3-27.
Aletti, J.-N.
    1990      'La présence d'un modèle rhétorique en Romains. Son rôle et son
              importance', *Bib* 71: 1-24.
    1991      *Comment Dieu est-il Juste? Clefs pour interpréter l'épître aux Romains*
              (Paris: Editions du Seuil).
Allo, E.-B.
    1937      *Saint Paul: Seconde Epître aux Corinthiens* (Paris: Etudes Bibliques).
Anderson, R. Dean
    1996      *Ancient Rhetorical Theory and Paul* (Kampen: Kok Pharos).
Aune, David E.
    1988      *The New Testament in its Literary Environment* (Cambridge: James
              Clarke & Co.).
Backus, Irena
    1996      'Bible: Biblical Hermeneutics and Exegesis', in *The Oxford Encyclo-
              paedia of the Reformation* (New York: Oxford University Press, 152-58).
Bailey, James L., and Lyle E. Vander Broek
    1992      *Literary Forms in the New Testament* (London: SPCK).
Barclay, John
    1996      *Jews in the Mediterranean Diaspora. From Alexander to Trajan (323
              BCE–117 CE)* (Edinburgh: T. & T. Clark).
Barthes, Roland
    1988      'The Old Rhetoric: An Aide-mémoire', in *The Semiotic Challenge*
              (Oxford: Basil Blackwell [original French version of this article was the
              result of a seminar in 1964–65]).
Baur, Chrysostomos
    1959      *John Chrysostom and His Time*, I (London: Sants ET of German original
              from 1929).
Beker, J. Christiaan
    1980      *Paul the Apostle* (Edinburgh: T. & T. Clark).
Betz, Hans Dieter
    1979      *Galatians: A Commentary on Paul's Letter to the Churches in Galatia*
              (ed. Helmut Koester; Hermeneia; Philadelphia: Fortress Press).
    1985      *2 Corinthians 8 and 9* (Philadelphia: Fortress Press).
    1992      'Paul', *ABD*, V: 186-201.
    1994      'Enthymemic Argumentation in Paul: The Case of Romans 6', in Eng-
              berg-Pedersen 1994c: 84-118.

Bieringer, R., and J. Lambrecht
1994        *Studies on 2 Corinthians* (Leuven: Leuven University Press).
Borgen, Peder
1987        *Philo, John and Paul. New Perspectives on Judaism and Early
             Christianity* (Atlanta: Scholars Press).
1994        ' "Yes," "No," "How Far?"': The Participation of Jews and Christians in
             Pagan Cults', in Engberg-Pedersen 1994c: 30-59.
Bünker, M.
1984        *Briefformular und rhetorische Disposition im. 1. Korintherbrief* (Göt-
             tingen: Vandenhoeck & Ruprecht).
Carrez, M.
1986        *La Deuxième Epître de saint Paul aux Corinthiens* (Geneva: Labor et
             Fides).
Clarke, M.L.
1996        *Rhetoric at Rome: A Historical Survey* (ed. D.H. Berry; London: Rout-
             ledge & Kegan Paul, 3rd edn [1953]).
Classen, C.J.
1991        'Paulus und die antike Rhetorik', ZNW 82: 1-33.
1995        'Melanchthon's First Manual on Rhetorical Categories in Criticism of the
             Bible', in L. Ayres (ed.), *The Passionate Intellect* (New Brunswick:
             Transaction Publishers): 297-322.
Chrysostom, John
1838        *Opera Omnia*, X (Paris: Gaine Fratres): 485-777; ET: in T.W. Chambers
             DD, *Chrysostom: Homilies on the Epistles of Paul to the Corinthians*
             (NPNF, 12; Peabody, MA: Hendrickson, 1995 [1889]).
Cohen, Shaye J.D.
1986:       'The Political and Social History of the Jews in Graeco-Roman Antiquity:
             The State of the Question', in Kraft and Nickelsburg: 33-56.
Cohen, David
1994        'Classical rhetoric and modern theories of discourse', in Ian Worthington
             (ed.), *Persuasion: Greek Rhetoric in Action* (London: Routledge): 69-84.
Collins, John J.
1983        *Between Athens and Jerusalem* (New York: Crossroad).
Combrink, H.J. Bernard
1996        'The Rhetoric of Sacred Scripture', in Porter and Olbricht 1996: 102-23.
Crafton, Jeffrey A.
1991        *The Agency of the Apostle* (Sheffield: Sheffield Academic Press).
Cuddon, J.A.
1991        *Dictionary of Literary Terms and Literary Theory* (Harmondsworth:
             Penguin Books).
Danker, F.W.
1982        *Benefactor: Epigraphic Study of a Graeco-Roman and New Testament
             Semantic Field* (St. Louis, MI: Clayton, 1982).
1989        *II Corinthians* (Minneapolis, MN: Augsburg).
1991        'Paul's Debt to the *De Corona* of Demosthenes: A Study of Rhetorical
             Techniques in Second Corinthians', in D.F. Watson (ed.), *Persuasive
             Artistry* (Sheffield: Sheffield Academic Press): 262-80.

Davies, W.D.
    1965        'Paul and Judaism', in Hyatt 1965: 178-86.
Di Berardino, Angelo, and Basil Studer (eds.)
    1996        *History of Theology: The Patristic Period* (Collegeville, MN: Liturgical
                Press).
Doty, W.G.
    1973        *Letters in Primitive Christianity* (Philadelphia: Fortress Press).
Dozeman, Thomas B.
    1992        'Rhetoric and Rhetorical Criticism', *ABD*, V: 710-19.
Egger, Wilhelm
    1987        *Methodenlehre zum Neuen Testament* (Freiburg: Herder).
Elliott, N.
    1990        *The Rhetoric of Romans: Argumentative Constraint and Strategy and
                Paul's Dialogue with Judaism* (Sheffield: Sheffield Academic Press).
Engberg-Pedersen, Troels
    1994a       'Introduction', in Engberg-Pedersen 1994c: 15-26.
    1994b       'Stoicism in Philippians', in Engberg-Pedersen 1994c: 256-90.
Engberg-Pedersen, Troels (ed.)
    1994c       *Paul in His Hellenistic Context* (Edinburgh: T. & T. Clark).
Fee, G.
    1987        *The First Epistle to the Corinthians* (Grand Rapids: Eerdmans).
Freund, Elizabeth
    1987        *The Return of the Reader* (London: Methuen).
Garuti, Paolo
    1995        *Alle Origini dell'Omiletica Cristiana: La lettera agli Ebrei* (Jerusalem:
                Franciscan Printing Press).
Gnilka, Joachim
    1996        *Paulus von Tarsus: Apostel und Zeuge* (Freiburg: Herder).
Grabbe, Lester L.
    1992        *Judaism From Cyrus to Hadrian*. I. *The Persian and Greek Periods*
                (Minneapolis: Fortress Press).
Grant, R.M., and D. Tracy
    1984        *A Short History of the Interpretation of the Bible* (London: SCM Press).
Group μ
    1981        J. Dubois, F. Edeline, J.-M. Klinkenberg, P. Minguet, F. Pire and
                H. Trinon, *A General Rhetoric* (Baltimore: The Johns Hopkins University
                Press).
Hastings, J., *et al.* (eds.)
    1898        *A Dictionary of the Bible* (Edinburgh: T. & T. Clark).
Heinrici, C.F.
    1896        *Der erste Brief an die Korinther* (Göttingen: Vandenhoek & Ruprecht).
    1900        *Der zweite Brief an die Korinther* (Göttingen: Vandenhoek & Ruprecht).
Hellholm, David
    1993        '*Amplificatio* in the Macro-Structure of Romans', in Porter and Olbricht:
                123-51.
Hengel, Martin
    1974        *Judaism and Hellenism* (London: SCM Press).
    1991        *The Pre-Christian Paul* (London: SCM Press).

Hester, James D.
    1996    'The Invention of 1 Thessalonians: A Proposal', in Porter and Olbricht
             1996: 251-79.
Horrell, David G.
    1996    *The Social Ethos of the Corinthian Correspondence* (Edinburgh: T. & T.
             Clark).
Hyatt, J.P. (ed.)
    1965    *The Bible in Modern Scholarship* (Nashville: SBL).
Jeanrond, Werner
    1992    'Interpretation, History of', in *ABD*, III: 433-43.
Johanson, Bruce F.
    1987    *To All the Brethren: A Text-Linguistic and Rhetorical Approach to 1
             Thessalonians* (Stockholm: Almqvist & Wiksell).
Keegan, T.J.
    1985    *Interpreting the Bible* (New York: Paulist Press).
Kelly, J.N.D.
    1995    *Golden Mouth: The Story of John Chrysostom, Ascetic, Preacher, Bishop*
             (London: Gerald Duckworth).
Kennedy, George A.
    1963    *The Art of Persuasion in Greece* (London: Routledge & Kegan Paul).
    1972    *The Art of Rhetoric in the Roman World* (Princeton, NJ: Princeton
             University Press).
    1984    *New Testament Interpretation through Rhetorical Criticism* (Chapel Hill:
             University of North Carolina Press).
    1994    *A New History of Classical Rhetoric* (Princeton, NJ: Princeton University
             Press).
Koester, Jelmut H.
    1966    'Paul and Hellenism', in Hyatt 1966: 187-95.
Kraabel, A.T.
    1992:    'The Roman Diaspora: Six Questionable Assumptions', in Overman and
             MacLennan 1992: 1-20.
Kraft, Robert A., and George W.E. Nickelsberg (eds.)
    1986    *Early Judaism and its Modern Interpreters* (Philadelphia: Fortress Press).
Lausberg, H.
    1990    *Handbuch der Literarischen Rhetoric: Eine Grundlegung der Literatur-
             wissenschaft* (Stuttgart: Franz Steiner Verlag [1960]).
Lemmer, Richard
    1996    'Why Should the Possibility of Rabbinic Rhetorical Elements in Pauline
             Writings (e.g. Galatians) Be Reconsidered?', in Porter and Olbricht 1996:
             161-79.
Lund, Nils W.
    1942    *Chiasmus in the New Testament* (Chapel Hill: University of North
             Carolina Press).
Mack, Burton
    1990    *Rhetoric and the New Testament* (Minneapolis: Fortress Press).
Majerik, R.
    1992    'Rhetoric and Rhetorical Criticism', *ABD*, V: 710-19.

Malherbe, A.J.
    1988    *Ancient Epistolary Theorists* (SBLSBS, 19, Atlanta: Scholars Press).
    1989    *Paul and the Popular Philososopher* (Minneapolis: Fortress Press).
    1994    'Determinism and Free Will in Paul: The Argument in 1 Corinthians 8 and 9', in Engberg-Pedersen 1994c: 231-55.
Malingrey, A.-M.
    1992    'John Chrysostom', in EEC, I: 440-42.
Margerie, Bertrand de
    1993    *An Introduction to the History of Exegesis*. I. *The Greek Fathers* (Petersham: St Bede's Publications [ET of French original from 1979]).
Martin, Josef
    1974    *Antike Rhetorik: Technik und Methode. Handbuch der Altertumswissenschaft II/3* (Munich: C.H. Beck).
Martin, R.
    1986    *2 Corinthians* (Waco, TX: Word Books).
Mitchell, M.
    1991    *Paul and the Rhetoric of Reconciliation: An Exegetical Investigation of the Language and Composition of 1 Corinthians* (Tübingen: J.C.B. Mohr [Paul Siebeck]).
Mortara Garavelli, Bice
    1994    *Manuale di Retorica* (Milano: Bompiani, 11th edn [1988]).
Muilenburg, James
    1969    'Form Criticism and Beyond', *JBL* 88: 1-18.
Munck, Johannes
    1966    'Pauline Research Since Schweitzer', in Hyatt 1966: 166-77.
Murphy-O'Connor, J.
    1979    *1 Corinthians* (Dublin: Veritas).
    1995    *Paul the Letter-Writer: His World, His Options, His Skills* (Collegeville, MN: Liturgical Press).
    1996    *Paul: A Critical Life* (Oxford: Clarendon Press).
Norden, E.
    1915    *Die antike Kunstprosa vom VI. Jahrhundert v. Chr. bis in die Zeit der Renaissance* (Leipzig-Berlin: Druck und Verlag B.G. Teubner [1915]).
Overman, J. Andres
    1992    'The Diaspora in the Modern Study of Ancient Judaism', in Overman and MacLennan 1992: 63-78
Overman, J. Andrew, and Robert S. MacLennan (eds.)
    1992    *Diaspora Jews and Judaism: Essays in Honor of, and in Dialogue with, A. Thomas Kraabel* (Atlanta: Scholars Press).
Palmer, Richard
    1969    *Hermeneutics* (Evanston, IL: Northwestern University Press).
Pascuzzi, Maria
    1997    *Ethics, Ecclesiology and Church Discipline: A Rhetorical Analysis of 1 Corinthians 5* (Roma: Editrice Pontificia Università Gregoriana).
Percy, Ernst
    1946    *Die Probleme der Kolossser- und Epheserbriefe* (Lund: C.W.K. Gleerup).

Perelman, Ch., and L. Olbrechts-Tyteca

    1971    *The New Rhetoric: A Treatise on Argumentation* (Notre Dame: University of Notre Dame Press [ET French original, 1958]).

Pitta, Antonio

    1992    *Disposizione e messaggio della Lettera ai Galati* (Roma: Editrice Pontificio Istituto Biblico).

Plummer, A., and A. Roberstona

    1911    *The First Epistle of St Paul to the Corinthians* (Edinburgh: T. & T. Clark).

Pogoloff, Stephen M.

    1992    *Logos and Sophia: The Rhetorical Situation of 1 Corinthians* (Atlanta: Scholars Press).

Pollastri, A.

    1992    'Libanius', in EEC, I: 484.

Pontifical Biblical Commission

    1994    *The Interpretation of the Bible in the Church* (Québec: Editions Paulines).

Porter, Stanley E., and Thomas H. Olbricht (eds.)

    1993    *Rhetoric and the New Testament: Essays from the 1992 Heidelberg Conference* (Sheffield: JSOT Press).

    1996    *Rhetoric, Scripture and Theology: Essays from the 1994 Pretoria Conference* (Sheffield: JSOT Press).

Reed, Jeffrey T.

    1993    'Using Ancient Rhetorical Categories to Interpret Paul's Letters: A Quesion of Genre', in Porter and Olbricht (eds.), *Rhetoric and the New Testament. Essays from the 1992 Heidelberg Conference* (Sheffield: JSOT Press): 292-324.

Roetzel, C.

    1992    '*Oikoumene* and the Limits of Pluralism in Alexandrian Judaism and Paul', in Overman and MacLennan 1992: 163-82.

Sanders, E.P.

    1977    *Paul and Palestinian Judaism* (London: SCM Press).

Schüssler Fiorenza, E.

    1987    'Rhetorical Situation and Historical Reconstruction in 1 Corinthians', *NTS* 33: 386-403.

Segal, Alan F.

    1990    *Paul the Convert: The Apostolate and Apostasy of Saul the Pharisee* (New Haven: Yale University Press).

    1994    'Universalism in Judaism and Christianity', in Engberg-Pedersen 1994c: 1-29.

Ska, Jean Louis

    1990    *'Our Fathers Have Told Us': Introduction to the Analysis of Hebrew Narrative* (Rome: Editrice Pontificio Istituto Biblico).

Smit, J.F.M.

    1989    'The Letter of Paul to the Galatians: A Deliberative Speech', *NTS* 35: 1-26.

    1991    'The Genre of 1 Corinthians 13 in the Light of Classical Rhetoric', *NovT* 33: 193-216.

1993      'Two Puzzles: 1 Corinthians 12:31 and 13:3 A Rhetorical Solution', *NTS*
          39: 246-64
1997      ' "Do Not Be Idolators": Paul's Rhetoric in First Corinthians 10:1-22',
          *NovT* 39: 40-53.
Stowers, Stanley K.
1992      'Letters (Greek and Latin)', in *ABD*, IV: 290-93.
1994      'Romans 7.7-25 as a Speech-in-Character (προσωποποιία)', in Engberg-
          Pedersen 1994c: 180-202.
Tcherikover, Victor
1979      *Hellenistic Civilization and the Jews* (repr.; New York: Atheneum
          [1959]).
Vanhoye, Albert
1963      *La structure littéraire de l'Epître aux Hébreux* (Clamency: Desclée de
          Brouwer).
Volkmann, R.
1885      *Die Rhetorik der Griechen und Römer in systematischer Übersicht*
          (Stuttgart: H.J. Teubner, 2nd edn).
Watson, D.F.
1988      *Invention, Arrangement and Style: Rhetorical Criticism of Jude and
          2 Peter* (Atlanta: Scholars Press).
Watson, D.F. (ed.)
1991      *Persuasive Artistry: Studies in New Testament Rhetoric in Honor of
          George A. Kennedy* (Sheffield: Sheffield Academic Press).
Watson, D.F., and Alan J. Hauser (eds.)
1994      *Rhetorical Criticism of the Bible: A Comprehensive Bibliography with
          Notes on History and Method* (Leiden: E.J. Brill).
Weiss, B. Bernhard
1897      'Beiträge zur Paulinischen Rhetorik', in G.R. Gregory *et al.* (eds.),
          *Theologische Studien* (Göttingen: Vandenhoeck & Ruprecht): 165-247.
Wellek, René, and Austen Warren
1986      *Theory of Literature* (repr.; Harmondworth: Penguin Books, 1986, 3rd
          edn [1963]).
Witherington, Ben
1995      *Conflict and Community in Corinth* (Carlisle: Paternoster Press).
Worthington, Ian (ed.)
1994      *Persuasion: Greek Rhetoric in Action* (London: Routledge).
Wuellner, W.
1995      'Death and Rebirth of Rhetoric', in T. Fornberg and D. Hellholm (eds.),
          *Texts and Contexts* (Oslo: Scandinavian University Press): 917-30.
Young, F., and D. Ford
1987      *Meaning and Truth in 2 Corinthians* (London: SPCK).
Ziesler, J.
1990      *Pauline Christianity* (Oxford: Oxford University Press, rev. edn).

# INDEXES

## INDEX OF RHETORICAL TERMS

# INDEX OF BIBLICAL REFERENCES

## OLD TESTAMENT

## NEW TESTAMENT

OTHER ANCIENT REFERENCES

| | | | | | |
|---|---|---|---|---|---|
| Demosthenes | | 36.1445a.27 | 137 | 4.22.30-31 | 109 |
| *Ep.* | | 37.1442.35 | 47 | 4.25.35 | 120 |
| 3.35 | 22 | | | 4.26.36 | 120 |
| | | Pseudo-Cicero | | 4.27.37 | 124 |
| *Syntax* | | *Herennium* | | 4.28.38 | 111 |
| 36 | 49 | 1.2.3 | 48 | 4.28.39 | 121 |
| | | 1.3.4-5 | 48 | 4.30.41 | 116 |
| *Ep. Char.* | | 1.3.4 | 132, 141 | 4.34.46 | 126 |
| 50 | 21 | 1.4.6 | 45, 136 | 4.39.51 | 119 |
| | | 1.4.8 | 45 | 4.45.58 | 119, 121 |
| Isocrates | | 1.6.9 | 136 | 4.45.59 | 123 |
| *Ep.* | | 1.7.11 | 45 | 4.49-62 | 123 |
| 2.13 | 21 | 1.9.14 | 46 | 4.53.67 | 126 |
| | | 1.10.17 | 46 | 4.54.68 | 124 |
| *On Style* | | 2.2.3 | 162 | | |
| 4.223-235 | 21 | 2.18.28 | 47, 132 | *Quintilian* | |
| | | 2.20.32 | 132 | 2.13.2 | 20 |
| Pliny | | 2.30.47 | 47 | 3.9.5 | 46 |
| *Ep.* | | 3.2.2 | 147 | 3.9.29 | 106 |
| 2.5.13 | 21 | 3.2.3 | 146 | 4.2.54 | 136 |
| 2.11.25 | 21 | 3.3.4 | 147 | 4.2.55 | 46 |
| | | 3.4.8 | 147 | 5.10.54 | 68 |
| Pseudo-Aristotle | | 3.10.18 | 145 | 8.2.10 | 115 |
| *Rhet. ad Alex.* | | 4.12.18 | 118 | 8.3.20 | 115 |
| 17.1432a | 152 | 4.13.18 | 105 | 8.3.82 | 124 |
| 18.1428a.16 | 47 | 4.13.19 | 107, 108 | 8.5.11 | 122 |
| 29 | 45 | 4.13.20 | 108 | 8.5.29 | 115 |
| 29.1437a | 45 | 4.13.213 | 112 | 9.1.6 | 115 |
| 29.1437b.15 | 45 | 4.14.20 | 112 | 9.2.26 | 126 |
| 29.143b.35 | 45 | 4.15.22 | 126 | 9.3.23 | 125 |
| 30.1438a.20 | 46 | 4.17.24 | 122 | 9.3.34 | 107 |
| 30.1438a.27 | 46 | 4.18.25 | 119 | 9.3.71 | 110 |
| 33.1439b.3 | 130 | 4.20.27 | 116 | 9.3.88 | 121 |
| 34.1439b.15 | 161 | 4.20.28 | 118 | 9.3.97 | 121 |
| | | 4.21.29 | 109 | | |

# INDEX OF MODERN AUTHORS

# JOURNAL FOR THE STUDY OF THE NEW TESTAMENT
## SUPPLEMENT SERIES